Feeling the Fleshed Body

the aftermath of childhood rape

Feeling the Fleshed Body

Brenda Downing

PETER LANG
Oxford • Bern • Berlin • Bruxelles • Frankfurt am Main • New York • Wien

Bibliographic information published by Die Deutsche Nationalbibliothek.
Die Deutsche Nationalbibliothek lists this publication in the Deutsche Nationalbibliografie; detailed bibliographic data is available on the Internet at http://dnb.d-nb.de.

A catalogue record for this book is available from the British Library.

Library of Congress Control Number: 2015955804

ISBN 978-3-0343-1970-6 (print)
ISBN 978-3-0353-0786-3 (eBook)

Hochfeldstrasse 32, CH-3012 Bern, Switzerland
info@peterlang.com, www.peterlang.com, www.peterlang.net

This publication has been peer reviewed.

Contents

Acknowledgements vii

Introduction 1

CHAPTER ONE
Philomela and me 9

CHAPTER TWO
The language and prevalence of sexual violence 35

CHAPTER THREE
What is somatics? 49

CHAPTER FOUR
Correspondences 75

CHAPTER FIVE
Somatic narratives: Participant somatic inquiry 113

CHAPTER SIX
Somatic narratives and meaning-making 121

CHAPTER SEVEN
Speaking of and with and through the raped body 149

CHAPTER EIGHT
Coming to knowing: A methodology of embodiment 167

CHAPTER NINE
Coming to knowing through embodied autoethnography 179

CHAPTER TEN
Coming to knowing through writing-as-inquiry 241

CHAPTER ELEVEN
Coming to knowing through performance-making-as-inquiry 257

CHAPTER TWELVE
Weaving the warp and weft of the aftermath of childhood rape 277

Bibliography 291

Appendix 1 315

Appendix 2 321

Index 323

Acknowledgements

My sincere and heartfelt thanks to the nine women who so generously offered their personal stories of post-rape trauma and placed their trust in me to hold their stories with sensitivity and care.

To Lekkie Hopkins, my loving thanks. Your deep feminist knowledge, insightfulness, and unwavering faith in me and in this book has been an invaluable support. Our many conversations overlooking the Indian Ocean helped breathed life into this project and helped sustain its momentum.

To Marilyn Metta, my loving thanks. Your belief in this project and your faith in my capacity to complete it with creativity and integrity has been invaluable. Your wise and generous counsel has sustained and nourished me throughout.

To Alice Cummins, my enduring gratitude and love for helping me find other ways to read, feel, and move with my body. Your involvement in this project and your presence in my life has been a gift.

My deep appreciation to a wide circle of friends and colleagues for their friendship, perceptiveness, encouragement, and good humour: Regina Downes; Debbie Marfleet; Danielle Brady; Julie Robson; the Magdalena Talks Back women; the Riddells Creek Body-Mind Centering women; Ross Colliver; Joy Scott; and Rashida Murphy.

To my siblings, who have only been aware of my story in recent times, my thanks for your continuing love and understanding.

And finally, to Jack, Lucy, and Beth, my tender love. These chapters will help you understand.

I would like to dedicate this book to the memory of my gentle and loving brother, Murray, whose tender words in the last days of his life will stay with me always. I would also like to dedicate this book to the memory of Susan. Her enthusiasm for life and the courage she showed during her illness will remain an inspiration.

Where does rape begin?

From the instant
the violating other
pierces the threshold
of personal boundary,

the body is there.

Even if the mind scarpers
the body remains, a loyal
scribe laying down memory
in the archives of the self.

Traumatic memory,
an intolerable always.

Don't be misled,
the body feels everything,
forgets nothing.

Cellular shelves bow
with the weight
of experience.

Once touched, the body
cannot
be untouched.

All rape begins with the body.

(2012)

Introduction

> The moment when a feeling enters the body is political.
> This touch is political.
> — ADRIENNE RICH

In the summer and spring of my final year of primary school, I was twice raped.

I was on the cusp of adolescence.

It was 1971, the year I turned twelve.

These rapes both took place at night at the home of a school friend. The first time it happened I thought I was going to die. The perpetrator's suffocating hand covered my nose and mouth. The terror I was experiencing made breathing almost impossible and prevented me from making any sound. My school friend slept on in another bed in the same room. The rapist was her older brother. Of course, given my age and the era, I did not have a framework of sexual violence in which to locate what was happening to me, but I knew it was a terrible thing and something she must not witness. I never spoke to her about the rapes, and as far as I know, she remains unaware of what took place in her bedroom on those nights. I lost touch with her after we left primary school.

I have written about these experiences of rape in great detail elsewhere: here it is enough to say that for many reasons I also kept this trauma from my family and chose instead to unburden my secret to a different school friend. While the intervening years have smudged my memory of the thought processes I must have undergone in order to choose this particular girl, I have reflected on this many times since and can make certain presumptions. I know that she wasn't a particularly close friend; I barely spent any time outside school hours in her company. My closest friend at that time, someone I have maintained a friendship with to this day, only became aware of my story in 2010 when we sat together on a hot West Australian summer's day, the deep shade of a Moreton Bay fig tree offering shelter from the sun as well as a sense of privacy and enclosure. We were reminiscing about our school years and the time seemed right. I quietly unfolded my story to her.

Perhaps it was a need to preserve this closest of friendships that drove me to choose to tell the other girl. It may be that my instinct for survival at that time prompted the need for schoolgirl normality. Perhaps I assumed that my story, if disclosed, would damage what I needed most. I do recall that the girl I disclosed to seemed somehow older and worldlier than the other girls in my class. Perhaps I thought she would understand what had happened to me because of this. Whatever the reasons, my judgement was poor and my intentions misguided. My disclosure was dismissed as a lie, and despite my protestations of truth, she refused to take me seriously. It had taken me weeks to build up the courage to tell this girl my secret. Her unanticipated dismissal crushed my schoolgirl hope.

I felt helpless and abandoned.

Not willing to risk such rejection a second time, out of a desperate need for self-protection and increasing feelings of shame, I took my secret and my traumatic memories, folded them carefully, wrapped them tightly in a pact of silence, and forced them firmly into the deepest recesses of my young body. I could not risk speaking of these rapes again.

For nearly thirty years I maintained my silence, apart from a fleeting and inadequate disclosure to someone I loved and trusted when I was twenty. During these years, I developed a difficult, tiring and tenuous relationship with my corporeal self. My mind and my body became embroiled in a battle of attrition, my mind an uncompromising and sadistic leader, my body a reluctant and rebellious custodian of my memories, an undisciplined, subversive, irrepressible, and noisy traitor.

For almost four decades I felt no compassion towards my body, merely a loathing that had its genesis in a darkened room in 1971, a loathing fuelled by a grief that remained unacknowledged yet ran deep and was ever present.

***

The point of propulsion for this book is my raped and censured body with its somatic aftermath narrative. The major focus of this book is my engagement with and reflection on the somatic manifestations of trauma I experienced in the aftermath of my childhood rape experience. The autoethnographic explorations I undertook as part of the research for this book spanned several years and involved a process I call somatic inquiry. During this period of embodied exploration, I immersed myself in the body-based therapeutic and experiential practice of Body-Mind Centering®[1] as a private client, workshop participant, and residential program participant. I was guided during this process by Alice Cummins, Body-Mind Centering practitioner, somatic movement educator, and dance artist. The somatic inquiry helped facilitate the identification and interpretation of the multiplicity of ways my body articulated my silenced and unresolved childhood trauma experience, and the ways in which sexual trauma shaped my life as a result. In addition, it helped facilitate a therapeutic engagement with my traumatised material self that led to the beginnings of a restored bodymind relationship and the cultivation of a deep appreciation for the intelligence present throughout my integrated self.

I also turned to other victims of sexual violence as part of my research process. The extracts from their stories appear in text boxes and often towards the margins of the page to remind the reader of the sociocultural and political containment of raped women's voices and of their marginal location within Western culture. Their inclusion adds greater depth to the book and creates a space of reverberation that not only resounds with my autoethnographic voice but also the voices of others raped in childhood. Our stories sit alongside one another to echo within the 'gaps and fissures' (Modjeska 1995, 31) in the existing sexual trauma discourses within the literature on childhood rape. Their inclusion will also: give these women a voice and presence in a book that focuses specifically on the somatic aftermath of childhood rape; serve to disrupt conventional discursive constructions of rape trauma; resist the erasure of the body and subjective experience

1 For reasons of aesthetics, the registered trademark for Body-Mind Centering will only appear on this page.

from universal and institutionally determined definitions of rape; reverberate against and amplify the material conditions of my autoethnographic aftermath story; reveal areas of experiential similarity and difference; and amplify the wider cultural experience of rape in childhood. The embodied voices of nine women join my own voice in the struggle to speak and be heard, and unite to bring the feminine language of our bodies into existence.

An additional, crucial, and highly innovative (within the social sciences) outcome of the original doctoral project was the performance work, *aperture*. Made in 2012 in collaboration with Alice Cummins, this creative piece emerged from my autoethnographic research to sit alongside the body of the thesis. *aperture* was a solo work performed in Perth, Western Australia. During the performance I used my body creatively as a site of intelligence, memory, and articulation to provide insight into the body's capacity to communicate the complex, fragmentary, and multi-layered nature of unresolved sexual trauma memory. Images included in several chapters are from the performance.

***

This book, with its feminist and materialist perspective, weaves together corporeal and discursive understandings of the long-term bodily response to the experience of childhood rape. As I gathered research, my conscious attention to the embodied impact and expression of rape trauma did not preclude me from exploring the literature surrounding discursive understandings of rape trauma. Indeed, to ignore these investigations would have meant denying myself access to a large and valuable body of scholarship. Maintaining my embodied focus however, consistently required me to dive beneath strong discursive currents to seek other, more multidimensional embodied ways of knowing and coming to knowing.

Two key insights emerged from my autoethnographic somatic inquiry in particular: that the trauma of rape begins with the body; and that the body in the aftermath of rape is not passive and inert. These insights are the central premise of this book. A crucial outcome of the project as a whole is the finding that responses to the experience of rape in childhood manifest at the level of the body irrespective of whether discourse exists to appropriately frame or 'explain' those responses, and irrespective of whether women, or treating healthcare professionals, make connections between rape experience and aftermath bodily symptoms. With or without discourse, as Vicki Kirby (1997) suggests, 'the pressing facts of bodily existence still endure.'

My autoethnographic inquiry additionally revealed that despite experiencing a sense of detachment from my body for several decades, the re-integration of my unresolved trauma memory into my personal narrative and the re-establishment of my body-mind relationship post-rape were possible. My extensive engagement in the therapeutic and educative practice of Body-Mind Centering was a profound and healing experience. Through touch, movement, experiential anatomy, and guided imagination, this practice encouraged deep exploration of my unresolved trauma memories at a micro cellular level, liberating them from the frozen and murky shadowlands of my body. The therapeutic effect of attending to these somatic memories with professional support and with conscious awareness helped re-pattern my habitual behaviours, re-integrate my memories into my personal narrative, and alleviate my somatic symptoms. The work simultaneously acknowledged and affirmed feeling responses to, and experiential understandings of everyday life and their relevance to the development of embodied consciousness. In combination, the multiple aspects of my somatic inquiry led to the formation of a more integrated body and mind relationship and, as a consequence, a greater sense of cohesion.

> *3 June, 2011*
>
> *'I have a body now, Alice.'*

It is on this basis that I argue for the multidimensional, complex, irrepressible, and often intangible somatic expressions of rape trauma to be given equal status to those that emerge as empirically supported psychological disturbance in order to encourage wider opportunities for integrative healing that embrace the mind *and* the body. As neuroscientist, Candace Pert (1999, 274) argues, 'the body and the mind are not separate, and we cannot treat one without the other.'

Based on the outcomes of both my autoethnographic somatic inquiry and the somatic inquiry of the other participants in the project, my research challenges and attempts to destabilise dominant discursive understandings of rape trauma that persistently position the psychological impact of sexual violence in hierarchical relationship to impacts that manifest in, and are expressed through the body. This hierarchical and binary positioning has, I believe, the effect of sustaining the already culturally entrenched and artificial Cartesian separation of mind and body. It is my argument, based on the findings of my research, that this separation has the additional effect of perpetuating the profound sense of bodily detachment that girls and women often experience as a response to the violence of rape. Within a therapeutic context, the tendency to diminish or refuse to acknowledge the legitimacy of somatic disturbances as multiple, multidimensional, and unresolved expressions of rape trauma positions these bodily responses as 'medically unexplained' and reduces them to the realm of the psychosomatic.[2] In doing so it frames these responses as by-products of mental instability, as 'imagined' and therefore 'not real'. Within feminist scholarship, the allegiance to poststructuralist discursive and linguistic modes of understanding has failed to support women who consistently experience somatic symptoms in the aftermath of rape. I argue that, whether within the therapeutic domain, or within the academy, the tendency to attenuate bodily responses and the practice of positioning the body as without agency, as inert, and as 'passive, plastic matter' (Alaimo 2008, 237), inflicts further damage on already traumatised girls and women.

These findings have implications for feminist theorising, for rape trauma research and pedagogy, and for professionals working in the area of women's health.

***

The book is organised into twelve chapters. My use of journal extracts throughout many of the chapters is a purposeful strategy designed to weave together the ontological and the epistemological. In this way, I amplify the interconnectedness of ways of knowing and ways of coming to knowing

2 My use of the term 'psychosomatic' is based on the following definition: 'of, relating to, concerned with bodily symptoms caused by mental or emotional disturbance.' This definition is found at: <http://www.merriam-webster.com/dictionary/psychosomatic>.

in embodied and autoethnographic rape trauma research. Chapter One, *Philomela and me*, sweeps through time, moving between ancient myth and the contemporary storying of rape. In this chapter, to underpin the somatic focus of the book, I give a brief account of the biological changes a human body undergoes when experiencing trauma. I provide some personal context to locate myself as both researcher and researched. And finally, I introduce the body-based practice of Body-Mind Centering and the first of many journal extracts to illuminate the somatic inquiry process undertaken as a major methodological component of the research. Chapter Two, *The language and prevalence of sexual violence*, introduces the multiple definitions used in rape trauma research and provides the rationale behind my own choice of language in this book. Chapter Three, *What is somatics?* foregrounds the body-based focus of the book and provides an *entrée* into my early interest in somatics and trauma memory. I give a comprehensive outline of the history of somatics and the various fields of study within somatics. Chapter Four, *Correspondences*, examines the literature surrounding disclosure, shame, and trauma memory. Chapter Five, *Somatic narratives: participant somatic inquiry*, is the first of two chapters focusing specifically on the nine research participants. It examines the ethics and rationale behind the choice of participant information gathering methods. Chapter Six, *Somatic narratives and meaning-making*, brings together and examines the findings from the participant somatic inquiry phase of the research and the understandings that emerged as a result. These two chapters provide the broad-brush macro somatic context for the micro, cellular somatic investigation that occurs in the embodied autoethnographic chapters to follow. Chapter Seven, *Speaking of and with and through the raped body*, is the first of five chapters to focus on the autoethnographic inquiry. This chapter outlines the dual difficulties I faced as a woman and as an autoethnographic rape trauma and somatic researcher. Drawing on the work of Virginia Woolf, Drusilla Modjeska, Hélène Cixous, Anne Michaels and other women writers, I reveal the struggles I faced in the attempt to shape experience into words when bound by the limitations of masculinist language. Chapter Eight, *Ways of coming to knowing: a methodology of embodiment*, gives an overview of the experiential and embodied focus that underpinned the methodological framework of the research and introduces the multiple and complementary methods of inquiry that supported the research. Chapter Nine, *Coming to knowing through embodied autoethnography*, is a substantial chapter to reflect the primary autoethnographic component of the research. The chapter is divided into three sections. In the first section, I establish the feminist ethics behind my research, and discuss the ways autoethnography contributes to knowledge-making practices. The second section focuses on the process of my embodied research during the somatic inquiry phase of the research. In the third section, I examine the findings from the material gathered for this phase. Chapter Ten, *Coming to knowing through writing-as-inquiry*, uses the first of two arts-based methods of inquiry to examine the potential of this method for meaning-making. Chapter Eleven, *Coming to knowing through performance-making-as-inquiry*, focuses on the second of the two arts-based methods of inquiry and the rationale behind the choice of performance-making as a method. The chapter includes understandings gained from the performance-making as well as a creative reflection on the performance itself. Chapter Twelve, *Weaving the warp and the weft of the aftermath of childhood rape*, closes the book by bringing together the findings and implications of my research.

CHAPTER ONE

Philomela and me

> The tragedy of violence is that it erases its own violent degrees, so that we may erase the first act of violence as trifling even though it was decisive. All violence has a history.
>
> — HÉLÈNE CIXOUS[1]

> When we tell a story we exercise control, but in such a way as to leave a gap, an opening. It is a version, but never the final one. And perhaps we hope that the silences will be heard by someone else, and the story can continue, can be retold. When we write we offer the silence as much as the story. Words are the part of silence that can be spoken.
>
> — JEANETTE WINTERSON[2]

This chapter is about bodily transformation. It is also about the significant role trauma plays in the transformation of bodies. The chapter begins with a brief overview of the neurobiological processes a body undergoes when experiencing and responding to a traumatic event. It then juxtaposes ancient myth and contemporary story. The inclusion of the Philomela myth amplifies the cultural presence of gendered and silenced sexual violence across time and reveals the potential for the unconventional communication of rape trauma. The primary focus of the book is my autoethnographic story of rape in childhood. This has already been revealed in the Introduction and will be explored in this chapter to further establish the motivations

1 From: Cixous, Hélène (1993). *Three Steps on the Ladder of Writing*. New York: Columbia University Press (47).

2 From: Winterson, Jeanette (2011). *Why be happy when you can be normal?* London: Jonathan Cape (8).

behind my interest in somatic research and in the material conditions of the raped body.

Trauma and the transformation of bodies

Candace Pert (1999, 189) reveals that 'every second a massive information exchange is occurring in your body'. She describes these sites of exchange as a 'vast super highway' (310), a complex network of microscopic pathways transporting chemical information across membranous tissue throughout the human body. This network is known within anatomy and the physiological and neurobiological sciences to help facilitate the easeful and continuous flow of information as chemicals are released from different system areas of the body, including the immune, endocrine, nervous and gastro-intestinal systems (Tortora and Derrickson 2009). Pert observes this process generally takes place at the level of the subconscious as the 'intelligent information travels from one system to another' (189) via the complex, extensive, interconnecting, and interrelated molecular and neural network. This flow of information is designed to assist and maintain the body in a homeostatic, or balanced state (Pert 1999, Tortora and Derrickson 2009). As these homeostatic adjustments occur, the microscopic movement of the tissues and fluids responding to these adjustments creates micro-movement, and this movement 'may be felt as an inner-body sensation' (Ogden, Minton, and Pain 2006, 15).

During a traumatic event, there is an abundance of sensory information entering the body (Ogden, Minton, and Pain 2006, Levine 1997, Scaer 2001). The neuroscience and psychological literature surrounding trauma is clear that during, and in the immediate aftermath of a distressing event, dramatic neurobiological changes occur (Nijenhuis and van der Hart 1999, Ogden, Minton, and Pain 2006) and molecular exchanges take place (Herman 1992, Levine 1997, Pert 1999, Scaer 2001, van der Kolk 1994). During a traumatic event such as rape, especially if the event is perceived as a threat to the individual's survival, the body goes into over-drive. The sensory systems and neural pathways become hyper-stimulated (Ogden, Minton, and Pain 2006, Levine 1997, Rothschild 2000). The body under threat is flooded with an influx of sensory information via the obvious organs of sensory input such as the eyes, nose, ears and tongue as well as through the sense receptors of the skin and muscles. These receptors register kinaesthetic and pain information before feeding it into the nervous system. Deep within the membranes and tissues of the body, at a molecular level, and without consciousness, stress hormones and neurotransmitters are released to assist with the processing of this sensory information (Scaer, 2001). The body under threat becomes engulfed with chemicals. The body under threat is forced, instantaneously, to manage a plethora of information on a multitude of levels.

Amidst this maelstrom, when feelings, sensations, and chemical responses bombard every cell in an attempt to preserve life, if the 'fight, flight or freeze' response is unconsciously imitated, the influx of information can overwhelm the body. The body under threat is then in a state of distress. When this occurs, the experience and responses to it can move beyond explicit or conscious verbal memory to register and reside within implicit or subconscious non-verbal memory (van der Kolk 2007).[3] This is the point at which temporal perception can slow (Rothschild 2000, Herman 1992), pain sensation can be modified (Herman 1992, Rothschild 2000), division of the memory into sensory or emotional fragments of the event can occur (Brison 2002, Culbertson 1995, van der Kolk, van der Hart, and Marmar 2007, Ogden, Minton, and Pain 2006), and the energy generated by hyperarousal during the event can become trapped and 'frozen' in the body (Levine 1997, Pert 1999). In a primitive behavioural manoeuvre intended to protect the individual from further trauma, the shift of state to below the level of awareness can precipitate a sense of separation between the body and the mind (Nijenhuis and van der Hart 1999, Ogden, Minton, and Pain 2006). This altered state is thought to act as 'a psychological escape mechanism from fear' (Scaer 2001, 98).

3 Explicit and implicit memory will be discussed in Chapter Four, *Correspondences*.

Unfortunately, although it offers a means of evading the fear of personal threat, the involvement of implicit memory in trauma processing can have lasting consequences (Herman 1992, Levine 1997, Pert 1999, Scaer 2001, van der Kolk 1994) with disturbing self-perpetuating complications. By consigning this information, even partially, to the subconscious as a means of self-protection, the body impairs its own ability to make sense of the event, particularly in relation to somatic disturbance. The dissociated and fragmented memory of the experience, the physiological re-living of the trauma when stimulated, and the somatic and non-linguistic memories which can linger, serve to '"tell the story" without words, as though the body knows what they [the individuals] do not know cognitively' (Ogden, Minton, and Pain 2006, 3). This somatic disturbance in traumatised individuals' bodies can be explained as them 'reliving in their bodies the moments of terror that they cannot describe in words' (Herman 1992, 239). However, although their bodies may be alive with such moments of terror, the dis-integration of body and mind can make it difficult for individuals to interpret and connect somatic symptoms, when they emerge, with the traumatic event itself (Goodwin and Attias 1999).

***

For women, the stories of sexual violence fill the archives of our existence; they are ubiquitous. Anchored in antiquity, these stories spiral up through time, coil around the present, and send out long tendrils into the future. Some of these stories come to us as tales of the imagination, others as narratives of lived experience. While the story of Philomela, which you are about to read, is considered myth, and therefore perhaps a work of fiction, there are those who study myths who consider these as 'early science' and an attempt to explain the social and cultural conditions of the day (Hamilton 1998, 13). For these researchers, myths are regarded as 'socially powerful narratives', that 'occupy a highly significant position within the societies that retell them, in that they embody and explore the values, not just of individuals, but of social groups, and even whole communities' (Buxton 2004, 18). Viewed through this lens, ancient stories such as Philomela's become chronicles of early civilisation, accounts drawn not simply from imagination, lavishly embellished with fantasy, but stories whose origins lie in the remembering of the everyday. These stories move through time and cultures, carefully passed from person to person, family to family, generation to generation, to take their place in mythology.

As you read Philomela's story, hold in your mind that it is written as a myth although, as is often the case with myths, hidden within the story lines are shards of the familiar, sharp hooks that extend beyond the edges of the page, barbs that can snag your clothes as you pass by and cause you to pause. And be aware as you pause, in that very moment of stasis, as you hang suspended between experience and action, as your senses take in all around you, one of those shards may penetrate the fibres of your flesh, pierce your heart and flood your body with a blood red resonance, filling you, perhaps, with the heat of the known.

Philomela: A Greek myth[4]

Tereus of Thrace, a descendant of the god Mars and a wealthy king, sails with his powerful army to Athens to help quell an uprising by barbarians. Pandion, himself wealthy and the king of Athens, has two beautiful daughters, Procne and Philomela. Always looking at ways to strengthen his position, Pandion is keen to form an alliance with Tereus and offers his daughter Procne to him in marriage. The couple wed without Juno, the Graces or Hymen, the traditional bearers of marital blessings, in attendance. Instead, their union is overseen by the Furies, the goddesses of vengeance. The couple return to Thrace.

In time a son is born to Tereus and Procne. He is given the name Itys.

4 This summary is drawn from Ovid's *Metamorphoses*, Book 6, 230–243, 2004 edition translated by David Raeburn, published by Penguin Books Limited.

Twenty seasons pass and Procne pines more and more for the company of her sister. She pleads with Tereus to travel to Athens and seek permission from her father for Philomela to join her in Thrace.

Tereus sails again to Athens to the palace of the king. As Pandion greets him, the virginal Philomela appears bedecked with jewels, her beauty unparalleled. Tereus, his lustful nature aroused, cannot take his eyes from her and knowing he must have her for himself, doubles his efforts to persuade Pandion to allow her to travel with him. Philomela, excited at the prospect of seeing her sister again, pleads with her father for permission. Pandion reluctantly agrees and the two set off on the return journey.

Disembarking in Thrace, Tereus takes Philomela not to the palace where her sister patiently awaits her return, but rather, he drags her to a hut in a forest and rapes her. Philomela, when she recovers her senses, threatens to tell all who will listen about the rape. Tereus, enraged, draws his sword and cuts out her tongue so she may never speak of the rape or anything else ever again. Now mute, her tongue twitching at her feet, she is raped over and over again by Tereus who then leaves her locked in the hut and returns to the unsuspecting Procne. When Procne sees he is alone, he tells her Philomela is dead. Procne is overcome with grief.

Four seasons pass during which Philomela finds a loom in the cottage. Taking white thread she strings a warp and begins to weave a cloth. Woven into the cloth are purple signs that tell the story of her rape by Tereus. She entrusts the cloth to a woman, who carries it to the palace and places it into the hands of her grief-stricken sister. Procne is able to decipher the signs and so learns with horror the story of her sister's brutal rape by Tereus, her tyrant husband.

Desperate to find her sister and free her, Procne attends a nocturnal festival held by young women to worship Bacchus, the god of wine and revelry. There is much wildly excited dancing and music. Procne mimics this frenzied movement and rushes through the woods and finds the cottage where Philomela is being held captive. Procne frees her sister and together, their sisterly ties drawn closer by the violation that has taken place, they return to Thrace to seek retribution.

Back in the palace Procne is in a state of fury as she considers the many means with which she could punish Tereus. In her rage her eyes fall on her son Itys, who bears the facial features of his father. She knows she has found her revenge. Brandishing a sword, she drives it into her son's chest, killing him. The sisters proceed to remove the child's head and carve up his body. They cook his flesh in a stew and deliver this to Tereus. As Tereus gorges on the meal, he calls for his son but Procne announces that his son is with him already, that the meat in the stew, and now held captive in his belly, is the meat of his own flesh and blood. As he cries out in disbelief, Philomela rushes into the room, holding aloft the decapitated head of his son. As Tereus reaches for his sword in order to drive it into the bodies of the sisters to kill them, all three are transformed into birds. Tereus becomes a hoopoe, an ugly and ungainly large-beaked bird. Procne becomes a swallow, fated to swoop in silent arcs across the sky. And Philomela? She is transformed into a nightingale, destined to a life of song, beautiful but mournful laments that caress the ear and fill the heart.[5]

***

The story of Philomela is undoubtedly one of metamorphosis in the aftermath of trauma. But it is not just Philomela's transformation into a bird that is significant here. Philomela's story is also one of resilience, persistence, and imagination in the aftermath of repeated rape and silencing. My experiential knowing, and my research, reminds me that the trauma of rape and the silencing that can accompany it in the aftermath, each have a major role to play in shaping bodily relationships and in the transformation of lives. My purpose for including Philomela's story here is to foreground her quest, in the aftermath of sexual violence, to resist silencing and find a means of articulation with which to transmit her story. Philomela's resolution to her

5 It should be noted that Ovid was a Roman poet and in his *Metamorphoses*, Procne becomes a swallow and Philomela a nightingale. Some Greek variations of this myth differ, reversing the transformations so that Procne becomes a nightingale and Philomela a swallow.

silencing lies in the embodiment of her trauma through semiotic representation and in the trust she held in her sister to decipher that representation. I am fascinated by the many ways rape trauma can be expressed, through linguistic and non-linguistic means. I include Philomela's story, despite its location in mythology, to amplify the human endeavour to give voice to trauma in the aftermath of silenced sexual violence, to help reconceptualise what counts as legitimate trauma responses, to illustrate the critical need for vigilance to trauma's many forms of articulation if rape trauma is to be more readily identified and acknowledged, and through this, for the cultural silencing of rape trauma to be cracked open. I turn now from Philomela's story to my own.

A metamorphosis of another kind

I look at the slightly crumpled photograph taken during the summer of 1962 in Perth, Western Australia. I see a child, a girl, about three years of age. She wears a white loose dress without sleeves, white socks folded at the ankle, black patent leather Mary Jane style shoes. A white crocheted bag hangs from her left hand. Her blonde hair is held back from her face by a ribboned bow. She looks towards the camera, her face open, her cheeks rounded with her smile. Her feet do not align; one is placed slightly forward of the other giving her the appearance of being on the verge of walking towards the photographer. She looks a confident child, unafraid to stand in a city street and be photographed by a stranger.

I look at another photograph taken during the summer of 1975. I see a teenage girl. She sits on shaded grass in a backyard, her body side-on to the camera. Her back is curved, her shoulders hunched. She glares at the camera, strands of hair fall forward into her eyes, a scowl darkens her face. She looks angry and sullen.

I look at the third photograph taken in 1998. I see a woman. Her eyes are empty, her skin pale, bleached of lifeblood. No smile plays on her lips. Her shoulders are rounded in defeat. She looks hollow, listless, and remote.

As I hold these photographs in my hand I feel the confidence of the girl child, I feel the anger of the teenager and I feel the defeat of the woman. I feel that confidence, anger and defeat deep within my cells.

I feel those things because that girl-teenager-woman is me.

Philomela, time, and me

In juxtaposing Philomela's story with contemporary stories of the aftermath of rape in this book, I am disrupting and subverting time. By telling the story of the rape of Philomela alongside my own in this chapter and including snapshots of other women's stories of the aftermath of childhood rape later in the book, I wish to simultaneously stretch and compress past and present. Through these stories, I wish to play with time as I would a concertinaed instrument, slowly collapsing time and expanding it. In my hands, the plaintive tone of the in-breath and the sighing strains of the out-breath carry the notes of these narratives across the centuries, an ageless temporal accompaniment of pain and sorrow, fear, anger and shame.

I am reminded at this point of Marianne Hirsch (2008) and her work on the intergenerational transfer of traumatic memory. Her term 'postmemory' describes the absorption of inherited traumatic experience by successive generations. 'Postmemory,' she argues, 'describes the relationship of the second generation to powerful, often traumatic, experiences that preceded their births but that were nevertheless transmitted to them so deeply as to seem to constitute memories in their own right' (1). Hirsch (1997) writes:

> In my reading, postmemory is distinguished from memory by generational distance and from history by deep personal connection. Postmemory is a powerful and very particular form of memory precisely because its connection to its object or source is mediated not through recollection but through imaginative investment and creation. This is not to say that memory itself is unmediated, but that it is more directly connected to the past. Postmemory characterises the experience of those who grow up dominated by narratives that preceded their birth … I have developed this notion in relation to children of holocaust survivors, but I believe it may usefully describe other second-generation memories of cultural or collective traumatic events and experiences. (22)

While Hirsch is referring specifically to the intergenerational transfer of holocaust memories, feminist philosopher and rape survivor Susan Brison (2002) argues the concept applies equally to multiple generations of girls and women in relation to sexual violence. Brison has appropriated the term *postmemory* and applied it to girls' and women's internalisation of cultural myths and rape stories. 'Girls in our society' she argues, 'are raised with so many cautionary tales about rape that, even if we are not assaulted in childhood, we enter womanhood freighted with postmemories of sexual violence' (87). Brison extends this concept further by suggesting that postmemories reach into the future, serving to create a phenomena she names 'prememory' (87). Brison writes:

> The postmemory of rape not only haunts the present, however, as do the postmemories of children of Holocaust survivors, but also reaches into the future in the form of fear, a kind of prememory of what, at times, seems almost inevitable: one's own future experience of being raped. Postmemories (of other women's rapes) are transmuted into prememories (of one's own future rape) through early and ongoing socialization of girls and women, and both inflect the actual experiences and memories of rape survivors. (87)

Expanding on the ways in which postmemories are transmuted into prememories, Brison discusses the impact of computer-generated imagery or simulated sexual violence (commonly seen in multiple forms of popular culture), on the internalisation of rape scripts. She cites depictions of sexual violence on television, film, video and electronic gaming as examples of mediums easily accessible by girls and women and argues these contribute to girls' and women's *postmemory of rape* and the creation of *prememories*. Brison acknowledges that the use of the term *prememory* (2002, 88) is a contentious one with its suggestion of prescience. She states:

> The idea is as baffling as that of backwards causation – or anticipation of the past. Memory follows time's arrow into the past, whereas anticipation, in the form of fear or desire, points to the future. So how can one possibly remember the future? One way of trying to make sense of this paradox is to note that fear is a future-directed state and that it is primarily fear that is instilled by postmemory of rape. The backward-looking postmemory of rape thus, at every moment, turns into the forward-looking prememory of a feared future that someday will have been – a temporal correlate to the spatial paradox of the Mobius strip, in which what are apparently two surfaces fuse, at every point, into one. (88)

While Brison's concept – of women embodying the memory of a feared future that someday will have been – may be controversial for its paradoxical and seeming prophetic quality, research consistently demonstrates that high on the list of women's fear is the possibility of being raped (O'Donovan, Devilly, and Rapee 2007, Easteal 1992a). Could it be that stories such as Philomela's enter the psyches of girls and women as postmemories to portend, as prememories, the terrifying future experience of rape?

The story of Philomela is certainly a cautionary tale. The resilience the story embodies by its continuing presence in mythology is testament to the relevance it still bears for generations who preserve the story by entrusting its transmission to future generations. Acts of gendered sexual violence cannot be viewed as simply a modern phenomenon, nor can they be attributed only to the barbaric behaviour of past ancient civilisations. There is no conveniently specific temporal or spatial location for trauma of this nature. The story of Philomela, the story of me, the stories of sexual violence against girls and women that have been silenced, and those that have not, these stories exist within the pleats and folds of global history.

In the folding and unfolding of the stories of Philomela and me, and the stories of others who have experienced sexual violence, in the expanding and condensing that plays out across history, I wish to allow the movement and the breath necessary to open our minds and our bodies, to draw attention to the pervasiveness of gendered sexual violence in our culture and to the lived experience of sexually traumatised girls and women throughout millennia and across differing social, cultural and geographical landscapes.

The removal of the tongue and the torture of silence

Silence and silencing each play a significant role in the story of Philomela, in my own story, and in the stories of the nine women whose stories appear in this book. Indeed, self-silencing and sociocultural silencing practices are a common, pervasive and highly damaging outcome of sexual violence against girls and women (Ahrens 2006).

You will recall that Philomela was silenced by Tereus after he first raped her; he drew his sword and sliced her tongue from her mouth when she threatened to disclose the rape. Philomela suffered the torture of imposed muteness for four seasons until, determined to find an alternative means to communicate her sexual violation and outrage, she discovered a loom. This loom became Philomela's tongue, her means of articulation. She found a voice through images woven into cloth, in white warp and purple weft, her fingers deftly working to create the symbols of her pain like blood seeping beneath pale virginal flesh to form deep bruises of story.

My own tongue, in relation to the sexual violence I experienced in 1971, was metaphorically torn from my mouth by the lacerating words of my school friend, her sharp accusations of untruth and her slicing dismissal. My own muteness from that point, both externally imposed and simultaneously self-imposed, lasted rather longer than four seasons. For too many years and to the eventual detriment of my health, I suppressed the memories of my traumatic experience from the moment my disclosure was met with disbelief, burying these deep within my body, and attempting to conduct my life as if they never existed.

Sadly, I was naively confident in my view that the self-imposed silencing of my experience would be enough to sustain my need for self-protection. In time, coupled with my despotic rule over my body, this conscious suppression of memory, albeit instituted and sustained as a form of self-care, became a form of torture in itself as the memories resisted constraint, wove their way through my cells, and played out through the loom of my body.

The twin burdens

I introduce at this point the first of many research journal extracts. The following extract was written several days after I attended a Body-Mind Centering hands-on session with Alice Cummins and eight months after I began my autoethnographic somatic inquiry process. Alice is the Body-Mind Centering practitioner, movement educator, and dance artist with whom I developed a close therapeutic relationship during the course of the somatic inquiry phase of my research. We also developed a creative collaborative partnership, working together on the development of *aperture*, which emerged as a solo theatre performance work. I include the following extract to graphically illustrate the irrepressible, enduring and distressing nature of the somatic impact of childhood rape.

9 March, 2011

I'm hesitating here in this writing. Although it is now Wednesday and the next experience I know I must describe was last Friday (the 4th), I can feel fear and dread spreading through my body. I (my psyche?) my body (my memory centre?) doesn't want to participate in the writing of this experience. I/we are simultaneously recoiling, united in the still raw and, as yet, only partially processed sensations and emotions.

It's difficult to distinguish between my two states, the somatic and the psychological. Each is clamouring for attention. Each is responding differently. Each is real.

My somatic state is one of extreme agitation. My body position has altered. I'm pressing back and away from the keyboard of my laptop. My breathing is shallower. I can feel the quickened beat of my heart beneath the fabric of my t-shirt. My skin is clammy. My neck muscles have tensed. My gut is clenched. The tick of the clock in the kitchen is irritating my ears. I want to throw something at it. I think of the 'flight, fight or freeze' response. I don't want to fight. I want to flee. My body is preparing for flight. I can feel my blood shrinking from my periphery. I can feel bubbles of oxygen rushing towards my viscera. My scalp is tingling. My flesh is alive. I feel dreadful and ill.

My mind is chaotic, my thoughts darting about like so many insects. My mind has no wish to settle and contemplate and taste. My mind is dodging the images that force their way into my consciousness as they rise from the semantic enveloping of this experience. Double images, triple images of the past and the present. The girl-child-me. The woman-adult-me. The girl-me within the woman-me. Inextricably linked, entwined, inseparable. Each lying on their backs. Each experiencing her own private terror. I must pause for a moment and breathe before I write of the hands-on session[1] which shifted everything.

***

Alice said that she felt she wanted to place her hands on the area of my collarbones. She asked if this would be okay. I said that I didn't know until she tried. She rested her hands lightly over my collarbones. She asked if this felt okay. Her hands immediately felt threatening. My body flooded with heat and cold. It roiled with fear as it became instantly overwhelmed with powerful tingling, sparking, sweeping, prickling, gurgling sensations. I wondered, fleetingly, how long I could tolerate having her hands there. Then, suddenly, without any conscious intention, my left hand whipped up from the floor and pulled Alice's hand away. I tried to throw it off but she held me. I was in a deeply distressed state.

I couldn't breathe. I kept swallowing the saliva that gushed up from my throat. I was trembling uncontrollably. I heard Alice's voice from somewhere above me.

'Brenda, can you tell me what's happening?'

I was gulping in air. I couldn't speak. I couldn't organise myself in any way other than to suck in air.

'Try'

I gulped and swallowed, gulped and swallowed.

'I thought I was going to die'

Trauma and memory researcher Cathy Caruth (1996) asks:

> Is the trauma the encounter with death, or the ongoing experience of having survived it? At the core of these stories … is thus a kind of double telling, the oscillation between a *crisis of death* and the correlative *crisis of life*: between the story of the unbearable nature of an event and the story of the unbearable nature of its survival. (7)

Clearly, what I experienced on those two occasions in 1971 were encounters I perceived as life threatening. Clearly, I survived these encounters with death. However, as Cathy Caruth (1996) observes, there is an oscillating movement that takes place in the space between the perception of imminent death and the survival that follows, a movement which is deeply unsettling and distressing. My own experience then, carries this twin burden of encountering a life-threatening event and surviving it. My survival, however, meant conscious denial and suppression of my traumatic memories, and conscious denial and suppression of my traumatic memories involved the imposition of decades-long self-silencing practices, all of which exacerbated my now fragile sense of self and affected how I viewed my place in the world. It also shattered my mind-and-body relationship. These twin burdens, of facing the possibility of death and surviving it, led to a life-long pattern of self-protection that had unintended consequences.

Rape narratives echoing in the aftermath

The literature is clear that witnessing or experiencing a traumatic event can lead to the eventual expression of the memory of that experience as a suite of somatic or body-based symptoms. These symptoms can emerge sometimes months or years after the event itself (van der Kolk 2007, Levine 1997). In relation to sexual trauma, particularly when experienced in childhood and especially if involving a need for secrecy, the silencing impact of this imperative can impair an individual's ability to integrate the experience fully. As trauma researcher Judith Herman (1992) notes, even if the individual has 'banished it [the trauma experience] from her mind, she continues to register its effects in her body' (Herman 1992, 108). Just as an echo continues to resonate long after the production of the original sound, body-held trauma memory can also continue to resonate long after the experiencing of the original event, especially if it has been silenced in some way or remains unresolved and dis-integrated.

In the autoethnographic component of the research, my deeply personal and complex story pivots on the conscious denial of trauma memory and its eventual expression in my body. It also pivots on silence. In addition to the externally imposed silencing that followed the trauma I endured in 1971, the self-silencing practice that I adopted as a response to this familial and sociocultural silencing has contributed to the complexity of my story. I believe silencing directly influenced the irrepressible and enduring unresolved nature of my trauma.

My evolving understandings of the somatic landscape of my rape aftermath was, at times, difficult research territory to navigate, reliant as it was on a process of trust (of the self and crucially, of others), deep inner listening through raised somatic awareness, conscious experiencing and re-experiencing of the ground of my trauma, the re-integration of my trauma memory, and self-reflexivity. During some of the autoethnographic exploration, I travelled across unchartered and shifting landscapes, an evolving topography featuring deep chasms and dark ravines, sheer-faced cliffs, raging swollen rivers, swallowing whirlpools, insurmountable ranges and vast desolate dunes. At other times though, this somatic landscape proved profoundly moving in its beauty, a complex and deeply intelligent cellular environment, breathtaking in its transformative potential and its capacity for resilience, renewal, and reciprocity. As I write, several years after I began the research for this book, my body remains in many ways a mysterious internal terrain, although I am less fearful of it now. By venturing into this cellular landscape through the somatic inquiry[6] process undertaken as a major part of the research, I am now able to perceive my body's miraculous capacity to hold paradox and contradiction alongside profound clarity. I

6 The somatic inquiry method will be examined in Chapter Nine, *Coming to knowing through embodied autoethnography*.

admire my body's ability to remind but also to reassure. I am in awe of the depth of knowledge to be found in my body. In a sense, the cellular landscape has itself become my most skilful teacher.

To help guide you through this difficult and complex somatic territory, I have chosen to use the naturally occurring phenomenon of the echo. I have adapted the characteristics and features of this phenomenon for two purposes. Firstly, as a mature aged woman, the echo metaphor acts as a descriptor for my own re-experiencing of body-held unresolved trauma memory first experienced in childhood. The repetitious nature of the echo will serve to symbolise the repeated dissonance I continue to experience decades beyond the nights of the rapes themselves. I have borrowed the use of the echo metaphor from the work of feminist academic Judith Greenberg (1998). In her research, concerning representations of trauma and memory, Greenberg draws a parallel between the common and persistent recurring symptoms of Post Traumatic Stress Disorder and the mythical story of Narcissus and Echo.[7] She argues that Echo's story is 'a story of separation from one's very body due to grief and the persistence of belated and fragmentary resonances in the aftermath of disembodiment' (319). It is also a story of incoherence through the loss of verbal autonomy.

In the myth, Echo's disembodiment was a response to her loss of free voice as well as the grief she incurred as a result of her humiliation and shame. In many ways, her story mirrors my own story of loss and grief in the wake of my trauma as I struggled to make sense of the violations I had endured. Echo's disembodiment mirrors too the mind and body separation I actively engaged in as a pragmatic and self-care response in the rape aftermath. The belated and fragmentary resonances I continue to experience as an adult I read as my body's unresolved and dis-integrated echoes of that original trauma. Although I have borrowed this metaphor from Greenberg, I would like to stress that I do not wish to examine my somatic memories and experiences, nor those of the other women in this book, through the lens of Post Traumatic Stress Disorder. Rather, my intention is to offer each

7 In this work, Judith Greenberg has drawn on the Allen Mandelbaum translation of Ovid's *Metamorphoses* (New York: Harcourt, Brace, and Company).

of the lived subjective experiences as illustrations of the diversity present within the range of somatic responses to amplify the pervasiveness and longevity of body-held rape-related childhood trauma and to amplify the breadth of its multiple and repeated manifestations. I do not wish to medicalise or pathologise these experiences. Rather, I want to allow them to reveal their complexity through multiple resounding voices. The mythical story of Echo's loss of free voice, her grief, her disembodiment, and her life of repetition seems entirely appropriate in this context.

Furthermore, the echo metaphor allows the imagination the space to hear my story and the stories of the other women as both acoustical and somatic reverberations of a gendered phenomenon. The stories of the nine women, all raped as children, have echoes of their own. For most of them, like me, the memory of their childhood experiences continues to resonate through their bodies long after the acts of violence themselves. By including these women's stories, held in the imagination as echoes, the book will resound with multiple voices, each echoing voice resonating with the somatic ramifications of sexual violence incurred in childhood. I wish to stress here that the inclusion of the women's stories is not intended as a mimetic strategy. I do not wish to diminish the specificity of their personal experiences or to universalise the aftermath experience of childhood rape through the use of a metaphor that implies exact replication and repetition. Rather, I wish to allow the chapters to ripple and reverberate with a cacophony of personal echoes which may, or may not overlap.[8] These echoes will help reflect the multiplicity of experience and the diversity of response to childhood rape. At times these echoes will bear no resemblance to one another, at other times they may appear to converge. I do not believe this is an attempt on my part to universalise experience. If at times these echoes reverberate and meet at an intersecting point, or if they begin to layer one upon another as an acoustical repetition might, this will serve to reinforce Herman's (1992) finding that the effects of (childhood) trauma

8 Chapter Six, *Somatic narratives and meaning-making* will examine the somatic symptoms experienced by the women in relation to my own suite of symptoms.

continue to register in (adult) bodies long after the event itself, even if the memory of the event has been driven from consciousness and lies in shadow.

Having made this point, the focus of this book being what it is, I feel it is impossible to ignore one strand of individual experience that winds, helix-like, around and through the multiple narratives I have gathered. That strand is tied of course to our experiencing of rape in childhood. This we have in common. However, this is the only point at which our stories intentionally intersect in a kind of universal coming together. The persistent and repetitious expressions and articulations of childhood trauma in the adult body, imagined and heard by the reader as a series of metaphoric echoes of lived experience, will provide an embodied entry point into the variety of responses to, and enduring impact of, childhood rape.

My story has already initiated the first reverberation. As the chapters progress, I draw in the stories of the other women to sit in the imagination alongside my own. My hope is, as the stories each touch and rebound, they eventually permeate the membrane of this book to synthesise with the multitudinous echoing stories of other women reverberating within our culture, across cultures, and throughout history. For now though, I continue with my own story and the path that led me to becoming a somatic researcher.

A somatic researcher emerges

On the eve of the new millennium, I knew without doubt that I was on the verge of collapse, rapidly losing my battle with the personal erosion and subsidence that had been destabilising me over time. Unlike the celebratory world around me whose escape from the chaos of global technological collapse was already clear, my own fall into chaos that champagne-midnight-hour seemed ineluctable.

The final decade of the previous millennium had challenged me deeply both physically and emotionally. I had given birth to three children, suffered the loss of two pregnancies to miscarriage, had surgery for a melanoma on my breast as well as treatment for cervical cancer, and was still living with the effects of an eating disorder that developed in my early twenties. Other, more minor illnesses had erupted from and resolved back into my body. I began to feel physically vulnerable. In 1997, I discovered a c the size of a golf ball in the side of my neck. After its removal in hospital and following a biopsy, the lump – a cyst – was found to contain a small secondary malignant tumour. Its primary parent was traced to my thyroid gland. Less than a week later I was back in a different hospital, on an oncology ward, having the butterfly-shaped gland removed, the tumour nestled in one of its wings.

I somehow held myself together following this surgery, although cracks were beginning to appear. I barely endured the follow-up treatment which left me on the edge of terror and alone in a large nuclear radiation isolation ward for four days. During this time my body had been filled with radioactive iodine and was highly dangerous to anyone who came near. The nurse who bravely attended me did so wearing a lead cover-all. My small number of visitors stood behind a thick lead screen, their bodies protected from the radioactivity emanating from mine. My clothing and books were destroyed after I was discharged.

In the aftermath of my treatment, it was a different story. With a large red scar stretching tight and angry across the base of my throat, I was reminded daily of my mortality. I suffered a complete loss of faith in my body. My reserves of strength grew exhausted, my confidence fell in tatters. I began to experience increasing feelings of hopelessness and helplessness and greater disconnection and detachment from my body. My grip on normality became tenuous, stability spilling through my fingers like fine sand. I was consumed with sadness.

I finally sought help when the fault-line of my internal landscape was wrenched apart by a sorrow so great I was unable to contain it. When grief eventually overwhelmed me, forced me sobbing to my kitchen floor and curled me into a foetal shape, it was the faces of my stunned and silent young children that drove me to my medical centre. My GP became the first professional person I 'officially' disclosed to. I had been going to him for some years but had never been able to tell him of my rape experience. He listened quietly and empathically and wrote out a referral to my first clinical psychologist. Subsequently diagnosed with severe clinical depression,

I tried to manage on weekly therapy sessions without any reliance on pharmaceutical intervention. When my depression became intolerable, I was eventually forced to concede that I needed the help of drugs in order to clear my mind and level my mood. I was a reluctant anti-depressant user. In time the drugs helped my thoughts feel less congested and dark and this helped my daily life become a little more manageable. It was necessary for me to take these drugs for three years.

During what became five years of almost weekly therapy, I was fortunate to have been in the care of two intelligent, empathetic and very patient female clinical psychologists. They had different therapeutic approaches. Towards the end of a very difficult first year of treatment, the first of these psychologists asked me if I had any unfulfilled dreams. I told her that I had always harboured a secret desire to go to university. She suggested that I give it a try. Having left school in year eleven, and with my self-esteem and self-confidence shattered, the suggestion seemed ludicrous. She gently persisted. After many weeks, I eventually set my self the task of returning to learning via evening classes at a local adult learning centre.

I cannot explain just how much courage it took to make this decision and to follow it through. I had become rather reclusive since developing severe clinical depression and knew that anything that took me out of the home would be extremely challenging. It had been twenty-four years since I had last been a distracted and disengaged adolescent student. Despite this, somehow I enrolled in two courses. These were being offered, ironically, at my old high school which seemed to have followed my own progression to adulthood and had grown into a college for mature aged students. My unit selections were driven by pragmatism and interest. I chose a unit in basic computer skills because I had none at all; and I chose Year 11 Human Biology because this subject had held my interest in high school.

I recall feeling deeply anxious in the first weeks of these courses. My hands trembled so violently in the computer class that I could barely hold the 'mouse', and the notes I took in my Human Biology classes were almost illegible. I persevered however, finding that the learning environment made me feel less hopeless. After surprising myself and successfully completing these units, the following year I enrolled in a Tertiary Entrance Examination course involving a year of part-time study. Again, I chose a Human Biology unit and added English. Despite my small success the previous year, my self-esteem and sense of self were still in poor shape at this time. During an early English class, when asked to write a page on ourselves, I couldn't bring my pen to the page. I was literally unable to find any words to describe myself. Things improved a little as the year progressed and I discovered a rekindled interest in writing. I passed my entrance exam that year well enough to convince myself that I could attempt that dreamed-of university degree.

In 2002, I enrolled part-time at Edith Cowan University in Western Australian in a Bachelor of Social Science degree majoring in Women's Studies. During my undergraduate years, and as a result of my psychotherapy, I made small inroads into my increasing desire to explore my childhood sexual trauma through writing. With a major in Women's Studies there was scope to attempt this, even tangentially, and I did so occasionally when opportunities presented themselves. By the end of my degree in 2007, although I hadn't spoken of my rape history, I found I was able to write a little of my experience when it seemed relevant. Each time I did this, however, I felt exposed, highly vulnerable and, on a somatic level, deeply agitated. When my assignments were returned, I was relieved to find that my limited disclosures were met with respect and empathy by my lecturers and I was gaining good marks. My self-esteem slowly grew and my self-belief developed. I finished my undergraduate degree in 2007 and, thrillingly, was invited to undertake an Honours degree.

I plunged into my rape trauma history and at the end of 2008, completed my autoethnographic Honours research. This reflective and reflexive feminist project examined the multiple ramifications of silenced childhood rape, locating my own experience within a broader socio-cultural-political narrative. The creative component of my research explored some of the short-term and long-term familial and social impacts of my rape experience in terms of the impact of silencing, as well as some of the physical and psychological manifestations that had emerged in the aftermath as a result of the silencing.

While the project was incredibly challenging, confronting and painful, and had, on occasion, left me feeling raw and exposed, it was also an extraordinarily empowering and complex period of research. By engaging an autoethnographic methodology and by choosing to explore my personal experience, in part, within a creative writing paradigm, I had also chosen a mode of enquiry that allowed me to write easily and, for the most part without struggle, thereby facilitating the liberation of my narratives from the corporeal fortress they had been imprisoned in. In doing so I was able to crack open the silence that had alternately whispered and roared within me since I was eleven years of age.

By weaving back and forth within memory both temporally and spatially, by exploring my interiority both through and with my body and mind via the lens of my silenced trauma, I was able to engage reflexively with my experience, gaining new insights and deepening my understandings. I found that on many occasions when I sat down to write, the words of my narratives erupted from me, like startled flocks of migrating birds flying across the landscape of my bodymind, my breath under their wings guiding them beyond my fingertips to rest and regroup on the page. These narratives flew from my body in no particular order and without particular direction from me, often leaving me breathless from the seeming effortlessness of their outpouring. I recall recording these eruptions with frantic diligence, as though I mustn't lose a word. It was as if my visibility, my credibility relied on them, as if the act of writing my story in ink could render my life indelible, impossible to erase again, and in doing so, it would be possible for me to exist fully, beyond the secrecy and darkness of my past.

Other passages required considerable effort and a more delicate touch. These I wrote in the third person. In doing this I was able to create a space for my body to breathe and calm itself, a buffer zone between the emergence of the languaged stories from my bodymind memory and the writing of them, an illusory space of relative safety. I was completely aware that by writing in the third person, I was engaging in a self-protective behaviour to guard against the re-traumatising potential of these trauma memories. I was aware, too, that the third person location deepened the illusion of safety allowing me to manoeuvre my story in other ways.

In removing the bodymind of the experiencing I/me from the intimacy of the personal and into the third person location, I was also taking the I/me of my bodymind away from direct disclosure. In other words, the fleshed, present, distinct and subjective I/me of the autoethnographic researcher/writer was able to slide into the shadows of the un-fleshed, indistinct and removed she/her of the viewed object, nudging these sections of the narrative into a more universal and less personal space, thereby masking the particularity of the event/s described. It seems that in order to write a personal narrative of sexual violation and disintegration with an uninhibited hand, I had to undergo a metamorphosis of sorts. The I/me/her/she writerly dance helped facilitate the choreographic movement necessary to undergo this transformation whilst also driving these narratives back and forth between the personal and the political.

Engaging these writing strategies during my Honours project meant that I was able to reveal the chaos present in my body and mind post-rape as well as the disconnection and detached behaviour that became entrenched in the aftermath. The writing disrupted chronology and mirrored shattered identity. Temporally and spatially my words became restless birds, unable to perch for too long, nor in one place (Mercer 2012). Slipping in and out of the first and third person, they struggled to maintain a fixed identity, or perhaps, refused one.

Tami Spry (2011, 28) speaks of the 'performative-I', 'performative-I disposition',[9] and 'performative-I persona' of autoethnographic writing and performance-making. Spry applies these concepts to the autoethnographic researcher/performer who moves between and through a series of stages of becoming as she interprets experiential knowledge, cultural context, and linguistic representation while seeking to embody the persona that emerges in performance. Although I did not discover the work of Spry until I took up my doctoral project, I recognise now that her formally captured performative states were precisely those I moved in and out of during my Honours work. The I/me/her/she dance I describe above offered a place of temporal pause as I engaged with my story and created the self-protection necessary to remain within my story long enough to write of it.

The multiple writing techniques I engaged in and strategies I developed and found essential in order to research and complete this Honours project equipped me with the skills to proceed to a more substantial exploration of

9 Chapter Eleven, *Coming to knowing through performance-making-as-inquiry* discusses these terms further.

childhood sexual trauma in 2009. The earlier project had cemented in me a continuing interest in the multiple impacts of childhood sexual trauma but had also sharpened my curiosity specifically in relation to the impact of the memory of childhood sexual trauma on the adult female body. The move from the broader familial, sociocultural, psychological, and physiological impacts of childhood rape to include a focus on the somatic aftermath in a doctoral project seemed a natural and increasingly desirable progression.

***

Early in 2010, still uncertain of how I would attempt to explore the autoethnographic component of my project, and during a conversation about my research with a colleague and friend, mention was made of the somatic practice of Body-Mind Centering and, more specifically, the work of practitioner, Alice Cummins. I'd not heard of either.

After a Google search for both the Body-Mind Centering Association and Alice Cummins to learn more about each, I read the homepages of their respective web sites and something inside me lurched. I was immediately and deeply moved by the words used to describe the work. Phrases such as *body-based language* and *embodiment* (BMC 2012), *cellular knowing*, *refined awareness* and *sensory integration* (Cummins 2012), burrowed comfortingly into me and I felt the curious and unexplainable stirrings of a sensation of conversance, of 'deep rememberings' (McLaren 2001b, 63). I experienced these sensations as loosely recognised though indistinct, entirely spontaneous and surprisingly visceral. I recall wondering at the time why it was that I felt so moved by this language, why these particular words held the power to evoke such a strong feeling response. In amongst the tangle of language and bodily response however, I intuitively understood this curious yet reassuringly familiar embodied response had confirmed for me that here was an approach to inquiry that would simultaneously hold me in my engagement with my somatic self, whilst also satisfying my requirement for intellectual and academic rigor.

I had found my researcher niche.

CHAPTER TWO

The language and prevalence of sexual violence

> The inclination for avowal, the desire for avowal, the yearning to taste the taste of avowal, is what compels us to write: both the need to avow and its impossibility. Because most of the time the moment we avow we fall into the snare of atonement: confession-and forgetfulness. Confession is the worst thing: it disavows what it avows.
>
> — HÉLÈNE CIXOUS[1]

This chapter includes many definitions: of sexual violence, of rape, of sexual assault, of sexual trauma. I have consciously included these definitions, with their explicit language and unsettling and confronting imagery, as a reminder of the focus of this book. This book is about the adult female body in the aftermath of childhood sexual violence. These definitions act as an *aide-memoire* for the range of sexual violations that lie behind the somatic aftermath narratives contained in these chapters.

Alongside some of these definitions, I have included extracts from the narratives of nine women. It is my multiple intention for these extracts to disrupt the accumulative narrative of the formal and clinical definitions, to illuminate the void beyond the definitions, and to help create embodied links between the de-personalised definitions and the subjective embodied reality of experience. The voices of the women help shed light on the space between the institutionalised and formal discursive constructions of sexual violence and lived reality to make connections between states of being, between existing discourses, and between what is said and what

1 From: Cixous, Hélène (1993). *Three Steps on the Ladder of Writing*. New York: Columbia University Press (45).

remains culturally silenced. The chapter includes discussion on the reality and impact of sexual trauma and concludes with a stark acknowledgment of the prevalence of sexual violence.

Terminology

The literature surrounding sexual violence is peppered with terms: rape, sexual assault, sexual abuse, sexual trauma, coerced sexual activity, unwanted sexual contact, indecent assault. Although the title of this book uses the term 'rape', in the body of the book I refer to crimes of a sexually violent nature variously as rape, sexual violence, sexual assault, sexual violation and sexual trauma. I use these terms interchangeably with full consciousness. By choosing to use multiple terms I acknowledge the multiple subjectivities present and the resulting broad range of interpretations possible in relation to the experiencing of violence of this sort. I wish to be sensitive to the subjective nature of sexually violent experience and have no desire to preclude readers from identifying with the topic of this book by insisting on the use of one term only.

My own preference is to describe my childhood experience as 'rape', although I also use other terms throughout the chapters depending on the context in which I write. Mary Koss (2005, 101) notes 'Feminist legal scholars have argued that the word *rape* is more explicit, politically evocative, and better at capturing the outrage and shame that is historically associated with sexual violation'. I choose to use this word not only for these reasons but also because it was the word 'rape' that provided me, four years beyond the year of my sexual violations, with a framework in which to locate my experience and thus understand what had happened to me. It is the word 'rape' that gathered together the many disturbing elements of my experience and offered me clarity. For me, it is a word resonant with meaning. It is one that enabled the eventual public expression of my experience although nearly thirty years elapsed before I was able to form this word in my mouth and launch it from my vocal chords. Because 'rape' is not the preferred term for other researchers and victims, wherever I refer to the literature and research material, I use whatever term appears in those sources. When I include information from the women, I use the term they have used to describe their own subjective experiences.

I also choose to describe myself as a 'victim' of childhood rape. The term 'survivor' does not adequately capture the space of vulnerability I occupied when I was raped, nor does it embody the trauma, both somatic and psychological, that I experienced and continue to experience in the aftermath. The longer terms, 'victim/survivor' and 'women who have experienced sexual violence', which sometimes appear in the literature, I find rather cumbersome and unwieldy. The former looks and sounds oppositional and the latter seems somehow to hold me in the past-tense (*women who have*) rather than extending the experience beyond the event itself and into the space of the aftermath. From my perspective, these terms ignore the aftermath of childhood rape. The experience did not end when the perpetrator left the room. I carried this experience through to adulthood, victim to its wanton vagaries and its cruel and controlling hand. My decision, then, is to use the term 'victim' in relation to my own experience. I do, however, use both 'survivor' and 'women who have experienced sexual violence' in the book. In doing so, I acknowledge the range of subjectivities and personal preferences of my participants and accommodate any ongoing legal or methodological requirements in place in other studies.

Multiple definitions of experience

There is no universal definition of rape (Fileborn 2011). Definitions vary depending on global location (WHO 2002) and the context in which they are used (Tarczon and Quadara 2012). While there may be no uniformity of definition, it is useful to have a general understanding of the range of definitions for these key terms. Multiple definitions are given below for sexual violence, rape and sexual assault, and sexual trauma.

Sexual violence

> *'I was orally raped repeatedly at age 4.'*
> — PATRICIA

Sexual violence is criminal violence that is perpetrated against an individual without their consent (CDC 2009) and covers a wide range of sexually specific acts. The World Health Organisation (WHO and PAHO 2012) states:

> Sexual violence encompasses acts that range from verbal harassment to forced penetration, and an array of types of coercion, from social pressure and intimidation to physical force. Sexual violence includes, but is not limited to:
> - rape within marriage or dating relationships;
> - rape by strangers or acquaintances;
> - unwanted sexual advances or sexual harassment (at school, work etc.);
> - systematic rape, sexual slavery and other forms of violence, which are particularly common in armed conflicts (e.g. forced impregnation);
> - sexual abuse of mentally or physically disabled people;
> - rape and sexual abuse of children; and
> - 'customary' forms of sexual violence, such as forced marriage or cohabitation and wife inheritance

> *'I have continuously experienced chronic pain & have PTSD. Had gynae problems, migraine & of course the inevitable long periods of major depression. I can now – this far on – put the majority of pretty much all those health issues down the events in my childhood.'*
> — PHILIPA

A report published by the Australian Institute of Criminology (Cook, David, and Grant 2001, ix) defines sexual violence as 'unwanted touching, sexual harassment and intimidation, coerced sexual activity, sexual assault and rape'.

Rape and sexual assault

Much of the literature surrounding sexual violence makes no distinction between rape and sexual assault. The two terms are used interchangeably. Neame and Heenan (2003) acknowledge the interchangeablilty of these terms and discuss a range of factors influencing their use. They note that some researchers will adopt the legal definitions provided by the relevant state or territories while others may choose wider definitions to enable a broader range of experiences to be gathered.

The Australian Bureau of Statistics (Australian Bureau of Statistics 2012) prefers the term *sexual assault* when conducting surveys. The following definition of sexual assault appears in its Crime Victimisation survey:

> An act of a sexual nature carried out against a person's will, through the use of physical force, intimidation or coercion, or the attempt to carry out these acts. Includes all incidents of a sexual nature involving physical contact and carried out without the victim's consent, any forced sexual activity such as rape, attempted rape or indecent assault (such as being touched inside clothing or intentional rubbing of genitals against the victim) and assault with the intent to sexually assault. Also includes any incidents that may have occurred at the victim's place of work. Excludes sexual harassment that did not lead to an assault. Only people aged 18 years and over were asked questions about sexual assault.

> *'I cannot eat tapioca or the other dessert which is similar without wanting to physically throw up because the texture and flavour is reminiscent of semen.'*
>
> — CAROL

The Sexual Assault Resource Centre in Western Australia (SARC 2013) gives the following definition for sexual assault:

> Sexual assault can be a violent, unexpected, traumatic and sometimes life threatening event or series of events. Sexual assault is ANY unwanted sexual act or behaviour which is threatening, violent, forced or coercive and to which a person has not given consent or was not able to give consent. Examples include:
>
> - Putting a penis, object or other parts of the body into someone's mouth, anus or vagina.
> - Being forced to give or receive oral sex – putting a penis into someone's mouth.
> - Being forced to masturbate or forced to watch someone masturbate.
> - Unwanted sexual touching – on private part of the body.
> - Sexual harassment – making inappropriate sexual comments
> - Voyeurism – someone exposing themselves to you.
> - Making someone watch a sexual act or pornography.

Sexual trauma

Roth and Lebowitz (1988) define sexual trauma as:

> rape, sexual assault, non-familial childhood sexual abuse, and incest. Rape and sexual assault are distinguishable in terms of the nature of sexual acts that occurred. This distinction is made largely for legal purposes, as there is no evidence that sexual assault and rape are different from a psychological point of view. (79)

Sexual violence researchers Yuan, Koss and Stone (2006) suggest that the term sexual trauma may be adopted by some women as it is 'less stigmatising' and for some 'may promote healing by acknowledging the violent act on the individual's well-being'.

***

As I have demonstrated, there is no single definition for sexual violence. Multiple definitions covering a range of sexually violent acts exist and are used by a variety of government and non-government institutions. The purpose of providing an overview of the range of definitions in current use is to remind the reader of the sorts of sexually violent experiences that have contributed to the bodily disturbance of the women in this book. The somatic aftermath narratives held in these chapters all emerged from these sorts of experiences. These definitions and the extracts that sit alongside them offer the imagination of the reader explicit information. I offer no apology for this. This is the reality of sexual violence.

Sexual violence: The gendered reality and impact

What hides beyond the margins of gender-neutral definitions is that rape is not simply a crime of a sexual nature carried out against a *person's* will. In reality, rape is a gender-based crime (Fileborn 2011). That is, it is a crime aimed almost exclusively towards girls and women (Brownmiller 1976, Freedman 2006, Rozee and Koss 2001, Cook, David, and Grant 2001).

In Australia in 2011–12, of the cases recorded by state and territory police, 85 per cent of sexual assault victims were female (Australian Bureau of Statistics 2012). In addition to being a crime that targets girls and women, rape is also a crime predominately perpetrated by men, and committed more often by a man known to the victim (Breitenbecher 2006, AIC 2007). It is a crime of violence that targets young girls in particular (Astbury 2006b) and occurs more often in private dwellings (AIC 2007, Cook, David, and Grant 2001). What also lies unseen within these definitions is that rape and other forms of sexual violence against girls and women are now recognised as human rights violations of the worst kind (Herman 1992) with consequences that can be far-reaching and devastating in their impact (Pennebaker and Stone 2004).

> *'I did not tell anybody after it happened. The first time I spoke to a health care professional about being raped as a child was 16 years later.'*
>
> — KATE

It is well established that sexual violence and its aftermath have the potential to cause prolonged and profound suffering in women and girls who are subjected to such trauma (Anderson and Doherty 2008, Astbury 2006b, Campbell and Wasco 2005, Chivers-Wilson 2006, Esposito 2005, Koss and Figueredo 2004, Morrison, Quadara, and Boyd 2007). The literature is clear that fear of rape or other forms of sexual violence is an everyday presence in the minds and lives of girls and women (Easteal 1992a, Yodanis 2004), while engendering the fear of sexual violence is considered by feminists to be an exercise of patriarchal power and social control (Brownmiller 1976, Maynard and Winn 1997). The literature unequivocally acknowledges the myriad and detrimental physical and psychological aftermath ramifications of sexual violence (ACSSA 2005, Anderson and Doherty 2008, Brison 2002, Campbell and Raja 1999, Campbell and Wasco 2005, Culbertson 1995). Multiple

> *'I need my house quiet so I can hear the cars in the street and everything around me so I know always what is going on.'*
>
> — CAROL

> *'I don't sleep longer than 2 hours ever. I am hypervigilant to sound and my environment. I notice everything.'*
>
> — CAROL

barriers to disclosure prevent or limit the capacity of girls and women to talk of their trauma experiences (Ahrens 2006, Feiring and Taska 2005, Lievore 2003, Littleton et al. 2006, Neame and Heenan 2003), while negative responses to disclosure can have a debilitating effect on victims (Ahrens et al. 2007, Anderson and Doherty 2008, Ullman et al. 2007). In short, sexually violent crime is 'a pervasive social problem that is linked with gender inequality, violates the right to live in freedom and without fear, and exacts costs from individuals, communities and governments' (Lievore 2003, 3).

A culture of gendered fear

> [T]he fact that all women's lives are restricted by sexual violence is indisputable.
>
> — SUSAN BRISON[2]

Cross-national research is consistent with the view that sexual violence is not gender-neutral and indeed, its presence reinforces a 'culture of fear' amongst girls and women confirming that 'violence against some can create terror and limit the behaviour of many' (Yodanis 2004, 672). This supports the belief that the 'world is fundamentally unsafe for women because they are women' (Freedman 2006, 114).

Sexual violence research findings indicate that women do not necessarily need to have been directly affected by violence in order to be more fearful (Yodanis 2004). Furthermore, the literature from this field suggests women are more afraid of being raped than they are of any other type of crime and as a result, engage in avoidance strategies and modified behaviours (Holgate 1989, Morrison, Quadara, and Boyd 2007, Hester 1992). A study by Patricia Easteal in the early 1990s found the threat of sexual violence resides within the psyche of all Australian women causing them

2 From: Brison, Susan (2002). *Aftermath*. Princeton, NJ: Princeton University Press (18).

to alter their behaviour in ways that restrict their freedom of movement as well as damaging their sense of personal safety (1992b).

While Brison's (2002) concept of *prememory*, discussed in Chapter One, may be controversial for its paradoxical and seeming prophetic quality, research consistently demonstrates that high on the list of women's fear is the possibility of being raped (O'Donovan, Devilly, and Rapee 2007, Easteal 1992a).

Sexual violence: Gender and age as determinants of victimisation

> While statistics tell us of rape's pervasiveness – one in four women, one every six minutes ... if the occurrence of rape were audible, its decibel level equal to its frequency, it would overpower our days and nights ... an insistent jackhammer ... we would demand an end to it ... we would refuse to live under such conditions.
>
> — KARYN L. FREEDMAN[3]

The literature surrounding sexual violence unequivocally identifies gender and age as primary determinants of sexual victimisation (Easteal 1992a, Klein 2004, Lievore 2003, Tarczon and Quadara 2012, WHO 2002, Cook, David, and Grant 2001).

The latest recorded crime report released by the Australian Bureau of Statistics reveals sobering figures surrounding sexually violent crimes (Australian Bureau of Statistics 2011). The report indicates that during 2011–12, of all major crimes

> *'I couldn't stand touching my own skin directly, and after my son was born I found it really hard to wash him because of my own fear that I would somehow tarnish him with my own filth. It took decades to be ok within my own skin.'*
>
> — MONICA

3 From: Freedman, Karyn L. 'The Epistemological Significance of Psychic Trauma.' *Hypatia*, Spring 2006 21 (2).

recorded by state and territory police (and rape is considered a major crime along with murder, attempted murder, manslaughter, and kidnapping/abduction), crimes of a sexually violent nature have the highest victimisation rates at 76 victims per 100,000 persons. The next highest victimisation rate for a violent crime is for kidnapping/abduction at 3 victims per 100,000 persons. The report revealed that of the recorded sexual assault crimes, 85 per cent of victims were females. Another Australian Bureau of Statistics release, the '4906.0 – Personal Safety Survey, Australia, 2006', supports the finding that females are more likely than males to be victims of sexual violence (ABS 2006). These figures have changed little since a major survey conducted in Australia in 1997 which found the overwhelming majority of victims of sexual assault were female (Cook, David, and Grant 2001). Clearly, gender is a primary determinant of sexual violation.[4]

In Australia, victimisation rates for sexual violence offences differ according to age (Cook, David, and Grant 2001). It is acknowledged through government funded research that young people less than eighteen years of age represent the most vulnerable age group in terms of sexual violence victimisation (Tarczon and Quadara 2012). A major study carried out by criminologist Patricia Easteal (1992a) supports this. Her survey questioned individuals who had experienced one or more incidents of sexual violence across their lifetime. Ninety six per cent of respondents were female. Almost half of the incidents occurred when the women were children or adolescents,

> *'After the childhood experience I wanted to never have breasts so I bound them for a long time.'*
>
> — MONICA

4 Australia is not unique in its female victimisation rates for rape. Globally, females experience similar rates of sexual violence (WHO 2002). Research in Canada, for example, found that female participants in a General Social Survey conducted in 2004 experienced rape incidents five times the rate of male victims (Brennan and Taylor-Butts 2008). Findings in the United States identified women and girls as almost six times more likely to experience sexual violence than men (Tjaden and Thoennes 2008). Findings in Britain reflect a similar picture (Myhill and Allen 2002, Roe, Coleman, and Kaiza 2009).

with most incidents occurring between eleven and sixteen years (Easteal 1992a). Although the Easteal study took place over twenty years ago, very little has changed. More recent Australian data has consistently found girls in the ten-to-fourteen age group record the highest rates of sexual assault (AIC 2007, Astbury 2006a).[5] These findings support the long-held feminist view that sexual violence is a gender-based phenomenon (Brownmiller 1976, Freedman 2006), with young girls in particular, at great risk.

> *'Most GPs seem too busy to discuss anything other than immediate symptoms and are often rude, abrupt, dismissing and make me feel like they couldn't care less ...'*
>
> — CAROL

Underestimates of prevalence rates

While national victimisation surveys and other information sources, such as police records, clearly indicate that in Australia and globally, crimes of a sexually violent nature overwhelmingly target females and young girls in particular, what we aren't able to determine is the true extent of these crimes. In general, victimisation survey data and administrative data (Tarczon and Quadara 2012), such as police records, have significant value in terms of providing information relating to a multitude of social issues. In relation to the pervasiveness of sexual violence however, methodological limitations (Myhill and Allen 2002, Lievore 2003, Tjaden and Thoennes 2008) and chronically low reporting rates to police (Ahrens and Campbell 2000, ALRC 2010, Clark and Quadara 2010, Easteal 1992c, Kong et al. 2003, Mouzos and Makkai 2004, Neame and Heenan 2003, Stanko 1985, Tarczon and Quadara 2012)[6] often mean that these sources of information can only

5 See Appendix 2 for an overview of global victimisation rates.

6 The Lievore (2003) report identifies a range of factors which act as barriers to the reporting of incidents of sexual violence to police. These factors include: fear that

provide a general indication of the actual extent of crimes of this nature.[7] For example, research conducted by Denise Lievore (2003, 15) for the Australian Institute of Criminology confirms that 'Official police statistics do not provide a comprehensive overview of the extent or nature of sexual victimisation, as they count only incidents reported to and recorded by police'.

Methodological constraints placed on sexual violence research contribute to 'the complexity of recording and counting such information' (Tarczon and Quadara 2012, 1), limiting data gathering as a result. In government survey research involving sexual assault, ethical limitations placed on the age of participants can have the effect of skewing public perceptions. The Australian Bureau of Statistics (ABS 2002) acknowledges that 'Surveys of individuals in the community provide a way of asking people directly about their experiences of crime, and therefore the victimisation rates from surveys are generally considerably greater than rates from administrative systems [such as police, hospitals and community service agencies]'. However, age restrictions which preclude young people less than eighteen years of age from participating in surveys involving sexual violence (ABS 2002) mean that any sexual victimisation data released will not take into account the incidents experienced by victims in this age group. As previously discussed, girls under eighteen years have the highest victimisation rates.

> *'I used to feel like I was here for sex, here to be used. I didn't have a sense of my body separate from how an abuser might view and value my body. It was something I blamed for what was done to me.'*
>
> — KATE

police would not believe the victim; a belief that police would not respond; a fear that the police and the justice system would be hostile to the victim; a fear or dislike of the police; fear of the legal process; a lack of proof that the incident happened; and uncertainty about how to report the incident to police. The '4530.0 – Crime Victimisation, Australia, 2011–12' (Australian Bureau of Statistics 2012) survey notes that less than a third of respondents reported the offence to the police.

7 See Appendix 2 for global statistical information regarding under-reporting to police.

With chronic under-reporting to police and methodological constraints limiting research data, it is critical to not lose sight of the fact that statistical information provides a profoundly conservative estimate of the pervasiveness of sexual violence, contributing to the formation of a partial and distorted cultural view of reality (Tarczon and Quadara 2012, Lievore 2003, UN 2007, Anderson and Doherty 2008).

CHAPTER THREE

What is somatics?

> Woman, who has run her tongue ten thousand times seven times around her mouth before not speaking, either dies of it or knows her tongue and her mouth better than anyone.
>
> — HÉLÈNE CIXOUS[1]

Before proceeding further, it is important to situate my research within an embodied field of inquiry. This chapter will present some historical background concerning the field of somatics, examine some of the factors influencing the evolution of somatics as a field of study, and provide a description of some of the component parts of this broad, body-focused area of study.

I begin by briefly examining the etymological origins of the word *somatic* and by providing an overview of contemporary reflections of the origins of dichotomous thinking and, crucially for this research, the separation of the mind and body that took place in Western philosophical traditions in ancient Greece and seventeenth-century France. The chapter then explores the post-Victorian puritanical era and the early twentieth century for its renewed interest in the body with the emergence of body-focused social movements, and the practice of classical dance which evolved to include the Modern Dance movement. The chapter then moves to the 1970s and the work of Thomas Hanna. The remainder of the chapter examines three major areas of study within the broad field of somatics: somatic

1 From: Cixous, Hélène, Clement, Catherine (1986). *Sorties*. In *A Newly Born Woman*. Minneapolis: University of Minnesota Press (95).

psychology; somatic bodywork (of which Body-Mind Centering forms a part); and somatic movement.

***

The Centre for Somatic Studies website (2012) describes somatics as 'an inquiry into our "lived body" by observing and exploring ourselves through sensing and moving. It is simply and most profoundly, the study of how human embodied experience unfolds' (Frank 2012, Young 2006). In current western usage, *somatic* describes something as 'of the body, not of the mind'.[2] It has its etymological roots in the ancient Greek word *soma*, meaning 'body' and is the English equivalent of the Greek form, *somatikos*.[3]

While ancient Greek culture may have acknowledged the body by naming it in their language system, a bias against the body appears early on in recorded western philosophical musings. Elizabeth Grosz (1994) notes that in the *Cratylus*, a dialogue written in the fifth century BC, the Greek philosopher Plato credits the introduction of the word *soma* to Orphic priests. The Orphic religion was an eschatological belief system, a system aligned with 'the part of theology concerned with death and final destiny' (Moore 2002, 373). The Britannica Online Encyclopaedia (2012) states that 'Orphic eschatology laid great stress on rewards and punishment after the death of the body, the soul then being freed to achieve its true life'. Orphic priests then 'believed that man was a spiritual or noncorporeal being trapped in the body as in a dungeon (*sema*)' (Grosz 1994, 5). Grosz (1994, 5) argues that 'Since the inception of philosophy as a separate and self-contained discipline in ancient Greece, philosophy has established itself on the foundations of a profound somatophobia' and as a result, 'The body has been regarded as a source of interference in, and a danger to, the operations of reason' (5).

2 This definition was obtained from *The Australian Pocket Dictionary* (5th ed), (2002, 1050).

3 Obtained from the Etymology Online website at: <http://www.etymonline.com/index.php?term=somatic>.

She goes on to note that in his musings in *Timaeus*, Plato used the term *chora*[4] to single out and denigrate the maternal body as 'a mere housing, receptacle, or nurse of being rather than coproducer' (5). Implicit in this, in procreative terms, Plato positioned man as an active producer of human life while simultaneously claiming and locating sole responsibility for production within the realm of the masculine. The passive female body-as-receptacle could just as well have been the equivalent of a modern day inanimate piece of laboratory equipment.

Brison (2002) argues that philosophers have traditionally distanced themselves from the body in order to maintain purity of thought. Focusing too on Plato and citing the work of Sara Ruddick (1989) she notes 'Plato praised philosophers for "despising the body and avoiding it," and urged that "if we are ever to have pure knowledge of anything, we must get rid of the body and contemplate things by themselves with the soul by itself". This rejection of the body,' she continues, 'has been most apparent in the disparaging of the female body, which has been presented as the antithesis to reason' (Brison 2002, 42). Patricia Moran (1996) concurs with this view, noting 'The body is the poor relative of the mind in Western thought: gross, animal, subject to decay and death, the body frequently figures not only as other but antagonistic to the aims of the soul and mind' (1). Philosopher Elizabeth Spelman (1982) agrees that western philosophical tradition has consistently aligned woman with corporeality and man with reason. She wryly notes that philosophy 'has not been noted for its celebration of the body' (111). She goes on to state, 'Plato's dialogues are filled with lessons about knowledge, reality, and goodness, and most of the lessons carry with them strong praise for the soul and strong indictments against the body ... the body, [according to Plato] with its deceptive senses, keeps us from real knowledge' (111).

If we turn our attention at this point to other, less conspicuous and less phallocentric, ancient cultural understandings of the mind and body,

4 The ancient Greek word *chora* refers to a room, or space of territory. This definition was obtained from the myEtymology website at: <http://www.myetymology.com/greek/chora.html>.

we see a different picture. In her research into the body and gender in ancient culture, Julia Asher-Greve (1998) explores early Mesopotamian understandings of the mind and body. Mesopotamia is considered one of the earliest known civilisations (c. 3000–1600 BCE) occurring alongside ancient Egypt (c. 3000–800 BCE) and pre-dating ancient Greece (c. 800 BCE). Like the Egyptians, Mesopotamians developed a system of writing conventions using symbols, or signs, to represent their Sumerian language and to reflect their culture. By grounding her work within a feminist paradigm and engaging with Mesopotamian art and literature from this perspective, Asher-Greve reveals that within this ancient culture an holistic approach was taken in relation to what constituted a human being. For Mesopotamians, no separation existed between the mind and body and no gendered hierarchy favoured one sex over another. Unlike the later ancient Greek concepts of gender and the dichotomisation of the body and mind, Asher-Greve argues 'The views expressed in Sumerian [...] sources [...] demonstrate that mind/body, mind/matter or spiritual/material dualisms are not all "universal", nor do they include a denigrating view of women' (9). Asher-Greve's interpretation of image and text, points to the notion that 'ancient Mesopotamians did not develop a system of binary gender equating male with positive and female with negative values.' Within this culture, she says, 'the body was the total self, the essence of humanity, equally matter and spirit, emotion and reason, both temporal and eternal' (29).

Similarly, Ioannis Grammatikakis (2011) points out, the Minoan civilisation (c. 2500–1400 BCE), which developed on the Aegean island of Crete and also pre-dates ancient Greek culture, did not hold negative views of women and the female body. Minoan culture, she argues, celebrated and worshipped, in story and art, the female body's fertility, childbearing and child-caring capacity. The reverence for women in this culture was such that they enjoyed a privileged and dominant position both socially and spiritually. Goddesses were in greater abundance than gods and women held a social status unequalled in later civilisations. Even Plato, rather grudgingly I imagine, was stirred to write that 'in Minoan Crete the important part played by women is discernible in every sphere' (972).

12 May, 2012

I've been reading Margaret Somerville's (1999) Body/Landscape Journals. I look down at my body as I sit at my writing table surrounded by texts on corporeality and sexual trauma, and I want to weep as I think of the opening quote from poet Anna Couani:

> *I begin with my body as you do with yours. It contains everything I am. I look downwards over my knees to my feet [...] downwards at my breasts and then across at my collarbone from shoulder to shoulder. This is not bleak, this is everything I am. (2)*

Like Anna Couani, my body is everything I am. I know this now; somewhere I have always known but my understanding of this has been subjugated and all but obliterated by the subliminal influence of masculinist dichotomous Western thinking coupled inextricably with my very conscious experience of childhood rape. Just one of these powerful influences would have been enough to wrench me away from my bodily self. As a raped female living within a patriarchal culture, the combination is formidable, needing an Amazonian effort to overcome.

In the reading of both Ioannis Grammatikakis and Julia Asher-Greve's research, I'm reminded that ideologies, doctrines and social frameworks can be pervasive and transient; they may come and go with greater or lesser degrees of frequency and influence. Nonetheless, they serve to effectively shape our thoughts, behaviours and responses to our selves, to our experiences, to others and to the worlds in which we co-exist. Generations of women globally have been infected with and restricted by binary oppositional thinking, separating them from their somatic selves. Generations of women too have suffered the aftermath of gendered sexual violence, the shame surrounding this and the detachment from their bodies this often creates. I have no desire to further compound this problem by being a part of a research community that perpetuates the division of mind from body. I don't wish to stand idly by as the bodies and somatic stories of other traumatised women are silenced through their absence on the pages of sexual trauma research. I will not consciously facilitate the erasure of the raped female body and the perpetuation of unwarranted feelings of shame.

Grosz (1994) points out that when we move through time to the seventeenth century we see the continuing separation of body from mind as we arrive at the door of Rene Descartes (1596–1650). This French philosopher took the separation of mind and body to a deeper and more pernicious level by characterising each in terms of their relationship to nature. For Descartes, Grosz

(1994, 6) argues, the body is subjective matter, an 'extended substance … a part of nature, governed by its physical laws and ontological exigencies'. The mind, by contrast, 'the thinking substance, the soul, the consciousness', is irreducible to nature. In other words, the soul *cannot* be linked to nature and subjectivity if it is to be the site of rational objectivity. By creating a binary opposition in which the mind (the masculine) is privileged over the body (the feminine), thought artificially and hierarchically elevated over subjective experience, Descartes further entrenched dichotomous thinking, the denigration of the body, and, by association, the feminine.

As Grosz (1994) and others argue, for Plato and Descartes, the body or *soma*, was considered antagonistic to reason and rationality and aligned with women, and women, with their insatiable and uncontrollable corporeal appetites, ample testimony to their threat to the effective functioning of the soul (Spelman 1982). By insisting then on the privileging of form over matter and corporeality, while continuing to position man as active-intellectual-transcendent being, and woman as passive-material-immanent being unreliably governed by her corporeality, these philosophers set the tone for a masculinist dichotomous philosophical tradition which in turn paved the way for the widespread penetration of enduring and profoundly somatophobic and misogynistic discourses in Western culture.

If we now move to the early twentieth century, we begin to see minute cracks appearing in these discourses and shifts occurring in attitudes towards the body. Exercise physiologist, movement therapist and dancer Martha Eddy (2009), notes that during this period in history, the largely puritanical and patriarchal constraints of the nineteenth-century Victorian era can be credited with the emergence of a renewed interest in the body and interactions with it. According to Eddy, 'there was a need to break free of Victorian strictures and also to embody the optimism the Victorian era offered' (6). Eddy cites 'free love'[5] and '*Gymnastik*' as examples of body-focused social movements which gained a stronger presence post the Victorian era. While

5 Advocates of the free love movement included feminists Mary Wollstonecraft (1759–1797) and Mary Gove Nichols (1810–1884), as well as the philosopher Bertrand Russell (1872–1970).

these were already established movements prior to the twentieth century, participation was limited to small numbers. However, by appealing to those wanting to experience the body in new and more liberated ways, participation rates increased around this time.

The bohemian 'free love' movement, thought to have been established in the eighteenth century, rejected the institution of marriage, believing that sexual and emotional relationships between individuals transcended the need for gender-biased social, religious and legal regulation (Hayden 2010). With a higher public profile in the early part of the twentieth century, 'free love' helped erode some of the taboos surrounding sex and sexuality, freeing the way for less puritanical considerations of the body and physicality.

Gymnastik teacher Elsa Gindler (1885–1961)[6] was an early pioneer of somatic bodywork and interested in the use of breath in the attainment of concentration. By 1913, Gindler, in her quest to achieve heightened concentration, had developed ways of focusing on inner awareness through breath to increase somatic awareness and consciousness (Gueter, Heller, and Weaver 2010). Gindler believed that it is 'only by means of concentration can we attain the full functioning of the physical apparatus in relation to mental and spiritual life' (Johnson 1995, 5).

In the early 1900s, the world of traditional classical dance was also undergoing change with the addition of a new focus on less structured ways of moving the body. Gill Wright Miller (2011), observes that Modern Dance had its genesis at this time, introducing a more fluid body into dance movement. Wright Miller tells us 'the front-and-back verticality of Ballet was giving way to the multi-dimensionality of a curved spine, as if the body were being allowed more options to move in space, to move more "naturally"' (271). Isadora Duncan and Mary Wigman (Gueter, Heller, and Weaver 2010) were early pioneers of expressive dance, and sowed the seeds for the emergence of Modern Dance, their styles helping to broaden the

6 Elsa Gindler became interested in the use of breath in consciousness after developing tuberculosis. By focusing on breathing with one lung only, Gindler was able to rest her damaged lung in order for it to repair to an extent that she was able to achieve greater comfort and improved health.

dance vocabulary to incorporate the natural body with its abundant capacity for self-expression through the language of free movement.

Eddy (2009) points out that in the first half of the twentieth century, interest in the body was further enlivened by theorists such as Maurice Merleau-Ponty, the French philosopher and phenomenologist. Merleau-Ponty's (1962) work rejected the mind/body dualism of his philosophical forefathers by offering an alternative view of the interrelatedness of the body and the mind. His view emphasised the pivotal role of the body in perception and helped 'return the body to the forefront of philosophy for the first time since Plato' (back cover).

In the 1970s a further shift occurred which helped validate subjective embodied experience. The word *soma* grew in meaning to describe 'the body in its wholeness' and symbolised 'a process of doing and being, rather than an abstract entity … a living process by which our bodily sensations, movements, perceptions, emotions and thoughts form a whole experience' (Frank 2012). Feldenkrais Method practitioner Olivia Cheever (2000) defines *soma* as 'body consciousness based on a sense of a whole embodied self interacting with our environment, human or otherwise, in a manner integrating body and mind' (17). The philosopher and somatic practitioner and educator Thomas Hanna (1928–1990) is given credit for redefining and broadening the word *soma* to include 'the body experienced from within, where we experience mind/body integration' (Somatics 2012). In terms of achieving an integrated self, with body and mind *not* viewed or experienced as separate entities, Cheever (2000) underscores the need to engage a holistic whole person consciousness by reminding us that 'one needs to develop a somatically based awareness from *inside* as well as *outside* the self' (17).

In 1976, Hanna developed the term *somatics* to encompass 'the field of study dealing with somatic phenomena, i.e., the human being as experienced by himself (or herself) from the inside' (Somatics 2012). Hanna (1988) believed that to engage in somatics required a shift in perspective to the first-person in order to view oneself from 'the inside out, where one is aware of feelings, movements and intentions, rather than looking objectively from the outside in' (20). By looking from the outside in, or the third-person perspective, Hanna believed only 'the phenomenon of the human *body* is perceived' whereas, 'when this same human being is observed from the first-person viewpoint of his [her] own proprioceptive senses,[7] a categorically different phenomenon is perceived: the human soma' (1986, 341). Jill Green (2002), notes that for Hanna, 'somatics is the study of the soma, not as an objective "body", but an embodied process of internal awareness and communication' (114). By further noting that *process* is intrinsic to the field of somatics, Green contributes to contemporary discussions on the body emerging in the area of new materialism (Alaimo and Hekman 2008b, Barad 2003, Hekman 2010, Kirby 1997, van der Tuin and Dolphijn 2010) which supports the validity of embodied experience in the expansion of self-knowledge and human potential.

Somatics then, is a paradigmatic term drawing together disparate communities whose common focus of inquiry is grounded in the body and embodiment. It is an umbrella term that serves 'to create possibilities of collaboration among communities that otherwise stand isolated from each other, often in competition and conflict' (Johnson 2012).

The components of the somatics field of study

What then, are the components of a field of study which values rather than denigrates the human body while placing *internal awareness and communication* central to its practice?

Dancer and somatic movement educator Susan Bauer (2012) tells us, broadly speaking, somatics is a 'holistic and interdisciplinary approach that connects body sciences, psychology, and movement to help each person understand more about his or her body/mind and move toward greater

7 Proprioception allows us to have a sense of spatial awareness during moments of stillness and movement. It is a process that involves the transmission and interpretation of stimuli, received from receptors in the muscles, tendons, joints and inner ear, transmitted through neural pathways to the central nervous system. Information obtained from: <http://www.online-medical-dictionary.org/definitions-p/proprioception.html>.

integration' (website). The somatics field is variously known as 'bodywork, body therapies, hands-on work, body-mind integration, body-mind disciplines, movement therapy, somatic therapy, movement awareness, or movement education' (Eddy 2002b, 47).

Eddy (2009, 7) acknowledges the interdisciplinary application of somatics and, for the purposes of a closer examination, proposes the field can be split into three main areas of study. These areas are: somatic psychology, somatic bodywork, and somatic movement. Those working in the field of somatics and somatic education may have differing views regarding Eddy's identification and division of these three areas of study. However, for the purpose of this book, I feel it is beneficial to divide the field as Eddy suggests for the sake of greater clarity. Because there is insufficient room in this chapter to give a detailed account of the origins and development of each of these areas of study, I will present only a brief history of each in order to provide a context and temporal framework for the work. To avoid confusion, I have also chosen to amalgamate somatic psychology and somatic psychotherapy. In the somatics literature, the distinction between the two seems fairly fluid with the terms 'psychology' and 'psychotherapy' used interchangeably.[8]

Somatic psychology/psychotherapy

In Western medicine in the eighteenth and nineteenth centuries, the body was thought to be the cause of the condition called hysteria, or 'womb disease.' Primarily occurring in women (Hustvedt 2011, Johnson 2008, Showalter 1998, Trimble 2004) and characterised by a range of often medically unexplained symptoms (Johnson 2008, Showalter 1998, Trimble 2004), hysteria was variously thought to have been precipitated by causes including, but not exclusive to, the presence of a 'wandering uterus' (Showalter 1998, Scull 2009, Trimble 2004), hereditary factors (Showalter

8 I'd like to acknowledge Dr Josephine Taylor for bringing clarity to my confusion surrounding the similarities and differences between somatic psychology and somatic psychotherapy.

1998), sexually traumatic experience in childhood (Scull 2009, Showalter 1998), or a lack of sexual gratification (Showalter 1998). Patients were often extensively treated with the use of touch, or massage (King 2011), itself often sexual in nature, with the express intent of inducing 'hysterical paroxysm' or orgasm, in patients (Bonitz 2008).

The French clinician Jean-Martin Charcot (1825–1893), was considered to have precipitated the 'golden age' (Showalter 1998, 29) of hysteria in the late nineteenth century at his clinic at the Salpetriere Hospital, Paris. Charcot was the first clinician to move away from the 'wandering uterus' basis for hysteria symptoms by identifying the central nervous system as the locus of disturbance. He also confidently described hysteria as 'a physical illness' (Showalter 1998, 30), and identified trauma as a causal factor (van der kolk, Weisaeth, and van der Hart 2007). Charcot understood that trauma played a role in the development of hysteria as well as acting as a catalyst for the emergence and expression of pre-existing and underlying hereditary conditions through hysterical symptoms (Showalter 1998). In 1886, the surgeon, John Eric Erichsen (1818–1896), introduced the notion of trauma manifesting in the mind, initiating a movement away from corporally-based conceptions of trauma to more psychologically-based considerations. However, although Erichsen preceded Sigmund Freud by a decade, it was Freud who was primarily given credit for this shift (Bourke 2012).

Freud (1856–1939) studied under Charcot, and along with his equally significant contemporary, Pierre Janet (1859–1947), originally worked with the body in psychoanalysis (Bonitz 2008, Young 2006). It was Freud, along with another contemporary, Joseph Breuer, who developed one theory of hysteria that located its origins in repressed and distressing childhood sexual experience.[9] According to Freud, the somatic expression of these experiences were '"mnemonic symbols" or physical metaphors of the suppressed trauma' (Showalter 1998, 38). Janet also understood that the origin of his patients' hysteria symptoms emerged from traumatic experience (Trimble 2004). Although both Freud and Janet originally considered the

9 Freud's position on repressed memory set the scene for the later, and contentious, growth of the 'recovered memory movement' (Showalter 1998, 45).

body as an integral element of treatment, Freud subsequently became less interested in corporeally-centred treatment, focusing instead on the verbal resolution of his patients' disturbances through psychotherapeutic treatment (Bonitz 2008, Young 2006). By the mid-1920s, 'Freud saw anatomy, physiology, and chemistry as demands on – resistances to – psychoanalysis' (Wilson 2004b, 2). Such was Freud's influence, there was a general turn away from the body and an increased focus on psychoanalytic talk-based therapy (Bonitz 2008, Young 2006).

While clear acknowledgement was made at this time of the influence of the psyche over the body, scant consideration seems to have been given to the reciprocal influence of the body over the psyche. Courtney Young (2006) tells us that during the period 1929–30, 'the body in psychotherapy became formally disowned' (20). He claims that as a result of this repudiation of the body and the inevitable change of direction from 'the more instinctual, organic, and drive-based models of understanding' towards 'a more object-relational understanding', the effectiveness of psychoanalysis, in isolation, was restricted (20).

While the mind/body binary persisted in conventional psychotherapy for decades (Young 2006), maverick psychoanalysts began experimenting with the re-introduction and re-integration of the body in therapy. One such person was the radical Austrian psychoanalyst Wilhelm Reich (Goodrich-Dunn 2004, Mead 2012). Reich, a protégé of Sigmund Freud, considered one of the most influential psychologists of the twentieth century, is credited with developing the branch of somatics known as somatic psychology. Reich is attributed with 'bringing the body into psychology at a time when others dealt with the mind and emotions' (Daniels 2008).

Early on in his career, Reich[10] began to question the effectiveness of psychoanalysis, or 'the talking cure'[11] as it became known. He witnessed

10 Reich began practicing as a psychoanalyst in 1919 at the age of twenty-two. By the 1930s his methods of treatment were considered highly controversial. He fled Nazi Germany for the United States in 1939, taking his radical therapeutic methods with him. Reich was imprisoned in 1956 for fraud and racketeering by the US Food and Drug Administration. He died just over a year later in prison.

11 The term *talking cure* was first used by Josef Breuer's hysteria patient Bertha Pappenheim. She was given the pseudonym 'Anna O' by Sigmund Freud in *Studies*

patients undergoing traditional psychoanalytic treatment appearing to show little improvement in their health, concluding that 'talk' alone was insufficient. On the strength of his observations, in the 1930s, Reich developed his own methods of treatment, considered unconventional at that time. These methods included an awareness of the influence of stored emotion in the body (Goodrich-Dunn 2004). Reich was the first psychoanalyst to overtly touch his patients during treatment sessions. He believed that patients, fearing the eruption of latent emotion, developed muscular and character armour. He created these terms to describe the blocking of the release of unwanted body-based emotion (Daniels 2008, Leijssen 2006, Young 2006). This is akin to contemporary understandings of trauma and the fear known to emerge and immobilise individuals in anticipation of re-experiencing symptoms (Levine 1997, 109). Reich considered the release of this emotion was integral to healing and to help facilitate the release, he physically touched his patients believing this in turn would help reshape the patient's entrenched behavioural responses to distress (Goodrich-Dunn 2004).

The use of touch remains a controversial issue within the psychotherapies (Bonitz 2008, Phelan 2009, Stenzel and Rupert 2004, Toronto 2001). Young (2006), however, suggests contemporary somatic psychotherapy still aims to achieve the body-inclusive ideals initiated by Reich by adopting a holistic approach to treatment in order to gain a deeper and richer understanding of the patient as a whole person. However, Young (2006) notes, 'this is only possible if the person's capacity for full intellectual freedom, emotional expression, free movement, and social connection is regained' (22).

In what ways then does contemporary somatic psychotherapy differ from traditional talk-based therapy? The Centre for Somatic Studies defines somatic psychotherapy as:

> The integration of somatic inquiry within the therapy session. Somatic psychotherapy emphasizes the process of dynamics within the session as primary to the work of therapeutic discovery, while the process of content is of secondary importance.

---

on Hysteria (1893). Freud adopted this term *talking cure* to describe psychoanalysis. Pappenheim went on to become a feminist activist and writer.

> Using somatic techniques as the means for exploration, the client is able to experience where spontaneity, creativity and deliberateness flow through his or her body and where flow is suppressed or blocked. With the body as locus of intervention, somatic psychotherapy uncovers early material as it lives in the here-and-now.

The Australian Somatic Psychotherapy Association (2012) states that in addition to working with clients in a traditional language-based mode, somatic psychotherapists also work with clients at the level of 'dynamic bodily experience'. They explain that the patient/therapist engagement 'includes patterns of breathing, posture, sensation and movement, and also working with body image and metaphor'. Therapeutic touch during sessions is not always implemented but rather, sits as a possibility. The association notes this form of therapy 'can be used to facilitate exploration and expression, to develop self-awareness, self-regulation and a sense of vitality and aliveness. This approach can help deepen a sense of connection to oneself and to others'.

The Australian College of Contemporary Somatic Psychotherapy (2012) web site differentiates somatic psychotherapy from traditional forms of psychotherapeutic work, stressing that the primary focus of any therapist-client engagement is 'very clearly psychotherapeutically based' (1). However, as with the description above, therapeutic touch can be utilised to augment talk-based therapy (1). They do note however that 'if body process is not included as an integral part of the psychotherapeutic process then we eliminate an opportunity to engage the significant transformative dynamic of the body' (2). Even if touch is not a technique used during sessions, the body remains a guiding presence within the therapeutic context.

The somatic psychotherapy field also acknowledges the influence of sociocultural context on the human body and health. The transformative dynamic of the body is seen to be 'a dynamic which impels us towards an eruption from the docile bodies in which culture has so frequently contained us' (Psychotherapy 2012, 3). Somatic psychotherapist Veronique Mead (2012) acknowledges that professionals working in the field of somatic psychology consider the multiplicity of influences on human health when engaging with patients. Mead's (2012) definition of somatic psychology reflects this whole person approach:

> [somatic psychotherapy is] the study of ways in which the environment influences our physiology, using the term 'environment' to include experiences of early life as well as the impact of ongoing experience. The influence of the environment affects not only our thoughts and behaviours, but also affects the body at the physiological level, and SP [somatic psychology] views thoughts, beliefs, and behaviours as being inherently a part of a bodymind continuum. (1–2)

The motivations for engaging as clients in body-inclusive therapeutic practices are multiple. Body-based psychotherapies may help individuals with a desire to re-enter into relationship with their intuition to gain a closer connection with this aspect of their embodied selves. It may assist too with the acknowledgement and validation of their emotions, as well as having the potential, as a result of these, to improve both intra and inter-personal relations (Stromsted 2007). Jungian analyst and dance/movement and somatic psychotherapist Tina Stromsted (2007) argues that for some individuals, traditional talk-based therapies may have inadequately attended to the complexity of their deeply held feelings. Stromsted (2007) notes that while insight can certainly be found in talk-based therapy, 'these insights are often *frozen in the intellect* [emphasis added], and people can feel unable to put them into action' (202). This is an interesting observation given that contemporary research has begun to uncover the ways in which trauma resides within the body (Rothschild 2000), resting in the cellular tissue in stasis, or *frozen* until it can be given conscious acknowledgement and reintegrated into the self (Levine 1997).

Somatic bodywork

There are a number of body-oriented therapies that fall under the umbrella term 'bodywork'. More familiar therapies include Alexander Technique®, Bowen Therapy, Craniosacral Therapy, Deep Tissue and Swedish Massage, Feldenkrais Method®, Reflexology, Reiki, Rolfing, Shiatsu, and The Trager® Approach (Hughes 2012). The practice of Body-Mind Centering also sits within this field.

According to bodywork educator and The Trager Approach practitioner Deane Juhan (1987), bodywork 'is a kind of sensorimotor education, rather than a treatment or a procedure in the sense common to modern medicine' (367). Like somatic psychotherapy, somatic bodywork has as its major foci, 'self-awareness, self-control, and the active application of the will to processes of growth and development' (367). Further, through increased awareness, bodywork can help individuals develop greater clarity and more intimate relationships with themselves, to 'discover strengths and joys that coexist with our weaknesses and pains' (367).

While all of the aforementioned therapies are considered 'bodywork', they may or may not include touch or manipulation of the client's body. Reiki is an example of a bodywork therapy where touching the client's body is optional. Developed in Japan in the 1920s, Reiki is considered a 'hands-on' healing practice and can involve the placement of the practitioner's hands directly on the client's clothed body or the practitioner's hands hovering just above the client's body (Reiki.org 2012). Similarly, Feldenkrais Method involves two approaches to treatment: Awareness Through Movement takes clients through a series of bodily movements via verbal guidance in group situations and involves no touch; and Functional Integration involves hands-on manipulation of the client's body by the practitioner in a one-on-one mode (Hughes 2012, Feldenkrais 2012, Johnson 1995).

Juhan (1987) observes that touch is the medium through which somatic sensation can be brought to consciousness and that it is through consciousness that improved physiological organisation and function can occur. Juhan doesn't underestimate the significance of touch in our lives. He cautions simply and unequivocally, 'Without touch you die' (356). 'Tactile input' he continues, 'is of primary significance to the organisation and successful function of a wide variety of physiological functions and physiological processes' (356).

In human development, touch is the first sense to develop in utero, at around six weeks gestation (Anxieu 1989, 14). Bonnie Bainbridge Cohen (1995) observes that the foetus in utero constantly receives tactile information as it moves. In the uterine space, 'its body parts rub against each other, against the wall of the uterus, and against the amniotic fluid. As the foetus moves, it pushes against the mother's organs, which in turn push back against the foetus' (200–201). Kinaesthetic information[12] 'begins *in utero* [author's own emphasis] through movement and touch' and helps prepare the foetus for birth as well as forming the foundation for movement patterns post-birth (Burns 2011, 24–25).Touch is also critical in child development (Benjamin 2012). Studies have found that cognitive development can be severely compromised in children if they are prevented from experiencing positive quality of touch at adequate levels (Field 2000).

For Juhan (1987), 'touch, more than any other mode of observation, defines for us our sense of reality' (368–369). 'Every time I touch something', he tells us, 'I am as aware of the part of me that is touched as I am of the thing I touched. Tactile experience tells me as much about myself as it tells me about anything that I contact' (368–369). Grosz (1994) notes too that when human to human bodily contact is made, as connection is registered through the skin tissue at a sensory level, 'the surface of the toucher and the touched must partially coincide' (98).

For Mary Starks Whitehouse (1911–1979), an early pioneer of dance movement therapy and the developer of Authentic Movement, touch becomes the conduit to the inner self. She argued that to touch another's body is also to touch the multiple levels and dimensions of that person's experience in all its subtlety and nuance. For Whitehouse, touch is the medium through which the whole person can be accessed (Frieder 2007). Touch is also an important medium of access to cellular consciousness in Body-Mind Centering. Bainbridge Cohen (2008) argues it is through touch that 'the subtle interplay between body and mind can be experienced' (6). Within the practitioner-client relationship in Body-Mind Centering, hands-on work via touch provides a way to enter the many levels of tissue within the multiple systems of the body to access cellular movement and memory. Through the hands of the practitioner, the experiences held in the client's cells are mutually explored. Through differing pressures of touch, attention can be focused within specific tissues in both client and practitioner. Touch, Bainbridge Cohen tells us, enables a cellular

12 Kinaesthetic information refers to information gained through sensory feedback and is related to the perception of our moving bodies in gravity.

conversation to begin between client and practitioner as 'each tissue of the client is explored by the corresponding tissue of the practitioner' (6). As Bainbridge Cohen (2008) notes, 'When we touch someone, they touch us equally' (6). Touch, then, is not only a point of connection helping to focus the client's attention on the area being touched, but is also a means of sensory communication.

In addition to touch, dancer and educator Andrea Olsen (1998, 8) argues that experiential anatomy 'enhances bodywork by providing an underlying awareness of body structure and function'. Developed alongside bodywork (Olsen 1998), experiential anatomy education relies on active physical and intellectual participation in one's own developing somatic understanding (Bauer 2012). It is a 'creative/humanistic approach' (Bauer 2013) that engages multiple modes of learning including 'movement, touch, imagery, and cognitive study' (Bauer 1999, 38) to 'embody and personalize learning' (Bauer 2013). In this way, 'One's experiences become the basis for understanding one's physical and movement potential' (Bauer 2013). Experiential anatomy is an essential element of all somatic training (Bainbridge Cohen 1993) and especially relevant to bodywork practices.

In terms of the role of the bodywork practitioner in the therapeutic relationship, according to Juhan (1987), the practitioner 'is not an interventionist' (366). Rather, he argues:

> [the practitioner is] a facilitator, a diplomatic intermediary between the physiological processes that have lost track of one another's proper functions and goals, between a mind that has forgotten what it needs to know in order to exert harmonious control and a body politic which increasingly utilizes disruptive demonstrations, terrorist tactics, and even all-out civil war to regain its governor's attention. (366)

Thomas Myers (1998) argues bodywork is an integrative and holistic practice which engages the client and practitioner in 'an equal partnership' with the intent of creating 'a harmonious unity within the entire spectrum of the person' (111). Within the therapeutic bodywork relationship, bodyworkers and somatic educators ideally draw on what Cheever (2000) calls 'somatic empathy'. She defines this as 'a special kind of empathy that involves a bodily based sensing of one's own and another's somatic experience' (16). Cheevers observes that somatic empathy allows practitioners to communicate with clients through sensory means using 'mindful and sensitive touch' (16). As noted earlier, the broad field of somatics focuses on more holistic understandings of human behaviour (Bauer 2012) and can include touch in addition to more traditional verbal interaction between client and practitioner. It is noted however, that verbal language can 'obscure intentions, [whereas] touch, with its kinaesthetic truth, goes right to our core' (19).

Cheever's view on the role of somatic empathy emerges from Moshe Feldenkrais' understandings of the direct nature and interconnectedness of sensory information and the unconscious. Feldenkrais (1995) argues that 'sensory stimuli are closer to our unconscious, subconscious, or autonomous functioning than to our conscious understanding' and as there is a less interrupted dialogue between sensory stimuli and the unconscious, communication is 'more effective and less distorted than at the verbal level' (139). Feldenkrais (1995) does point out however, that this form of communication, occurring as it does at the sensory level, may not be easily understood or articulated by the client or student through semantic language, relying instead, through the medium of touch, on non-language based sensing and feeling.

Like Bainbridge Cohen, Feldenkrais (1995) supports the view that when we touch we are also touched and suggests a 'new entity' emerges through the exchange of sensory information. He notes, 'Through touch, two persons, the toucher and the touched, can become a new ensemble; two bodies when connected by two arms and hands are a new entity. These hands sense at the same time as they direct. Both the touched and the toucher feel what they sense through connecting hands' (139). To help give a multi-dimensional illustrative understanding of Feldenkrais' *new ensemble* term, Olivia Cheever (2000) utilises the image of the Mobius strip a length of paper joined at each end with a 180 degree twist in the middle. Due to its unique construction, the strip 'appears paradoxically to have two sides yet no longer has a clearly identifiable inside or outside surface' (18). Cheever suggests when somatic empathy is present between practitioner and client or student, as sensory information oscillates between the two, in a continuous indistinguishable flow, the relationship is 'synergistic in that the whole [...] is greater than the sum of the parts (the individuals)' (18).

The third entity that emerges from this flow, according to Cheever, is what Feldenkrais refers to as *a new ensemble*, with touch enabling its creation. The Mobius strip, for Cheever, is a symbolic representation of this new entity, capturing for us in image, the continuous, though indistinguishable flow of sensory information between client and practitioner in the therapeutic bodywork relationship.

Somatic bodywork then, as a therapeutic body-oriented practice, engages holistically with individuals to expand and deepen understandings of the embodied self through refined awareness and increased consciousness. The therapeutic interaction between client or student, and practitioner involves the use of direct or indirect touch, with both practitioner and client or student engaging in an integrative relationship using sensory awareness processes, or *somatic empathy* (Cheever 2000). The interaction may incorporate, though does not rely on, verbal language as a means of communication. Somatic bodywork is an educative practice that 'teaches us to be exquisitely sensitive' (Myers 1999, 115) to our inner cellular life. This refined inner awareness can help mitigate the effects of body and mind separation and sense of detachment often present in the aftermath of body-based experience (Cheever 2000, 22).

Somatic movement

Somatic movement can be described as 'movement that is sensed and shaped from within, rather than from an external source' (ISMETA 2012). A central and guiding principle underpinning the spectrum of somatic movement practices is the specific focus on sensory awareness and inner feeling. Through refined sensory awareness it is possible for heightened experiential consciousness and the resulting inner impulses and sensations to drive and be expressed in movement.

As previously discussed, those working in the area of free expressive dance in the early 1900s made a significant contribution to the field of somatics and towards establishing the body as a site of experiential and emotional intelligence. We can recall that at this time, the body was excluded from many spheres of western culture and thought. The body was being driven from the field of psychoanalysis, mind/body dualism was firmly entrenched in western philosophy, and the remnants of the sexually repressive and patriarchal Victorian era were still reverberating within western culture. To resist contributing further to the cultural marginalisation of the body and to reinvest in the potentiality of somatic awareness in movement practices was to walk against the tide of established and powerful traditions. But walk they did.

Leading pioneers in the field of free expression included Rudolph Laban (1879–1958), Isadora Duncan (1878–1927), Mary Wigman (1886–1973), and Margaret H'Doubler (1889–1982) (Eddy 2009, 10). Eddy (2009) argues these embodied artists' work was ground breaking. By 'paying careful attention to bodily sensation' (10), they helped pave the way for additional and alternative ways of working with the body to help initiate and support movement.

This close attention to sensing and the felt experience of the body was an unconventional approach to movement at that time and very different to more traditional dance forms which relied on technique and imposed choreographed movement. These artists' pioneering interest in 'deep internal reflection' introduced and helped establish somatic awareness as an additional dimension to movement work and is currently applied in a diverse range of contemporary body-based practices including 'acting, martial arts, exercise, physical education, physiotherapy, and dance' (Eddy 2009, 11).

With regard to the practitioner-client relationship and the self-educative aspect of somatic bodywork, the International Somatic Movement Education and Therapy Association (ISMETA 2012) is clear that 'Registered practitioners guide individuals and groups into inner experiences of their bodies' rather than instruct. Practitioners of somatic movement education and therapy employ a range of skills and approaches to guide clients and students towards increased sensory-motor awareness. This range includes 'diverse qualities of touch, empathic verbal exchange, and both subtle and complex movement experiences' (Eddy 2009, 7). Practitioners, as with bodyworkers, also draw on experiential anatomy knowledge to understand more fully the systems of the body to facilitate greater inner consciousness.

In 1958, Mary Starks Whitehouse (1995) warned, 'The less the body is experienced, the more it becomes an appearance' (245). Andrea Olsen

(1998) supports experiential somatic education through her international work as a dancer and teacher of anatomy. She notes however, with a sense of dismay some forty years after the words of Whitehouse, that 'one of the most thoroughly neglected areas of body education is the awareness of what is happening inside: the dialogue between inner and outer experience in relation to the whole person' (11). As I have already established, somatic movement relies on this inner-outer dialogue in order to become an integrated form of expression. As Andrea Olsen (1998) tells us, 'The body is our guide, all we need to do is learn to listen' (7).

As in somatic bodywork, the relationship that develops between practitioner and client or student is one of reciprocity, based on the exchange of somatic knowledge (Eddy 2002a). It assists in the discovery of 'the natural movement or flow of life activity within the body' (Eddy 2009, 7) with the aim of achieving for the individual 'self-organization, self-healing, or self-knowing' (8). In this way, somatic movement education and therapy aligns itself with other somatic practices, with a focus on reciprocity and to transformation and empowerment with the aim of working towards refined perception, inner understanding and self-affirmation.

Authentic Movement is a somatic movement practice that relies on and encourages respect for the inner life and intelligence of the body. Authentic Movement emerged from the Movement-in-Depth work of Mary Starks Whitehouse. Whitehouse studied dance at a school in Germany founded by the expressive movement pioneer Mary Wigman. She was also taught by Martha Graham (1894–1991), influential modern dancer and choreographer. Starks Whitehouse also studied at the Jung Institute in Zurich (Chodrow 1999). Jung's psychoanalytic method of 'active Imagination' (Chodrow 1999, 305)[13] was used by Starks Whitehouse in the 1950s and 60s to help develop her 'Movement-in-Depth' approach. This work was

13 Jung developed 'active imagination' as an analytic tool around 1916. Joan Chodrow (1999) interprets the process of 'active imagination' as being able to be 'open to the unconscious and give free rein to fantasy. At the same time, you maintain an alert, attentive, active point of view' (305).

further developed by her students into what is today known as Authentic Movement (Chodrow 1999).

As Authentic Movement is readily described by Nancy Chodrow (1999), Janet Adler (1999) and others, all Authentic Movement involves a person moving and a person bearing witness to that moving. The mover positions themselves in the movement space and, with eyes closed, begins a process of deep inner listening, sensing and feeling, easing from a state of outer awareness towards the unconscious and inner self. Adler (1999, 142) describes this process as movers 'descending towards themselves'. The mover then responds with spontaneous movement to whatever arises from this inner state. As the mover moves, each occasion different from the last, she opens herself to experiencing 'deeper levels of her kinaesthetic reality' (Adler 1999, 142), responds to new sensations and impulses, and without conscious direction, moves from them.

Starks Whitehouse (1995) describes the moving experience as the following:

> The core of the movement experience is the sensation of moving and being moved [...] Ideally, both are present in the same instant, and it may be literally an instant. It is a moment of total awareness, the coming together of what I am doing and what is happening to me. It cannot be anticipated, explained, specifically worked for, nor repeated exactly. (243)

The crucial point here is that the movement cannot be specifically worked for, nor repeated exactly but rather the mover responds in the instant to 'body-felt sensations, emotions, memories, movement impulses, and/or images' (Stromsted 2009, 202). In other words, the movement 'has to be "found" in the body, not put on like a dress or a coat' (Starks Whitehouse 1999, 53). The movement, then, is the unique result of the perfect moment of alignment of feeling and action. It is this uniqueness that forms the basis for the use of the term authentic in the naming of this particular movement practice.

Witnessing is critical to this movement practice. The witness holds responsibility for providing a 'safe, contained, and receptive presence' (Stromsted 2009, 202) to enable the inner listening to occur within the movement space. Sitting to one side of the space, the witness brings a particular quality of presence that holds the mover and enables full freedom of expression. As she witnesses, she brings all her attention to both the mover's 'bodily expression as well as her own embodied experience' (Stromsted 2009, 202). She does so with deep respect for the mover as well as for herself as witness, witnessing without judgement and without projection of her own feelings onto the movement (A. Cummins, personal communication, 4 June, 2010).

When the movement draws to a close, creative expression is given to the tracked movement through language or drawings as the mover creates images on paper or describes the details of her embodied experience to the witness. When the mover articulates this experience, 'she begins to see herself, hold herself, take herself seriously, attending to the detail, every precious detail of each physical movement and the concomitant inner experience' (Adler 2007, 28). The witness, without judgement, describes the movement she witnessed as well as describing 'sensations, images and feelings' present in her own body as she witnessed the mover (Stromsted 2009, 202). This exchange of experience can be a deeply affirming one. Janet Adler (2007) emphasises the centrality of the mover-witness union. She suggests that intra and inter-relationships lie at the heart of Authentic Movement: 'between a mover and an outer witness, between the moving self and an inner witness [...] This gift, this work, this challenge of being a person is about relationship' (29). Adler talks of the ways in which moving and witnessing the mover's expression and articulation of inner experience broadens understandings and leads to new discoveries. She tells us 'the literal force of moving and witnessing the embodiment of sensation, emotion, and sprit infuses relationship with new ways of knowing the self and the other' (Adler 2002, xviii).

Engaging in both inner and outer witnessing during Authentic Movement is not without risk. As an individual embarks on the journey of articulating sensation and emotion before a witness, she places her trust in the ability of her witness to see her in this process, and risks the possibility of experiencing herself as not being seen (Adler 2002). However, as Alice Cummins (2012) argues, when risk is present it acts as 'provocation towards realization'. Adler (2002) notes too, 'In the right circumstance and the right time this risk is essential, because in human development it is only when one does feel seen by another that one can see oneself' (6). Clearly, in the seeing and being seen, where risk is undoubtedly present, gestures of possibilities reside.

***

Having established a trans-disciplinary location for my embodied sexual trauma research within the field of somatics, the next chapter discusses some of the literature I engaged with during the research process.

CHAPTER FOUR

Correspondences

> When I write, I read-write, I know that the works of others are being resurrected in translation. When I write, I rewrite; of course I write my own work, but my own work is already a gathering of other works. An answer; if I write, it's because I have received a letter. My writing is the letter that answers the letter I have received, and the correspondence goes on.
>
> — HÉLÈNE CIXOUS[1]

During the years of research for this book, I read widely in the areas of rape trauma, the psychophysiological ramifications of rape, the sociocultural impact of rape, trauma memory, somatics, and embodiment. I have been especially influenced by the writings of Susan Brison, Brene Brown, Bonnie Bainbridge Cohen, Tami Spry, and Hélène Cixous on the topics of rape aftermath, shame and vulnerability, embodiment and experiential anatomy, performative autoethnography, and embodied writing. However, word limitations precludes the inclusion here of all the reading I have done, consequently, this chapter situates itself as a partial archival holding place. To extend Cixous' metaphor, it is the location for only some of the correspondences from theorists and researchers that I engaged with during my research. My responses to the writings of Cixous and Spry, for example, do not appear in this chapter although references to their work are made elsewhere. Rather than offering a comprehensive gathering together of the overall literature examined, my focus here will be on three major themes:

1 From: Cixous, Hélène (1990). 'Difficult Joys.' In H. Wilcox, K. McWatters, A. Thompson, and A. Williams (eds), *The Body and the Text: Hélène Cixous, Reading and Teaching*. Hemel Hempstead: Harvester Wheatsheaf (26).

disclosure of sexual trauma; the role of shame; and trauma, memory, and the body. Much of my reading within these themed areas took place early in my research, overlapping with and informing the autoethnographic somatic inquiry work. As a body of reading, the literature provided a firm foundation for the autoethnographic component of the research. Throughout the chapter I have included extracts from the material gathered from the women research participants.

***

Brison (2002) was an influential presence throughout my research. More than any other autoethnographic research, her work propelled me into deep and thorough exploration of the literature concerning disclosure, shame, and trauma memory. I encountered her work, *Aftermath: Violence and the Remaking of a Self*, in the early stages. In this powerful text, Brison, a philosopher, articulates the shattering of self she experienced following a brutal act of rape and attempted murder in France in 1990. Drawing on established philosophical assumptions and feminist theory, she traces the complexities of her ongoing attempt to re-build an identity and sense of place in the world in the aftermath of her encounter with violence including her confrontation with the material conditions of her existence. Her work challenges the relevance of philosophy to gendered sexual violence and lived experience and questions its effectiveness in relation to ethics and social justice.

Brison's work guided and supported me in many ways. As an autoethnographic work it was shocking and courageous in its candidness and admirable for its lack of self-pity. It was also deeply affirming. Brison describes many of the aftermath ramifications of sexual trauma that I too have experienced. She writes of her sense of loss of control over her life; the fragmentation of the chronology of her experience; the disruption and frustration this caused in her attempts to create a coherent narrative of her experience; and the periods of verbal incoherence and 'fractured speech' she suffered (114). She talks of her shifting relationship with and mistrust of her body in the chaos of the aftermath as she grew to perceive her body as the 'enemy' (44). She chronicles her states of hypervigilance, her heightened startle response, chronic insomnia, her sense of a foreshortened future, and feelings of increased vulnerability. Each time I came across a reference to one of these responses in her text, all recognised in the rape trauma literature as predictable responses to the violence of rape (ACSSA 2006, Campbell and Wasco 2005, Crome and McCabe 1995, Foa and Rothbaum 1998), my body responded with a thrill of gratitude at encountering the familiar. But it was her telling of the slide into psychological dis-order in the absence of cognitive stability and her eventual understanding of this that left me weeping: 'I wasn't crazy. I was *traumatized*. My responses were normal, to be expected, after such a terrifying event' (111). Brison had captured in three sentences what I had struggled to acknowledge and then articulate during my own slide into and climb out of psychological dis-order. At various periods in my life, I had felt *crazy* without appreciating that I was *traumatised*. It was deeply moving and affirming to read a personal account of something so devastatingly familiar.

Brison writes extensively about the pervasiveness of gendered sexual violence, 'a problem of catastrophic proportion' (19), and the importance of personal testimony to the changing of public perceptions. In relation to this last point, Brison cites Bertoldt Brecht who writes: 'When evil comes like falling rain, nobody calls out "stop!" When crimes begin to pile up they become invisible. When sufferings become unendurable the cries are no longer heard. The cries, too, fall like rain in summer' (98). Brison responds with the following:

> And so we must come forward and report that evil has been done to us. Doing so does not turn us – or others – into victims. It may be that the most debilitating postmemories are those instilled by silence. It is only by remembering and narrating the past – telling our stories and listening to others' – that we can participate in an ongoing, active construction of a narrative of liberation, not one that confines us to a limiting past, but one that forms a background from which a freely imagined – and desired – future can emerge. (98–99)

Brison refers here to the potential for a new type of freedom for women victims of sexual violence which hinges on disclosure. For Brison, this freedom is tied to the consciously held memory of sexual violence, is bound to the notion of solidarity, and is facilitated by collective disclosure. Brison's freedom also refers to both the personal and collective empowerment to be found in the storying of rape trauma experiences. She suggests that it is through the telling of personal accounts of rape and other crimes of sexual violence, that we can draw greater attention to both the personal and the political aspects of rape, to the ramifications of sexual violence on both an individual and global level. Brison argues that if the stories of sexual violence remain untold or are told in isolation and if the voices of the victims central to those stories are hushed or fragmented, then the crimes themselves will indeed pile up and remain invisible and no-one will call out 'stop!'

I feel there is great hope in Brison's vision of the future and I want to be swept along by her optimism, but I fear that her hope has sprung from the experience of having her own story met with belief. It's possible to imagine that the disclosure of her brutal rape and near-death experience must have seemed inevitable. Given the injuries she sustained, it's also possible to imagine that those who came into contact with her immediately following the attack (a farmer on his tractor, the medical staff at the hospital, the police) would have had no trouble in accepting her disclosure as plausible. While the aftermath of her terrifying experience undoubtedly left her profoundly damaged and altered on many levels, the reassurance of having her story met with belief, with each telling, must surely have shaped her in other ways too. It's possible to speculate that the reassurance of knowing that her story had been accepted as a truthful account of her experience from the outset, as well as a plausible explanation for her injuries, must have allowed her personal integrity to remain intact. I imagine this has been pivotal to her ability to hold such hope for the future and to place this hope in the hands of disclosure.

Even so, Brison also notes that she was 'initially reluctant' to tell her family and friends that she had been raped fearing 'the word "rape" would have conventionalised what happened to me, denying the particularity of what had happened' (90). Brison was orally raped. Her reluctance to disclose was motivated partly by shame as well as a desire to avoid labelling herself a victim. Further, because her work as an academic involved in researching pornography and violence against women, she was concerned her disclosure would be 'dismissed as the ravings of an "hysterical rape victim"' (91). The word 'rape' also lacked specificity for her and she was concerned that it would implant false understandings of what happened in the minds of those around her, understandings based on postmemories that did not accurately reflect her reality. The term *postmemory* perhaps needs further clarification. As already noted, Brison has appropriated this term from the work of Hirsch (2014) and applied it within the context of gendered fear of rape violence. Hirsch developed this term to describe the generational transmission of memories inflicted on the children of Holocaust survivors:

> 'Postmemory' describes the relationship that the 'generation after' bears to the personal, collective, and cultural trauma of those who came before – to experiences they 'remember' only by means of the stories, images, and behaviours among which they grew up. But these experiences were transmitted to them so deeply and affectively as to seem to constitute memories in their own right. Postmemory's connection to the past is thus actually mediated not by recall but by imaginative investment, projection, and creation. To grow up with overwhelming inherited memories, to be dominated by narratives that preceded one's birth or one's consciousness, is to risk having one's life stories displaced, even evacuated, by our ancestors. It is to be shaped, however indirectly, by traumatic fragments of events that still defy narrative reconstruction and exceed comprehension. These events happened in the past, but their effects continue into the present.

Clearly, if we dwell for the moment on the impact of culturally absorbed postmemories of rape and their influence on her assumptions about how her story would be received, disclosure was a complex site of negotiation for Brison. It was possible though for her to at least negotiate this complexity from the platform of already established credibility.

Disclosure of sexual violence

My immersion in the work of Brison has drawn my attention to the role of disclosure in healing and to the deep gulf between her experience of disclosure and my own. For many of us who have experienced sexual violence, disclosure has either not been possible, or our disclosures have been treated with contempt and rejected as fabrications. My own desire to contribute to cultural change by reaching out with the story of my own experience of childhood rape and its aftermath, arises from a deeply held conviction that propels me to also make space, to help clear a path for the stories of other girls and women. Like Brison, I too feel the 'ethically and politically imperative' (91) for me to now tell my story and in the doing of telling, to make such stories less difficult in the future for girls and women to disclose. Like Brison too, I am cautious about adding further to girls and women's *prememories* by doing so. Unlike her though, my hope for a future of freedom in terms of ease of disclosure feels more tentative, somehow more fragile.

I lived for many years following my own experience of sexual violence with my personal integrity in pieces. The phrase 'You're a liar', tossed so casually into the intersubjective space between my young self and the girl I chose to disclose to, was a blow that added profoundly to my already shattered sense of self. This has shaped *me* in particular ways.

I long for a future free of sexual violence against girls and women, but I know this is naive and utopian. I long too for a future which will allow the voices of all girls and women whose bodies and lives have been violated by sexual trauma, to have the freedom to articulate what has been done to them, freedom bolstered by the knowledge that their stories will be treated with respect and care; a future in which girls and women are not shamed into silence, and in which disclosure and formal reporting of sexual violence is as culturally normalised as talking of other forms of personal violation. But I know that it may take several generations and intensive work by feminists and those interested in social justice to re-pattern entrenched sociocultural beliefs and expectations. I'm not without hope for change, it's simply that my hope emerges from my own shattering and silencing experiences and consequently, my hope balances on less stable ground. I am inspired by Brison's call to break open the silencing that surrounds sexual violence to create a *narrative of liberation*, and empathise with her when she says she is 'no longer afraid of what might happen if I speak out about sexual violence. I'm much more afraid of what might happen if I don't' (19). I'm acutely aware however, of the risks involved in disclosure and the consequences of negative responses to speaking out, especially for a child.

The rape trauma literature is clear that disclosure of a rape experience is not without risk for victims and acknowledges that there are a number of factors preventing victims from speaking out (Ahrens et al. 2007, Neame and Heenan 2003, Starzynski et al. 2005). These will now be explored.

Barriers to disclosure

As I have indicated in my personal story which opened the book, and as my own research with other women amplifies, disclosure of a rape experience is not without risk for victims. When deciding whether to disclose an assault and to whom, victims face a dilemma. While the desire for support undoubtedly drives the victim towards disclosure (Ahrens et al. 2007), the literature tells us there are a number of factors that act as barriers to disclosure (Ahrens et al. 2007, Neame and Heenan 2003, Starzynski et al. 2005). When deciding to disclose a sexual violence experience, victims risk not being believed; having their experience trivialised; and being made to feel responsible or to blame for the assault (Ullman et al. 2007). Furthermore, research suggests that sexual violence experienced specifically in childhood has a significant impact on disclosure, given the social stigma attached to such experiences as well as the child's fear of how their disclosure might be met (Feiring and Taska 2005).

We know that disclosure rates to formal support providers are low. Approximately two-thirds of victims disclose to some type of informal support provider such as friends or family members (Ullman and Filipas 2001). However, anticipated responses to sexual trauma disclosure can greatly influence decision-making for victims (Ullman 1996). There are several other factors which act as barriers to the disclosure for girls and women who have experienced sexual violence. These include a fear of destabilising the family unit; a sense of responsibility for other children in the family (if the victim is a child and the perpetrator known within the family); fear of further personal harm (Neame and Heenan 2003); self-blame; embarrassment; wanting to keep the experience private; and wanting to protect the perpetrator (Lievore

2003). With specific regard to self-blame, when this is incorporated into a victim's personal storying of their sexual trauma experience (as a means of making sense of the event), a further barrier is raised. This involves the victim doubting if they can in fact name the event as sexual violence, thereby rendering it less plausible and making disclosure less likely (Ahrens 2006, Littleton et al. 2006). This latter point is particularly relevant for children who have limited frameworks in which to place their experience, and, as indicated in Chapter Two, was certainly relevant to my own situation.

How a disclosure is responded to can have damaging ramifications for the victim. Studies suggest that different disclosure responses by support providers impact on a victim's recovery depending on whether these reactions are perceived by the victim as positive or negative. Somewhat surprisingly, positive responses have a limited impact; conversely and predictably, negative responses to disclosure, not uncommon particularly from formal support providers (Ahrens 2006, Starzynski et al. 2007), can have an extremely detrimental impact on the victim's future recovery and healing (Ahrens et al. 2007, Ullman et al. 2007, Anderson and Doherty 2008). Negative responses to disclosure can exacerbate feelings of shame, already identified in the previous chapter as a common response post-rape (Feiring and Taska 2005, Seu 2006, 2008, Vidal and Petrak 2007, Weiss 2010). Negative responses can lead to maladaptive coping strategies such as self-silencing behaviours, further serving to disempower the victim (Ahrens 2006). Anticipation of negative responses to disclosure may ultimately prevent girls and women from speaking (Ullman and Filipas 2001). The literature tells us that maladaptive coping strategies such as self-silencing practices place victims at an increased risk of subsequent physical health issues (Pennebaker and Stone 2004), as well as placing victims at an increased risk of developing Post Traumatic Stress Disorder and other health conditions (Ullman et al. 2007, Ullman and Filipas 2001, Feiring and Taska 2005, Seu 2006, Vidal and Petrak 2007, Weiss 2010). I believe self-silencing behaviours were central to the development of my unstable health in the aftermath years.

Negative responses to disclosure can also function as a form of revictimisation, serving to stigmatise the victim further (Klein 2004, Kaukinen and DeMaris 2009, Starzynski et al. 2005), and help create what has been termed 'secondary victimisation' (Ahrens 2006, Anderson and

Doherty 2008). This term is used to describe the impact of negative and judgemental responses by support providers to a victim's disclosure (Campbell and Raja 1999). Unsurprisingly, research is clear that victims already find an assault experience 'dehumanizing and humiliating' (2010, 286). When the treatment of the victim following disclosure lacks sensitivity and involves victim-blaming attitudes this can lead to secondary victimisation (Campbell and Raja 1999). With specific regard to formal support providers, Jill Astbury (2006a, 6) states unequivocally that 'Secondary victimisation by service providers is a major preventable form of harm to the survivor'. Implicit in this statement is the argument that it is critical to provide professional support providers with adequate levels of training if re-traumatisation is to be avoided. I argue, based on the experiences of myself and the other women in the book, that training which encompasses a focus on empathic, non-judgemental engagement with disclosing victims is essential to the prevention of secondary victimisation as well as necessary to avoid the exacerbation of feelings of shame.

> *'When I go to the dentist I have to spend a great deal of time convincing them that having things in my mouth is traumatic and then they have to hold me in the chair because I try to get away from them even though I am an intelligent woman and aware of my problem I still kind of dissociate.'*
>
> — CAROL

Given one of the components of my research was a survey of women's healthcare providers in relation to professional understandings of somatic responses to sexual violence, an Australian study by Mazza, Dennerstein, and Ryan (1996) offers up significant information with regard to disclosure rates to healthcare providers. The study found that despite previously attending medical practices, only 9 per cent of respondents had ever disclosed a rape experience to their healthcare professional with most saying that they had never been asked about a past history of sexual violation.

Clearly, disclosure of sexual violence is complex, full of risk, and freighted with difficulty. It is clear too that fear, in its many guises, plays a major role in determining whether a girl or woman will disclose. The literature confirms that victims fear a suite of possible consequences to disclosure: further harm (Neame and Heenan 2003); being made to feel responsible for the assault (Ullman et al. 2007); having their story dismissed

(Ahrens et al. 2007), or trivialised (Ullman et al. 2007). My own experience, following the rejection of my disclosure in childhood, included all of these factors, and is echoed in the stories from the other women.[2] Collectively, I believe these factors contributed to the strong feelings of shame I developed in relation to the rapes and to my rejected disclosure in the aftermath. The influence of shame in the context of rape trauma and disclosure will now be discussed.

The role of shame

Extract from my Honours thesis

[...]

You see, I didn't even have a name for what happened to me. The perpetrator's suffocating hand and urgent and harsh whispering had told me that what he was doing to me was seriously wrong, [...]. I thought that what he had done must have been sex, that nebulous, embarrassing thing we sometimes talked about with schoolgirl giggles in the corner of the playground. But, in amongst the giggling and the gaping gaps in my knowledge, I thought that this thing called 'sex' was something only adults did, so although this partially satisfied my need for an answer, in many ways it merely compounded my confusion. I was a young girl, not an adult and I had definitely not been willing, so where did that leave me? [...] Having decided to myself that 'sex' was the name for what I had experienced and the playing of games the cause, what other avenue was open to me but silence? I certainly couldn't talk to my parents about sex, especially if I had brought it on myself. The shame I felt was too great. And on reflection, perhaps this is why the girl in the garage had rejected my story too. Perhaps, by framing my experience as a sexual one (the only option available to me at the time), I had rendered my story shameful or improbable from the start.*

[* The 'games' I refer to here were 'Spin the bottle' and 'Postman's knock'. I became convinced fairly soon after the first rape that my participation in these games had brought about my own violation.]

2 Chapter Six, *Somatic narratives and meaning-making* provides a close examination of this.

Shame played an enormous role in the silencing I experienced post-rape. The shame I developed following my rejected disclosure and my imagined responses by others to any disclosure I might have been brave enough to attempt continued to silence me. The shame became self-perpetuating. The research has revealed to me that the profound feelings of shame I carried with me for so many years, and understood as particular to my own experience, are not uncommon in the aftermath of sexual violence. It also tells me feelings of shame are frequently associated with feelings of self-blame (Vidal and Petrak 2007, Weiss 2010). Feminist psychotherapist Bruna Irene Seu has written extensively on the role of shame in women's lives. Drawing on the work of Wumser (1981), Seu (1996) argues:

> the experience of shame can be triggered by a number of different situations, however in most cases, it seems to involve exposure in circumstances where the subject is perceived as weak and failing, dirty or defective (both physically and psychologically) and/or having lost control (either in terms of feelings or body functions). (40)

Feminist philosopher Cheshire Calhoun (2004, 131) notes how 'fears attached to shame are fears of being ridiculed, made the subject of gossip, subjected to demeaning treatment, and of being ostracized or abandoned'. I certainly felt all of these things; all were relevant to my own experience with many also relevant to the experiences of the women participants. But how does shame come to hold such sociocultural power? Calhoun argues that philosophy questions the worth of feelings of shame precisely because of the ways in which it diverts attention away from morally acceptable collective standards of behaviour to socially sanctioned individual modes of conduct. She argues:

> [...] shame seems to shift attention away from what *morality* requires to what *other people* [author's emphasis] require us to do or be like. In shame, we see ourselves through others' eyes and measure ourselves by the standards that we may not share. We take seriously the prospect of being subjected to ridicule, demeaning treatment, or social ostracism for falling short of other's moral standards. And we fear being exposed as the less worthy beings they might take us to be. (128)

Philosopher Sandra Bartky (1990) takes up this internalisation of shame. She argues shame can emerge in the aftermath of an experience as a perception not only of the failure to reach normalised social standards but also of the failure to meet personal standards of behaviour. She notes:

> Shame is the distressed apprehension of the self as inadequate or diminished: it requires if not an actual audience before whom my deficiencies are paraded, then an internalized audience with the capacity to judge me, hence internalized standards of judgement. Further, shame requires the recognition that I *am* [author's emphasis], in some important sense, as I am seen to be. (86)

Following both Calhoun's and Bartky's argument, shame invokes a complex form of social and self-punishment leading to perceptions of the self as deficient, inadequate, flawed and unworthy. While the experience of childhood rape alone could induce such perceptions, the desire for connection can perpetuate these feelings and reinforce the need for silence. Lee and James (2013, 46) understand the impact of shame within a social context as a 'social threat'. They define this as 'the sense of being rejected by the people who matter to us'. In this sense, shame functions as a form of social castigation and self-rebuke leading an individual to navigate the difficult territory between the desire to maintain connection with existing support systems and the retreat into the silence brought about by shame in order to protect those support systems. As already discussed, my own experience of wanting to preserve my closest friendship as a schoolgirl led me to disclose to someone I was not close to. The consequences of this decision had lifelong ramifications, although in reality, I could not have anticipated a positive response from my closest friend either, nor could I have assumed this from my family. And this was the immobilising conundrum. Silence seemed the only option. However, as my research revealed, both non-disclosure and anticipated negative reactions to disclosure are associated with poorer health outcomes (Ahrens, Stansell, and Jennings 2010). Clearly, there is little room to manoeuvre within this claustrophobic predicament. With shame playing a significant role in decision-making in relation to disclosure (Lievore 2003, Feiring and Taska 2005), where is a raped child supposed to take her story?

17 May, 2013

My understanding is that the 'flight, fight or freeze' response is innate. It is a reflexive behaviour aimed at aiding survival. Fear, however, is a learned response. It can be generated following a traumatic experience. It can be inherited transgenerationally through family stories. Or, it can be absorbed culturally. Fear is of course useful in terms of helping to recognise potential danger. But it can also paralyse voice and immobilise movement, creating a kind of rigor mortis. Shame is a cultural and discursive construction, it is not innate. Shame can offer self-protection but it can also be profoundly damaging. Fear and shame are almost always present in the aftermath of rape.

The work of scholar and social researcher Brene Brown (2010) has had a significant impact on me as both a sexual trauma researcher and someone who has experienced childhood rape. While Brown doesn't write specifically about the influence of shame within the context of rape trauma, the clarity she brings to her interpretation of shame and vulnerability cuts through complexity in ways that allow the work to resonate with me strongly on both a professional and personal level. Brown's (2012) twelve years of research into shame and vulnerability found that 'vulnerability is the core of shame and fear and the struggle for worthiness'. She understands shame as 'the fear of disconnection' as well as an individual's concern that if something about them is known, it will render them 'unworthy of connection' and leave them with feelings of 'not [being] good enough'.

'As I have been able to let go of various bits of shame about my past, I've felt less need to "punish" my body, in a sense.'
— KATE

Other researchers agree that vulnerability, understood as feelings of being unable to meet the standards of imposed sociocultural norms and/or self-imposed standards, is problematic for individuals and a major contributor to feelings of shame in contemporary western culture (Metcalf 2006, Jordon 2008). In her work however, Brown (2012) dispels any notion of vulnerability being a pejorative behavioural trait aligned with weakness, instead positioning vulnerability as 'emotional risk,

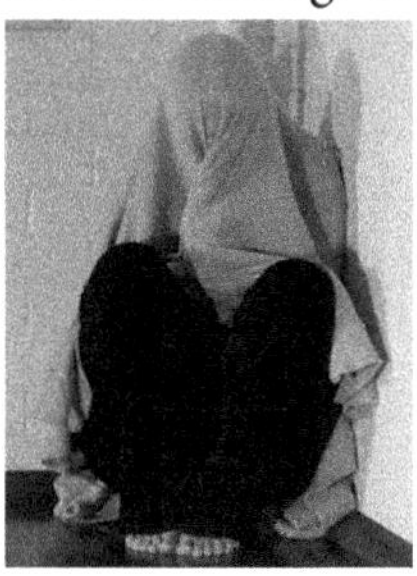

exposure, uncertainty. It fuels our daily lives [...] vulnerability is our most accurate measurement of courage – to be vulnerable, to let ourselves be seen, to be honest'. This view is supported by psychologist and scholar Judith Jordon (2008, 213). Jordon suggests reframing vulnerability as 'an experience in which we are open to the influence of others at the same time we are open to the need for others. We feel we can bring ourselves more and more into relationship. There is openness to mutual impact, a sense of being safe enough to move toward connection with others'. While this is a laudable position to take up, as someone who made the move toward connection to others as a child and suffered rejection, it is still difficult for me to perceive of states of vulnerability as anything other than places of great personal risk. Despite my years of psychotherapeutic intervention and my more recent body-based work for this research, I move in and out of acknowledging the potential benefits of allowing vulnerability to foster greater connection with others, and the retreat into less interpersonally connecting but personally and historically reliable states of self-protection.[3] It may be that my reluctant though persistent retreat into these states is fed by the remnants of an enduring perception of myself as both responsible for (guilty) and flawed by (shamed by) my rape experience.

Shame and guilt are often mistakenly brought together as facets of the same state. Brown (2012) however, is very clear about the distinction between feelings of shame and feelings of guilt. 'Shame,' she argues, 'is a focus on self, guilt is a focus on behaviour'. She notes that feelings of shame create a whole-of-person self-assessment, leading an individual to conclude 'I am bad' whereas feelings of guilt direct individuals towards the experience that precipitated those feelings, leading to the assessment that 'I did something bad'. Feiring and Taska (2005, 338) make a similar distinction between the two terms, noting 'Guilt concerns one's actions. Shame concerns one's entire being'. While these researchers differentiate between the two terms, they do not insist that the two are mutually exclusive. In

3 See Chapter Ten, *Coming to knowing through writing-as-Inquiry*, for a series of journal reflections relating to further contextualise my ongoing struggle with feelings of vulnerability.

relation to childhood sexual violence, my experience tells me that feelings of both shame and guilt can arise simultaneously during and following a rape experience, emerging from states of vulnerability that create feelings of both I am bad and I did something bad. My experience also tells me that harbouring such powerful self-critical feelings of shame and guilt leads to self-silencing behaviours.

The literature supports my understanding, telling us that shame, with its attendant self-silencing potential, is linked to an appreciation of concealment. Maureen L. Mahoney (1996, 605) cites Donald L. Nathanson (1992), who states, 'Shame teaches us the value of privacy: the privacy that protects us from shame, and the private place to which we must repair when humiliated. Just as shame follows the exposure of whatever we wished to keep private, the wish to withdraw provides a reasonable compensatory stratagem'. Calhoun (2004, 131) supports this view, suggesting that feelings of shame are 'strongly connected with the desire to conceal failings from others' view, with fear of exposure, and with anxiety about "how it will be for one's life with others" if one acts shamefully'. Furthermore, Mahoney (1996) suggests that a 'split subjectivity' (608) (one external, one internal) that can emerge from perceptions of difference and a desire to conform, holds particular types of experience in silence. She argues that 'Silence about difference is propelled by the threat of public humiliation' (607). This certainly reflects my own desire across the years for the protection silence gave me. While I continually feared the potential disclosure held for further humiliation and greater harm, I also longed to be like other people; not [self] judged or [self] damned for my rape history. I wanted to be free of feelings of shame, guilt and self-loathing.

Regrettably, although reassuringly for victims who carry shame, such feelings in the aftermath of sexual violence are not uncommon. A UK study found that two thirds of respondents harboured feelings of shame following a sexual assault experience with a high correlation between feelings of shame and feelings of self-blame and self-condemnation (Vidal and Petrak 2007, Weiss 2010). Brison (2002, 74), however, notes the ways self-blame can be misunderstood in the aftermath of sexual violence. In the context of the loss of control that victims experience, she writes:

> Whereas rape victims' self-blaming has often been misunderstood as merely a self-destructive response to rape, arising out of low self-esteem, feelings of shame, or female masochism, and fuelled by society's desire to blame the victim, it can also be seen as an adaptive survival strategy, if the victim has no other way of regaining a sense of control. (74)

Lee and James (2013, 48) differentiate between the shame that emerges from the perceived risk of judgement from those around us and the shame that emerges from self-imposed judgement. They position 'external shame' as the fear associated with 'how we exist in the minds of others'; the origin of external shame sits beyond the boundaries of self. They credit the potential for external shame with the power to silence any disclosure bound in shame. They apply the term 'internal shame' to shame experienced as a result of self-judgement, its genesis lying in contemptuous thoughts and critical self-evaluations. This ties in with the work of Metcalf (2006, 27) who draws on Freud's writing on shame and trauma in which Freud positions shame as a form of 'anticipatory vigilance [...] that offers protection'.

The literature has already established that experiences of shame can emerge from, and are linked to, a range of perceived human failings (Seu 1996). Working on Nathanson's premise that the retreat into shame offers a reasonable compensatory stratagem (Mahoney 1996) and taking Freud's concept of anticipatory vigilance (Metcalf 2006), shame can be understood in terms other than as a response to unconsciously and uncritically absorbed socially constructed and stigmatised views of experience. Metcalf suggests that if we take up Freud's position, it is possible to then consider shame as an agentic behavioural response 'that [...] protects against [...] traumatic vulnerability'. Viewed through this lens, the attachment of feelings of shame to particular experiences serves as a form of conscious self-protection, albeit a form impotent to effecting change in terms of altering entrenched socio-cultural attitudes through disclosure and formal reporting.

My own experience tells me that feelings of shame are a limiting factor in terms of inhibiting the re-integration of my trauma story, thus restricting the parameters of healing. The literature confirms this to be the case. Feiring and Taska (2005, 346) highlight the dangers of retreating into forms of self-protective behaviour. Their longitudinal research examined feelings of shame arising from childhood sexual trauma. The study found that shame acted as an impediment to the integration of trauma memory and trauma-related thoughts, determining that 'shame-motivated suppression of traumatic events is unsuccessful and contributes to high levels of intrusive recollections and memories'. They argue that intrusive recollections and memories, grounded in an inability to 'emotionally and cognitively' process the trauma, became symptomatic of the development of conditions such as Post Traumatic Stress Disorder. Other studies have also found that shame, especially when precipitated by the experience of a violent and traumatic event such as rape, can contribute to the development and severity of psychopathological conditions such as emotional stress and depression, as well as Post Traumatic Stress Disorder (Lee and James 2013, Robinaugh and McNally 2010, Vidal and Petrak 2007). Lee and James (2013, 48) consider both external and internal shame to be damaging states to carry but note that harbouring feelings of internal shame can be particularly detrimental to health. They argue that in the case of individuals who have experienced a traumatic event, harbouring internal shame can re-stimulate trauma memory in the form of flashbacks by 'continually stimulating our threat system'.

I'm reminded at this point of Brison's concept of the 'prememory of rape' (2002, 87–88). This hinges on the argument that girls and women's fear of rape is a cultural phenomenon and stems from their absorption of other people's stories and memories of rape (Hirsch's postmemories). This absorption works to presage the likelihood of their own rape in the future (prememories) and the fear of this holds girls and women in states of heightened vigilance. If we draw together Brison's prememory of rape, Freud's anticipatory vigilance, and Nathanson's reasonable compensatory stratagem and hold them alongside one another, it is possible to see how these concepts are temporally positioned, always projecting into the future in acknowledgement of the potential for future harm to all girls and women while also emerging from a victim's concomitant, immediate, and agentic desire for self-protection stemming from their already experienced past.

Undoubtedly, feelings of shame in the aftermath of a traumatic event are freighted with complexity and contradiction. The literature uncovers several crucial understandings. It makes the link between shame and the silencing that can emerge in its shadow. It reveals that shame can act to create self-protective behaviours through the silencing of victims' stories. And it shows that silencing, whether imposed or self-imposed, by inhibiting the re-integration of the trauma story, can have a largely detrimental impact on victims' physical and psychological health. My experience of harbouring feelings of shame in the aftermath of childhood rape resonates with the literature, echoing its complexities and the paradoxes. Shame is also present for some of the women in this book. Clearly, shame and its attendant consequences is a significant and powerful by-product of trauma, holding the capacity to impact in self-perpetuating ways on an individual level as well as at the broader cultural level.

Trauma, memory, and the body

> [T]rauma is not, will not, and can never be fully healed until we also address the essential role played by the body. We must understand how the body is affected by trauma and its central position in healing its aftermath. Without this foundation, our attempts at mastering trauma will be limited and one-sided.
>
> — PETER LEVINE[4]

> The sum total of experience, and therefore all memory, begins with sensory input.
>
> — BABETTE ROTHSCHILD[5]

The trauma literature is clear that trauma remains in the body if the experience remains unresolved (Herman 1992, Levine 1997, Rothschild 2000, Scaer 2001). As I have indicated in the previous chapter, Post Traumatic Stress Disorder is a common and devastating health outcome for victims

4 From: Levine, Peter (1997). *Waking the Tiger*. Berkeley, Cal: North Atlantic Books (3).

5 From: Rothschild, Babette (2000). *The Body Remembers: The Psychophysiology of Trauma and Trauma Treatment*. New York: W.W. Norton & Company (38).

of sexual violence (Ullman and Filipas 2001). It is critical to note however, that Post Traumatic Stress Disorder is unlikely to be the only way in which post-rape trauma manifests.

A study by Jacqueline Golding (1994) found 'women with a medical history of sexual assault were significantly more likely than women without a sexual assault history to report poor health status, several chronic diseases, and a variety of somatic symptoms, whether or not medically explained' (135). The study notes 29.3 per cent of women with a history of rape reported a minimum of six medically unexplained symptoms in contrast to only 15.8 per cent of women with no history of rape (133). The study focused on a range of medically unexplained symptoms, including gastrointestinal problems, pain, cardiopulmonary symptoms, neurologic, sexual, and reproductive dysfunction (134).

A further study conducted in the same year by Kimmerling and Calhoun (1994) found the most frequently reported physical symptoms of women who had experienced rape included tension headaches; stomach pain or nausea; back pain; allergies; cardiac arrhythmia; menstrual symptoms; weight changes; skin disorders; high blood pressure; and migraine headaches. The findings of these two studies are consistent with other more contemporary studies (Martin et al. 2007, Waldinger et al. 2006, Thompson et al. 2002). Many of the symptoms identified are consistent with the findings of this research, although I argue, they are not necessarily 'medically unexplained'.

Extract from my Honours thesis

The girl felt that if she wrapped the sheets and heavy blankets tightly around her body this would somehow protect her. She strained her eyes in the gloom, willing them to stay open. The effort made them feel dry and scratchy and swollen. She told herself she wouldn't fall asleep and that the blankets would keep her safe.

When the male silhouette appeared in the doorway, the blankets offered no protection and her body flooded with a darkness so impenetrable that it would be impossible for the girl to recall later the details of this night. She was, however, left with the image of the male silhouette burned into her memory with the force of a branding iron and it would be this image that would return as nightmares, year after year, to terrify and remind her once again.

I entered my research driven by the intuitive sense that my unresolved somatic memories of the events of 1971 were at the heart of the bodily dissonance I had experienced across the intervening years. It seemed apparent therefore, that before I could embark on a project that focused specifically on the bodily expression of the memory of sexual trauma, it was imperative that I first have a grasp of the attributes of memory as well as the impact of trauma on memory storage. Prior to the project, my reading within the field of memory research was minimal. Once immersed in the literature, I found my reading helped untangle the many disparate and knotted threads of my post-rape experience to enable me to perceive these not as a messy incoherent mass but rather as 'normal' responses to childhood trauma. Once again, the literature brought clarity, resonance and affirmation. The following section focuses on memory and trauma, briefly outlining memory's distinctively selective storage capacities, its ability to disrupt temporality, and the implications of this for trauma healing.

***

Trauma therapist Peter Levine (1997, 206) notes 'One of the most profound and challenging aspects of healing trauma is understanding the role played by memory'. Trauma specialist Babette Rothschild (2000, 26) describes memory as:

> [...] the recording, storage, and recall of information perceived from the internal and external environments. All of the senses are integral to how the world is perceived. The brain processes perceptions and stores them as thought, emotions, images, sensations, and behavioural impulses. When these stored items are recalled, that is memory. (26)

Attempts to understand the role and physiology of memory go back to ancient classical times when Plato imagined memory was akin to a tablet of wax into which impressions (memories) of experience were made and stored for later retrieval (Foster 2008). It wasn't until the 1960s, within the fields of medicine and the biological sciences, that interest in the function and mechanisms of memory systems began. Within these fields, as well as the neurosciences and psychology, the 1980s and 90s brought with them the recognition that memory was dynamic and involved multiple systems, leading to the recognition and identification of 'explicit' and 'implicit' memory. These discrete and contrasting systems differentiate between types of information, how they are stored, and how they are recovered (Rothschild 2000).

Explicit memory, sometimes referred to as declarative memory (Rothschild 2000, Scaer 2001), is information that is held with consciousness and cognition and which relies on language for both 'storage [...] and retrieval' (Rothschild 2000). Explicit memory records experience sequentially as it occurs (Levine 1997), holds episodic information (Rothschild 2000), and semantic information (Scaer 2001) allowing the chronology of events to be stored along with factual information surrounding events. Explicit memory moves from the present time backwards towards past events (Fuchs 2004). The activation of explicit memory is suppressed during a traumatic experience or during the re-experiencing of a traumatic event (Rothschild 2000). Implicit memory, sometimes referred to as non-declarative memory (Rothschild 2000, Scaer 2001), is memory that remains beyond consciousness and does not rely on language (Rothschild 2000). Implicit memory is reliant on past experiences (Foster 2008), is experientially, or somatically focused and relies on sensory information. Implicit memory 'does not re-present the past, but re-enacts it in the course of the body's performance. [...] implicit memory is our *lived past* [author's own emphasis]' (Fuchs 2004, 2). Implicit memory is compromised by trauma experience (Rothschild 2000).

There is a growing body of literature surrounding the impact of trauma on the body emerging from the fields of psychiatry, psychology, somatic psychotherapy, and the neurosciences (Goodwin and Attias 1999, Levine 1997, 2008, 2009, Rothschild 2000, Scaer 2001, van der Kolk 1994, 2007, Herman 1992). It is now accepted within these fields that 'somatic disturbance' (Rothschild 2000, 7) is central to disruptions in psychophysiological health (Nijenhuis and van der Hart 1999, Ogden and Minton 2001, Scaer 2001). It has been identified that symptoms continue to impact on victims via intrusive and often involuntary memories long after the traumatic event itself has passed (Rothschild 2000).

As mentioned in Chapter One, the literature from the psychiatry/psychotherapies tells us that during a traumatic event, while registering and responding to the experience, the conscious mind can separate itself from the actively engaged sensory body (van der Kolk 2007) thereby locating the traumatic event and responses to it either 'fully or partially [...] out of normal consciousness' (Nijenhuis and van der Hart 1999, 40) but still within the body. In this way, the storage of trauma memory differs from the storage of other types of memory (Mechanic, Resnick, and Griffin 1998). It is often fragmented (Culbertson 1995, Brison 2002, van der Kolk, van der Hart, and Marmar 2007), predominately sensory, and often non-linguistic (Hovdestad and Kristiansen 1996, Nijenhuis and van der Hart 1999, van der Kolk 2007, 1998). Consequently, people who experience a traumatic event often are unable to provide a cohesive or coherent account of the experience because the event itself has failed to register as explicit memory, thereby fragmenting the memory in both temporal and spatial terms (Rothschild 2000), making verbal accounts difficult.

The memories I carry of my two separate experiences of rape offer examples of the ways in which memory detail is selectively stored, can become fragmented, as well as temporally and spatially distorted. The memory of my first rape experience is dense with sensory detail although limited visually. I hold this memory as a series of predominately viscerally-felt experience fragments; when I replay this event my limited visual memories have an interrupted, staccato quality like a badly edited film, jumping from scene to scene with large blank gaps between each. Alongside the few images, I can feel in my body the many sensory elements of the experience and the fear and powerlessness I felt.[6] If I recall my second rape experience, my visual memory stops at the silhouette of the perpetrator standing in the semi-lit doorway of the bedroom but my somatic memory does not end there. I can still feel the terror that went ricocheting throughout my entire child's body as I waited, frozen with fear, for what I knew was inevitable.

The 'flight, fight, or freeze' response offers an explication of partial or incoherent trauma memory. Levine (1997) writes extensively on this response to trauma with special attention given to the ways in which the

6 Chapter Ten, C*oming to knowing through writing-as-inquiry*, holds the poem 'rape', written largely from my sensory memory of the first rape experience.

freeze response impacts on the nervous system. The freeze response, also called the 'immobility' response by physiologists (Levine 1997, 16), or 'tonic immobility' by psychotherapists (Rothschild 2000, 9), is an involuntary behavioural response intended to protect 'reptiles and mammals when faced with an overwhelming threat' (Levine 1997, 16). Levine illustrates the duality of the strategic usefulness of this response using a young impala and a cheetah as an example. Firstly, if the impala 'freezes' or plays 'dead', the cheetah might begin to drag the impala to its den with the intention of consuming it with its young. If the cheetah's attention is diverted for some reason, the impala might emerge from its frozen state and escape. Once in a place of safety, it will 'literally shake off the residual effects of the immobility response and gain full control of its body' (16). Secondly, while in its frozen state, should the impala not be able to escape and should the cheetah begin to feed on it, the impala's consciousness is altered to such an extent that it will experience no pain.

Humans, as mammals, drop into this same involuntary response when faced with life-threatening situations. For example, when the human body freezes, like the impala, the altered state ensures that 'Time slows down and there is no fear or pain. In this state, if harm or death do occur, the pain is not felt as intensely' (Rothschild 2000, 10). The difference, however, between humans and other living creatures, Levine (1997) argues, is that some human brains rationally override the instinctual body, interrupting the primal necessity for the energy to move into and out of the body through shaking off in order to create resolution and restore equilibrium. When interruption occurs in humans, it leaves the unresolved and residual energy frozen in the body. Levine observes that if the memory of the event is subsequently stimulated and somatic responses are felt and re-experienced, this is the trapped and frozen residue of energy in the nervous system. If it remains trapped, he cautions, 'it can wreak havoc on our bodies and spirits' (19). It is not, therefore, that the body feels no pain, but rather, the memory of the pain sits at a somatic level and below consciousness in a kind of rigor mortis state.

The physiological impact of shock or trauma on the nervous system of the body is discussed in terms of 'nerve reversal' within the Body-Mind Centering paradigm (Bainbridge Cohen 2013). Bainbridge Cohen observes that during a non-traumatic event, sensory information enters the body via the somatic and autonomic nervous systems, finds its way into the spinal cord via the 'dorsal root', or 'posterior horn' as it is sometimes referred, at the back of the spinal cord and flows out via the motor nerves of the 'ventral root', or 'anterior horn', at the front of the spinal cord. Drawing on experiential theory, Bainbridge Cohen observes that during a traumatic event, 'when more information comes in than can be processed [...], we refuse the information into the posterior horn [dorsal root].' The theory goes that when refusal occurs, the information reverses back along the sensory nerves of the dorsal root where it is stored in the cellular tissue. This reversal is thought to have the effect of 'slowing down time' (Hartley 1995, 257). With the information in stasis, it cannot be processed in the usual way via the output of energy through the motor nerves (Bainbridge Cohen 2008). Linda Hartley (1995) takes up Bainbridge Cohen's experiential understandings:

> When a person goes into a state of shock, she is unable to process information coming in and an appropriate motor response cannot be made. [...]The initial response to traumatic events is one of numbness and disbelief. The information is rejected and time stops; there is a freezing that, when extreme, can ultimately lead to death or be witnessed as a kind of living death. A part of us may stay there for a whole lifetime, unconscious to the shock effect, as the trauma hasn't yet been fully experienced. (256–257)

Similarly, Levine (1997, 21), with specific reference to 'war veterans and victims of rape', also points to the long-term impacts of unresolved and frozen sensory information. Levine argues when information 'remain[s] stuck in the traumatic maze', it creates symptoms of physiological unrest and distress in victims' bodies for 'months or even years.' He cautions that when somatic symptoms are experienced in the aftermath, they can be frightening. The answer, however, to the resolving of physiologically frozen states, he argues, lies in 'uncoupling the immobility [...] from the fear associated with it' (109). Given the 'overpowering surges of emotion' that can be unleashed when un-freezing occurs, 'fear of violence to self and others reactivates the immobility, extending it, often indefinitely, in the form of frozen terror. This is the vicious circle of trauma' (109).

Within the Body-Mind Centering approach, Bainbridge Cohen (2013) refers to the re-integration and resolution of stored cellular memory as 'de-reversal'. Hartley (1995) expands on this:

> It is important to reach the actual point of experiencing the full impact of the shock. This means getting in touch with the emotions or actions that were felt to be unacceptable or overwhelming. If we can hold ourselves within the experience without responding in our habitual ways, it is possible to begin to 'de-reverse' this patterning. (258)

Bainbridge Cohen (2013) makes a crucial point with regard to de-reversal by stressing the importance of attempting the process slowly so as not to 're-enact' the experience but to 'resolve' it. Hartley (1995, 258) also cautions that de-reversal needs to take place within a trusting and contained therapeutic space or other environment where the individual feels safe and supported enough to sit with the emotions of the experience. When this safe space is established, she says, the individual 'can begin to process the experiences that have been held unconsciously within the spinal cord, enough energy will be released to make some motor response possible through the front of the cord, and the de-reversal can begin to happen.'

In addition to the resolution of frozen cellular memory stored in the spinal cord through a process of de-reversal, Bainbridge Cohen (2008) also makes specific reference to the impact any disruption to the autonomic nervous system can have on the enteric, sympathetic and parasympathetic nervous systems. Each of these systems is implicated in responses to trauma. The autonomic nervous system, and more especially, the enteric nervous system, is of particular interest. Concerned with the gut, the enteric nervous system is the earliest nervous system to develop embryologically (Bainbridge Cohen 2008). Although autonomous, it has extensive connections with the sympathetic and parasympathetic nervous systems (Tortora and Derrickson 2009). The enteric nervous system has a higher concentration of neurons than any of the peripheral organs and is thought to have a similar number to those contained in the spinal cord (Furness 2011). These neurons run the length of the gut from the oesophagus to the anal sphincter (Bainbridge Cohen 2008, Pert 1999, Tortora and Derrickson 2009). Aside from the already established understandings of the role the enteric nervous system plays in digestion (Tortora and Derrickson 2009), Bainbridge Cohen's experiential understandings consider that it also determines 'whether we feel safe or not' (180). This is a view shared by Pert (1999, 188). She argues the enteric nervous system has the ability to 'feel our emotions.'

Bainbridge Cohen (2008) argues that the impact of trauma on the body can affect the autonomic nervous system by interrupting the wave-like rhythm created by the movement of fluid between the parasympathetic and the sympathetic neural pathways. This 'autonomic rhythm' (186) moves on a horizontal plane throughout the cells of the body, running perpendicular to the longitudinal nerves of the somatic nervous system. Her understanding is that the autonomic rhythm 'underlies the flow and activity of the somatic nerves' (186). When an interruption occurs, such as during a traumatic event, the autonomic rhythm is 'restricted' (186) and this then impacts on the functioning of the somatic nerves which serve the muscle systems of the body. The restricted functioning of the somatic nerve pathways 'can cause secondary stress in the autonomic rhythm' (186), and thus creates a self-perpetuating disruption which impacts negatively on the balance of the parasympathetic and sympathetic nervous systems. When this occurs, according to Bainbridge Cohen, it manifests in an individual's 'ability to "move" through the world with or without symptoms being overtly expressed in the skeletal muscles' (186). Further, Bainbridge Cohen argues that 'disruptions in the autonomic rhythm can manifest as physical, emotional, perceptual, and/or cognitive difficulties' as well as becoming 'key factors in chronic conditions' (186).

Levine's psychotherapeutic understandings of the freeze response, and Bainbridge Cohen's experiential observations and understandings surrounding trauma, nerve reversal, and the disruption to the autonomic rhythm, each offer explanations for the long-term bodily dissonance I have experienced. Additionally, it clarifies for me the underlying physiology of the re-stimulation of cellular memory I experienced on several occasions during private Body-Mind Centering hands-on sessions with Alice.[7] It is

7 See Chapter One, *Philomela and me* for the journal extract concerning one of these private sessions with Alice. From what I have come to understand from this research,

interesting to note here that, given Levine's example of the impala shaking off the residual effects of its frozen state in order to carry on, I endured long bouts of trembling on each of these specific private sessions, as I did from time to time during other hands-on and deep cellular work. I now draw two likely explanations for this. Firstly, I was experiencing a much delayed although spontaneous drop into the primal behavioural pattern of 'shaking off' in order to regain equilibrium following the shock of re-experiencing the feelings and sensations in my body, something that quite possibly failed to take place when fear overwhelmed me both during and following the original rapes. And secondly, the anticipatory fear I held with regard to the re-experiencing of feelings and sensations associated with the original rapes initiated a fight or flight response within my sympathetic nervous system. This response increases the heart rate and respiration and reduces blood supply to the skin and peripheral regions redirecting it to the muscles in preparation for fight or flight (Rothschild 2000). The reduction in blood supply to my periphery would have had the effect of making me feel very cold, while the trembling, in addition to shaking off residual energy to restore equilibrium, would also have served to restore warmth and thermostatic balance to my body.

I have drawn these conclusions from the literature already mentioned and from my experiential explorations and understanding. Further to this, I believe it was absolutely necessary for me to re-experience my unresolved and frozen cellular memory in order to process and re-integrate the information and eventually find greater somatic balance. Critical to this though, is my certainty that I could not have released my hold on my body to allow my cellular memory to rise up and consciously meet me without the unwavering trust I built up over time within the therapeutic space with Alice. Her depth of experience as a Body-Mind Centering practitioner, coupled with her intelligence, sensitivity and support in the therapeutic relationship were crucial elements, I believe, to the ongoing resolution of

---

the hands-on work precipitated re-stimulation of frozen sensory information held in my body since my childhood rape experiences.

my unprocessed trauma memory at a cellular level and were vital to the containment of the feelings and sensations that form part of this process.

Returning to the memory research of Levine (1997), drawing on the work of researchers Israel Rosenfield (1988), Gerald Edelman (1989) and Akhter Ahsen (1968) from within the fields of medicine, neuroscience and psychotherapy respectively, Levine presents a view to challenge prevailing understandings of memory. These researchers each posit the concept that memory is partial and selective rather than supporting the prevailing notion that memory is a linear and sensorially accurate record of an experience. Based on their findings, Levine cites memory as 'a particular type of perception' (208) rather than 'an accurate imprint of an event'. He supports this view with the often dramatic variation in eye witness accounts of the same incident as an example. Further to this, he says, memory becomes a 'process by which the organism creates a gestalt (functional unit) of the experience' which can be either 'a faithful representation of an actual event or it can just as easily be a rendering consisting of unrelated data from several different events [...].' Levine admits that presenting memory in this way is contentious, turning 'conventional notions upside down and backwards' (210) but defends these researchers' work by suggesting this concept 'offers a reprieve to traumatized people who are caught on the endless treadmill of trying to piece together a coherent movie of what happened to them' (1997, 210).

This desire for such a reprieve could account for my own repeated replaying of the fragmented film of my rape experiences and my frustrated efforts to fill in the gaps to produce a flowing account of each. Regrettably, the suggestion that the memory-film I replay could be either unreliable or inaccurate, possibly a direct record of one event or maybe a composite of both events is a suggestion I find surprisingly disturbing. On the one hand, Levine's understanding of memory appears to offer me a means of interpreting and understanding memory that could shift the frustration of partial and fragmented memory recall away from my own inadequacies and onto the underlying mechanisms of memory storage and recall itself. On the other hand, it flings me into the realm of self-doubt once again, despite my frustrations. These memories, held in my body and now re-experienced as somatosensory and visual, fragmented and partial, are my only 'evidence' to those events. If doubt is cast over their accuracy, and with no perpetrator coming forward to admit to the rapes, where does that leave me? I prefer to honour my embodied processes and instead consider the fragmentation and incoherence of my trauma memory as experientially accurate, or an accurate measure of the level of embodied terror I experienced. This is a complex minefield. I am fascinated by my own response to Levine's work here, in particular his suggestion that my own series of fragmented visual and somatic memories may somehow be flawed, or 'inaccurate' in a rational, logical sense.

Roberta Culbertson (1995) provides an elegant account of the embodied response to a traumatic event. Her writing, which begins with her re-framing of trauma as a form of wounding, helps bring alive what could become disembodied information in a less somatically sensitive hand:

> Wounding produces in the body particular neurological responses; these are retained as the memory of the event – largely as it was experienced and responded to, whether understood or not. Such memory is generally full of fleeting images, the percussion of blows, sounds, and movements of the body – disconnected, cacophonous, the cells suffused with the active power of adrenalin, or coated with the anesthetizing numbness of noradrenalin. The action of adrenalin and noradrenalin at the time of traumatic events functions to make the event a certain sort of experience (in which one fled or went numb or fought back) which may later be recalled. It also makes the experience qualitatively different, limiting it sometimes merely to the reflexes; siphoning senses of fear and panic off into other parts of the brain so as not to destroy the potential for action as required. Thus events and feelings are simply not registered, but this does not mean they are forgotten; they are located in other parts of the mind and the parts of the body affected as well, though separated from the continuing integrated story of the self. Such memories – of abject fear, pain, anguish – are left apart from the story of the self because if included in it they would destroy it, being so counter to the self's conception of itself as whole as to be inimical and threatening to it. Thus the body and mind conspire to protect the self from overwhelming awareness of its permeability, to deny in important ways the terror of the experience. This does not necessarily suggest some ulterior altruism of the mind or some sort of super-knowledge of harm. It may simply be the consequence of the body's purpose – to sustain the body at nearly all costs. The body is designed to focus in extremity on what can be done, or how best to avoid injury – the rest of what remains a human experience is cut off or not processed by the brain otherwise engaged. Such defences

> may continue, even though, like much healing, they may ultimately be incomplete or even likely to result in more harm to the body. (174)

Culbertson (1995, 174) goes on to articulate a rarely discussed ramification of post-rape trauma that holds a great deal of interest for me. She identifies and offers a possible explanation for the presence of gaps in recall, or blank periods in everyday life, sometimes experienced by victims of trauma, including me. These blank periods, she tells us, can occur when under stress, during moments when the repressed memories of traumatic experiences are triggered by stimuli, or when victims attempt to retrieve the trauma memory. She calls these blank periods 'temporal blanks', positing they could be the manifestation of the original memory itself, too traumatic to recall but present nonetheless through absence. This intriguing concept is consistent with other research already mentioned which acknowledges the exclusion of some information from storage in the explicit memory system following a traumatic event (sitting as repressed memory), the subsequent fragmentation of the original memory of that event, and the incoherent narrative that can emerge as a result of that fragmentation (Rothschild 2000, van der Kolk 1994). Culbertson's concept of temporal blanks offers both an explanation for, and a jolting reminder of, the enduring presence and persistence of unresolved embodied trauma memory, one that resonated strongly with me, as the following journal extract attests.

13 April, 2012

I've been reading again the Roberta Culbertson (1995, 175–176) journal article that has become so important to me. I'm particularly interested in the section where she talks about 'blank' periods that can arrive, sometimes triggered, sometimes spontaneously, in the aftermath of trauma. She understands these 'blanks' as the resurgence of the trauma experience itself without any of the imagery, the periods when the mind erased the memory of the experience, went blank, in order to protect the self. I've of course heard of people suffering amnesia following trauma. But this is quite different. She's suggesting these ongoing 'blank' periods that arrive are the manifestation of the splitting of conscious awareness at the moment when one is experiencing the threat to survival. In going blank, one is re-experiencing the moments of terror without the actual memory.

It's a stunning concept and when I first read this I was completely astounded, firstly, to read about blank periods and secondly, to have an explanation for something that has plagued and frustrated me since the rapes because it's something for which I have never had a satisfactory explanation.

I have always viewed these 'going blank' periods, as I've described them to myself, as simply the manifestation of whatever anxiety I was feeling at the time they occurred. Most often they happen when I'm talking to people, am asked a question, become self-conscious and literally lose language and thought with stunning abruptness and can't go on or retrieve what it was I wanted to say. The notion of the 'blank period' being the memory without the details of the actual memory is extraordinary and utterly affirming.

My reading within the field of memory research overlapped with my pursuit of information that could provide links between trauma memory and the somatic manifestations of rape. I found the literature emerging from the field of sexual trauma consistently told me that when memories of traumatic events are not able to be integrated there is a risk of biobehavioral[8] adaptations manifesting as a result. While literature surrounding mental health outcomes dominates sexual trauma research (ACSSA 2005, Anderson and Doherty 2008, Campbell and Wasco 2005, Thompson et al. 2001), research emerging from some areas of the psychologies supports the view that rape and other forms of sexual violence have more than a psychological impact and indeed commonly compromise the physical health of victims (ACSSA 2006, Crome and McCabe 1995, Thompson et al. 2002).

'Quite often, I fear that something will go wrong in my body that will be fatal, but I know this is part of a sense of foreshortened future which is part of PTSD.'
— PATRICIA

While I have stated elsewhere that I do not wish to view this research through the lens of Post Traumatic Stress Disorder, it must be noted that Post Traumatic Stress Disorder is commonly cited as a

8 The term *biobehavioral* is defined as: 'Of or relating to the interrelationships among psychosocial, behavioural, and biological processes, as in the progression or treatment of a disease'. Obtained from: <http://medical-dictionary.thefreedictionary.com/biobehavioral>.

predictable and devastating health outcome for victims of sexual violence (Ullman and Filipas 2001). Indeed, prevalence rates of Post Traumatic Stress Disorder amongst victims of sexual violence are higher than for those who have experienced combat trauma (Esposito 2005). For the purposes of this research however, it is important to note that Post Traumatic Stress Disorder, while commonly considered to be so, is not just a mental health condition, rather, it is a complex disorder with significant somatic elements. Rothschild (2000, 6–7) states unequivocally 'somatic disturbance is at the core of PTSD' and those who develop this condition in the aftermath of trauma commonly experience 'visual, auditory, and/or other somatic reality' in the form of sensory flashbacks as well as 'chronic hyper-arousal in the autonomic nervous system'.

A number of studies on the health outcomes of women who have experienced sexual violence found women often report similar physical symptoms (Kimerling and Calhoun 1994, Martin et al. 2007, Thompson et al. 2002, Waldinger et al. 2006). A study by Jacqueline Golding (1994, 135) is consistent with these findings although she makes the point of adding that somatic symptoms may or may not be 'medically explained'.

We know at this point of the risks involved in disclosing a rape experience. We know of the impact of trauma on the body and the concomitant selective nature of trauma memory with its full or partial storage potential. And we know somatic symptoms are not always connected by victims to their trauma experience (Goodwin and Attias 1999). With these established understandings in mind, the possible link between these understandings and the emergence of aftermath symptoms in the body, whether medically explained or otherwise, begins to reveal itself. With research in the fields of psychiatry (van der Kolk 1994) and the neurosciences (Pert 1999, Damasio 1994, Doidge 2007) now acknowledging the physiological links between the mind and the body, it seems apparent that while the strategic storage of trauma memory acts 'as a psychological escape mechanism from fear' (Scaer 2001, 98), the feeling body has no escape mechanism.

The literature discussed thus far has established that trauma is felt in the body (Culbertson 1995, Herman 1992, Levine 1997, Rothschild 2000, Scaer 2001). My experiential observation is that my body was at the frontline of my rape experiences and as such, continued to store, or freeze, sensorial information related to the rapes until such time that it was able to be brought to consciousness, processed, and re-integrated. Until this complex processing was made possible through my experiential research, the unresolved and silenced trauma memory continued to play out in my body. Herman (1992, 1) argues that 'remembering and telling the truth about terrible events are prerequisites [...] for the healing of individual victims' although she cautions that the often fragmentary nature of traumatic memory can discredit victim accounts of trauma, leading them to adopt secrecy behaviours. Herman notes that when this occurs, 'the traumatic event surfaces not as a verbal narrative but as a symptom'.

Within the fields of medicine and psychiatry, the term somatisation[9] is given to traumatic mental distress expressed through physical symptoms. Somatisation is a gendered phenomenon that occurs globally and primarily in females. It can be defined as 'the tendency to experience, conceptualise and communicate mental states and distress as physical symptoms or altered bodily function' (Singh 2009, 90). It's important to note the chronology suggested by this definition: the change in physicality expressed as dysfunction occurs after the trauma is experienced at the level of the psyche. My own research challenges this chronology by examining the ways in which sexual trauma is experienced first at a bodily physiological level with subsequent somatic and/or psychological dysfunction/disturbance the direct expression of this bodily experience. The literature already discussed, derived as it is from the fields of psychology, psychotherapy, and trauma studies, consistently supports the chronology I have adopted and identifies 'somatic disturbance' (Rothschild 2000, 7) as central to compromises in psychological and physical health (Scaer 2001, Ogden and Minton 2001, Nijenhuis and van der Hart 1999).

This is an important point for professional healthcare practitioners. Health research suggests that practitioners are likely to encounter amongst their female patients those who have experienced violence of various kinds (Klein 2004). Of the women patients attending healthcare

9 This use of the medical term *somatisation* is not to be confused with the use of the same term within the practice of Body-Mind Centering. See Appendix 1 for a definition of the term within this context.

practices, it is estimated that over the course of their lifetime, up to one third will have experienced sexual violence in particular (Astbury 2006b). Additionally, an estimated 30–60 per cent of patients 'in primary healthcare settings' present with somatic symptoms that have 'no known medical basis' (Waldinger et al. 2006, 129). These findings suggest, when viewed in combination with the findings from the field of psychology which indicate that victims themselves do not always associate their physical symptoms with past sexual violence (Calhoun and Atkeson 1991, Goodwin and Attias 1999), there is a pressing need for professional healthcare providers not to dismiss physical complaints as simply somatisation[10] or somatoform disorders[11] for which 'no organic cause is readily apparent' (Singh 2009, 90). Indeed, Bessel van der Kolk (2007) urges clinicians to make themselves aware of the possibility of a patient's trauma history if they are to treat their patients effectively, a view underscored by others in the field who suggest that routine questioning of a possible sexual violence history of patients by professional healthcare practitioners may better assist the treatment and recovery of victims of sexual trauma (Hurst et al. 2003, Ahrens et al. 2007, Havig 2008). This is especially relevant given that we now know that victims, as patients (van der Kolk, van der Hart, and Marmar 2007) do not always volunteer details of past sexual trauma (Forbes et al. 2007, Esposito 2005), even if they are experiencing distress during something as routine as a gynaecological examination (Robohm and Buttenheim 1997).

The sexual trauma research confirms that somatic symptoms may persist for some victims only in the short term, while for others, symptoms

10 'Somatisation disorder' is the contemporary name for the suite of unexplained symptoms once referred to as hysteria (Showalter 1998). Somatisation disorder is sometimes referred to as 'somatoform disorder'. Chapter Six: *Somatic narratives and meaning-making* explores this further.

11 These conditions are also sometimes referred to as 'somatisation disorder'. Somatoform disorders are defined as: 'Any of a group of psychological disorders marked by physical complaints for which no organic or physiological explanation is found and for which there is a strong likelihood that psychological factors are involved.' Found at Merriam-Webster Online Dictionary, <http://www.merriam-webster.com/medical/somatoform%20disorder>.

may continue for many years (Calhoun and Atkeson 1991). Indeed, the separation of mind and body that can occur post-rape, either consciously or unconsciously, can be a continuing source of disturbance for girls and women. Mills and Daniluk (2002), in a study of dance therapy and its impact on victim recovery, found that female patients who felt detached from their bodies following a rape experience, sought dance therapy specifically to satisfy their desire to cultivate a sense of reconnection with their bodies. The women in the study saw dance movement as a means of 'getting back into their bodies' (80), and a way to facilitate the process of re-integration.

The somatic manifestations of trauma have profound implications for healthcare professionals in relation to the care of girls and women who may have experienced sexual violence. Information drawn from a large US study highlights the need for healthcare providers to be alert to the physical manifestations of sexual trauma when dealing with patients (Thompson et al. 2002). This point is underscored in a study by Martin, Young, Billings and Bross (2007) which found that 42 per cent of victims displayed physical health conditions. The complex combination of self silencing and fragmented and/or repressed trauma memory previously discussed means that victims experiencing traumatic stress may not have awareness of links between their trauma history and what they are experiencing. This can make it difficult for victims to interpret somatic symptoms and connect them to the traumatic event itself (Goodwin and Attias 1999). When this occurs, women may often seek help for somatic complaints without mentioning a history of past sexual violence (Forbes et al. 2007, Esposito 2005).

Another US study (Robohm and Buttenheim 1997) found 82 per cent of participants had never been questioned by their gynaecological healthcare professional about a possible history of sexual violence despite a significant number experiencing distressing responses, including disturbing somatic memories, during examinations. This is consistent with the Mazza, et al study (Mazza, Dennerstein, and Ryan 1996) already mentioned and is supported by a New Zealand/Australian study conducted in 2003. The Hurst, MacDonald, Say and Read (2003) study drew on the earlier work of Shew and Hurst (1993) which found 90 per cent of patients at a sexual health clinic had never been asked about a past history of sexual violence by any healthcare professional. The Hurst et al (2003) study surveyed professionals working in the field of sexual health. Their research revealed that only 67 per cent of New Zealanders and 44 per cent of Australian respondents 'mostly, or routinely' asked patients about a past history of sexual violence. This is despite 93 per cent of respondents acknowledging the appropriateness of such questioning within a sexual health setting (2003, 331).

The findings from these studies are consistent with my experiential observations which confirm that it is unlikely a healthcare practitioner will enquire after a woman's history of sexual trauma. I have been a patient at a great number of medical centres since 1971, for a variety of health concerns, some major, some minor, and some medically unexplained, both here and in the UK. I have sat in front of numerous healthcare practitioners unable to communicate the difficulties I was experiencing, hoping they would notice my distress and ask what was troubling me. I finally poured out my rape history to a GP, and later to the psychologist I was referred to, only when I eventually sought help for my severe depression in 1997, and only when exhaustion, desperation, and the sheer weight of the trauma and grief I was carrying was making my life intolerable. These were the only occasions I ever voluntarily disclosed my rape history. I had not been asked by any healthcare professional if I had a history of sexual trauma prior to 1997 and nor have I been asked this since. I can only now, some forty-five years after the events, disclose to others without feeling physically ill.

***

Throughout this chapter I have actively drawn attention to the ways the literature I have encountered does or does not resonate with my own experience. The more nuanced our understanding of the connections between sexual violence, somatic memory, shame, and ongoing trauma, the more likely it will be that girls and women who, like me, have experienced rape violence, will not have to struggle to disclose until they reach breaking point.

The literature discussed in this chapter is clear: we know that rape is a gender-based crime; we know that women fear the possibility of rape above all other crimes; we know that the category ten-to-fourteen-year-old girls consistently registers the highest victimisation rates; we know that rape and other crimes of sexual violence are chronically under-reported; we know that sexual violence itself impacts in multiple ways on both the body and the psyche; we know that disclosure, both formal and informal, is axiomatic to Brison's (2002) narrative of liberation through the telling of our stories and by listening to others while at the same time, telling our stories is full of risk; we know that shame plays a significant role in decision-making with regard to disclosure; we know that shame and feelings of self-blame can silence disclosure leading to the development of self-silencing practices; we know that carrying silenced trauma experience has further significant and detrimental health ramifications at the level of the physiological as well as the level of the psychological; and we know that healthcare professionals do not always ask women about a possible history of sexual violence despite women acknowledging the appropriateness of such questioning.

My immersion in the literature was often bleak and confronting and weighed heavily on me. However, this weight also lengthened my spine, squared my shoulders, lifted my chin, and filled my body with renewed strength and the motivation to continue the research journey.

CHAPTER FIVE

Somatic narratives: Participant somatic inquiry

Your words and your life no longer separate, after decades of hiding in your skin.

— ANNE MICHAELS[1]

'... fear about their [health care workers], responses fear I'd be forced to report the abuse'

— NINA

'I only remember trying to tell my GP once, & being totally discounted, & being told not to make up silly stories'

— PHILIPA

'I can't breathe if I watch people in confined spaces [...] I can't have my face underwater or held under a blanket'

— CAROL

'I felt disconnected from my body when I was growing up, it felt like a stranger's body'

— KATE

'There are many things I realised over time that were the result of the Childhood Sexual Abuse'

— NANCY

'Flashbacks can induce a sense as though somebody is painfully entering my body'

— PATRICIA

'Push thought back of mind. Never think about it'

— FELICITY

'I love massage but am not good with trust so have found the chairs in shopping centres to be the best alternative/compromise'

— MONICA

'On one of the rare occasions that I have discussed the childhood rape with a health care professional, it was at my antenatal booking appointment and I received a pamphlet about childhood abuse and was advised to seek professional counselling, no personal interest was shown'

— ROS

1 From: Michaels, Anne (1997). *Fugitive Pieces*. London: Bloomsbury Publishing (267).

This is the first of two chapters to focus specifically on other women's experiences of childhood rape and the somatic impact of those experiences. The bulk of my research involved an autoethnographic investigation of the cellular level of somatic response to childhood rape and is explored in later chapters. The somatic narratives of nine women explored here and in Chapter Six provide a contemporary and specific context for this. As with my autoethnographic exploration, I see my work with the nine women as somatic inquiry. Although the exploration carried out by them differed from my own, each revolved around somatic understandings of the aftermath of childhood rape. My own inquiry involved many hours of exploration at a micro and cellular level, as well as at a macro level. The inquiry carried out by the women, while still focusing on the somatic, was based not on cellular responses but on more general observations of their physical health since their childhood trauma experience/s, prompted by questions and accessed through self-reflection. As with other chapters, I have included extracts from the women's responses to allow their voices to resonate within the discussion.

An overview

In 2011, following an exhaustive ethical approval process and extensive training in online information gathering techniques at my university, I conducted an Australia-wide recruitment campaign to invite into the research other women who had experienced childhood rape and to provide an updated Australian context through which the specificities of my autoethnographic account would resonate. The nine participants were female, had experienced rape in childhood, were over the age of eighteen years, and resided in Australia.

All the women completed the first survey phase. Four of them agreed to continue into the second interview phase. University ethics requirements made it necessary to protect the identities of the nine women through the adoption of pseudonyms. Some of the nine women took up the option to choose their own pseudonyms. Others stated they were not ashamed of their stories and felt a pseudonym was not necessary but understood the ethical need for compliance. The ages of the women varied. One of the women (Philipa) stated her age as sixty-eight years; five women (Carol, Felicity, Monica, Nancy, Patricia) fell into the forty-five- to fifty-four-year age range; and three women (Kate, Nina, Ros) were in the twenty-five to thirty-four-year age range.

Designing the shape of the information gathering

Before commencing the information gathering, I established a series of central research questions each grounded in the embodiment of the aftermath of sexual trauma. These included: Do women who have experienced childhood sexual violence make connections between the body and the trauma? In what ways do women who experience sexual trauma understand their own bodily responses? What are our cultural understandings of somatic responses to sexual trauma? What is it that healthcare professionals might need to know about somatic responses to sexual trauma in order to respond adequately to women who have been silenced by the experience of sexual violence?

These questions were pooled from three sources, each flowing from the lifeblood of personal experience, and each forming another layer of conceptual support for the methodological connective tissue of my research. The first source flowed from the persistent bodily detachment I experienced as a mature-aged woman/researcher in the wake of my silenced childhood rape. I was interested to discover if other women experienced this sense of detachment and disconnection. The second source concerned my inability (failure? resistance?) firstly as an adolescent then through to my mid-thirties, to make connections between the trauma of childhood rape and my declining physical health as well as to the constant sense of bodily dissonance I carried. I had already made connections between my precarious mental health and the rape experience by my mid-thirties but had not made specific associations between my bodily disturbances and my rape experience. The third source grew out of my experience of being silenced by the rape experience, the negative response I received when I disclosed to a friend, and my resulting inability to disclose to others. This led (after many years of visiting a range of healthcare professionals hoping they would see in my eyes the trauma history I carried in my body but couldn't speak), to a perception of feeling 'let down' by the medical system whose professionals weren't able to consider that my deteriorating health might be linked to the possibility of underlying trauma, nor recognise my inability to speak of my rape trauma history. These sources helped sculpt the methodological shape of this somatic inquiry component of my research and form the arterial network of questions through which the women moved. Overarching the shape that formed was my conviction that it was essential that I develop a means of information gathering that embraced my strong sense of ethnical responsibility towards the women. This purposeful strategy was designed to reflect several important considerations.

My primary concern in this component of the research, along with the concerns of my university's ethics committee, was to offer as safe and supportive inquiry environment as possible for the women to give voice to their experiences without causing unnecessary distress. The McAndrew and Warne (2005, 174) study of self-harm behaviours of women who have experienced sexual violence reminded me that 'Feminist research recognizes that power is an ever-present dynamic just as it is for women who live their lives in a patriarchal society'. I extend this argument to suggest this is particularly relevant for raped women in cultures in which an imbalance of power dynamics is the cause of gendered violence and where dominant psychological discourse stifles or ignores the full range of aftermath responses to sexual violence. The McAndrew and Warne study also reminded me that 'The participants' experience of trying to communicate but no one hearing their voices only condemns them to a position of powerlessness' (175). In the field of trauma research it is noted that re-establishing a sense of personal empowerment is critical to healing in the aftermath of a traumatic event or events (Herman 1992). Having experienced firsthand the effects of disempowerment through sexual violence, I certainly didn't want to contribute to feelings of powerlessness or impose further silencing on other women through an inappropriate inquiry method.

Self-reflection and reflexivity became particularly necessary and ethically responsible during this time as I began to shape the information gathering method. I deeply reflected on what kind of research I would be prepared, or able, to take part in as the researcher. I considered how it might be to step into the shoes of other women. Being an autoethnographic sexual trauma researcher placed me in a unique and delicate position. I could easily imagine how it might feel to take part in a range of possible information gathering methods; my bodily responses to these imaginings were strong and immediate, emerging directly from my viscerally-held trauma history. As a researcher then, my experiential knowing played a significant role in determining the eventual use of an online method.

The participant somatic inquiry questions

Starting from the premise that responses to trauma of a sexually violent nature can be both complex and multi-dimensional (Ahrens et al. 2007, Astbury 2006b, Campbell and Wasco 2005, Ullman 1996), I gave careful consideration to the questions offered to the women to sensitively support and reflect these complexities and to minimise the risk of re-traumatisation. As the research was qualitative in nature, I designed open-ended questions to encourage a spacious and dynamic self-reflective exploration of the women's somatic aftermath stories rather than risking narrowing down the potential for self-reflection through the use of more heavily structured and exploratively restrictive closed questions. The Campbell et al (2010, 77) rape trauma study, which focused on the impact for rape survivors of participation in interview research, found the women 'appreciated that several sections of the interview were open-ended so that they could decide, construct, and control what they wanted to talk about'.

The questions, then, reflected the original research questions outlined earlier, propelled by my interest in the particularity of the somatic expression of trauma memory following childhood rape, as well as the use of bodywork practices as alternative means of accessing trauma memory and facilitating its re-integration. While not asking the women to explore their somatic responses at a cellular level, the questions were designed to initiate a close examination of the women's physical health since the rape event/s.

Responding to the responses

I had looked forward, with an uneasy anticipation, to the survey material. When the responses began to arrive, despite commencing my own autoethnographic somatic inquiry the previous year and already reaping the benefits of it in terms of my resilience, when I read the responses from the women, the catastrophe of their accumulative experiences was painful to absorb and left me deeply emotionally challenged.

3 November, 2011

My first two responses are in. Although I was half anticipating it, it's been a shock to find that the women's somatic stories echo my own in so many ways. Their grief and sadness, anger and resignation sit in their words. It is palpable. Reading them has been distressing. I've wept long and deeply. I felt such immediate empathy and compassion for these women who find themselves, like me, still reeling from the cumulative ramifications of events in their childhood, their adult bodies betraying them at every turn, their trust in others destroyed, their desire for touch and intimacy overshadowed by their fear … it's too much. But I also felt the purity of my rage towards the men who commit such brutal and appalling acts of violence on children then walk away leaving their victims to somehow piece together their shattered lives and carry on. This is a challenging time for me. I hope I have the resources to open myself to what these women can teach me in order for me to pass this on to others. I'm living right now in my body the reason I delayed sending out the questions … I've feared what I would feel when the responses came in … the stories of other women, their suffering, the trauma in their bodies … it's so painful … and yet I feel such rage too that it strengthens my resolve and drives me on to raise awareness of these stories, our stories, the stories of generations of women. I mustn't be silenced by my response and their stories mustn't be silenced as a result.

Often fragments of the women's stories would return to me in my daylight hours as well as via my subconscious in my dreams. Warr (2004, 586) describes this return of the research material as '"voices in the head" that are difficult to forget'. She suggests that 'keeping the stories close and managing their impact' is a question of balance and if this balance is found, it can lead to 'powerful' research. By way of finding this balance, I talked at length with my supervisors when I felt it necessary to do so. I wrote in my research journal. And I walked. Walking was particularly helpful. The movement of my body through space and across the quiet landscape of the bushland near my home, or on the nearby coast with the ocean beside me, helped integrate the stories into my research praxis and reconcile my feelings in response to the women's suffering. As I walked, I often thought of my privileged position as the new custodian of these stories and the overwhelming debt of gratitude I felt towards the women for entrusting them to me. As distressing as I had found their stories, my conviction to include them in my project grew stronger each time a line or a fragment of their words returned to me.

> *'I cannot make noise of any kind during sexual activity; I fear being heard [...] I cry and cry but I am silent.'*
>
> — CAROL

> *'I am overweight because food is comforting and is the only thing I can put in my mouth without fear.'*
>
> — CAROL

In amongst the swirl of these emotional responses, I hadn't anticipated that I would also take comfort from the women's stories. An advantage of online and asynchronous methods of information gathering is they allow the time and the opportunity to individualise interactions between the researcher and the participants (James and Busher 2006). In the context of my research, the asynchronous nature of the electronic information gathering method allowed me the time to process the women's often candid words. It allowed me to sit with their stories without the need to continue with a conversation as I would any face-to-face interaction. With the time to give their words a close reading and to sit in my own feeling responses to them, I was able to bring to consciousness, and reflect upon, some aspects of the women's somatic aftermath stories which overlapped with my own. Sherry Gorelick (1991, 463) uses the term 'pathology of the normal' to describe what can be revealed when exposure to knowledge, sometimes as a result of 'crises or ruptures' in the everyday, creates openings to the discovery of self-affirming information. In addition to my encounter with Brison's work, to also read in the women's responses of feelings of claustrophobia, chronic insomnia, unexplained stomach pain, and eating disorders, allowed me to begin to see that much of the somatic dysfunction I had experienced across the years was possibly a range of 'normal' responses to rape trauma. This was, as with the reading of Brison, deeply affirming. Of course this affirmation may have been possible should I have pursued the information gathering via face-to-face interactions with the women. I was thankful, however, to have had the privacy, the time and the space to move through my feeling responses. I was reassured as a result, that as an autoethnographic sexual trauma researcher, I had made the right choice of information gathering medium.

> *'My first sexual assault was washed under the carpet [...] one little girl was not important [...]. When I was raped [again], at 18 I scrubbed and scrubbed with a scrubbing brush but I could not get clean [...]. A social worker (male) said he didn't believe my story and that I didn't have my facts straight.'*
>
> — MONICA

CHAPTER SIX

Somatic narratives and meaning-making

> Was Poppy saying with her body what she couldn't say with words, what couldn't be said with words? Perhaps she lost control of herself, or her body, when she lost control of the sense we depend on language to provide for us. It was not that she would not speak, but that she could not. Her silence was a symptom and a cause. Words literally failed her. The voice she needed hadn't been invented yet, or if it had, it hadn't been heard in the south of England.
>
> — DRUSILLA MODJESKA[1]

In this chapter I bring together the somatic narratives and findings from the participant somatic inquiry component of the research. Given the more macro non-cellular focus of the women's inquiry, I examine these narratives in relation to my own more general non-cellular experience of the somatic aftermath of childhood rape. I explore both in relation to the literature.

To briefly reprise my research objectives in this component of my research, my aims were multiple: to establish a sense of the relationship the women now had with their bodies after significant periods of time had elapsed since their childhood rape experience/s; to discover how they thought their bodies had responded since their experience/s; to determine whether the women had made connections between their physical wellbeing in the aftermath and their childhood experiences; to find out if they had discussed any of their bodily responses with healthcare professionals; and to ask whether they had attended any sessions of bodywork and, if they had, how they felt this had impacted on them.

1 From: Modjeska, Drusilla (1996). *Poppy*. Camberwell: Penguin (83–84).

The self-identified somatic consequences of rape: The findings

The women identified a range of somatic symptoms across their lifetime including anxiety and tension (Carol, Kate, Monica, Nina); pain (Nina, Patricia, Philipa, Ros); symptoms associated with Post Traumatic Stress Disorder (Kate, Patricia, Philipa); insomnia (Carol); claustrophobia (Carol); concerns about sexual intimacy (Carol, Monica, Nancy); eating or weight problems (Carol, Monica, Nancy, Patricia); panic attacks (Carol, Patricia); headaches and migraine (Patricia, Philipa); sustained periods of severe depression (Philipa); general illness (Monica); chronic gynaecological issues (Philipa); nausea (Patricia); digestive issues (Nina); and an exaggerated startle reflex (Carol, Nancy). Other states identified included hypervigilance (Carol), and fear (Carol, Patricia, Ros).

The symptoms the women self-identified sit comfortably with my own. I too experienced the suite of somatic symptoms observed by the women, at some point since my childhood rape experiences, with varying degrees of persistence and intensity. I have been overweight and underweight, have experienced symptoms associated with Post Traumatic Stress Disorder, have had headaches, pain, intimacy problems, digestive concerns, general illness, and severe depression. I continue to suffer from insomnia, anxiety, and panic attacks. I am claustrophobic and can't tolerate having my face, particularly my nose and mouth, covered. I am hypervigilant at night, and when I feel unsafe, and I respond with an exaggerated startle reflex to loud and unexpected sound.

The self-identified somatic consequences of rape: The meaning-making

It is a significant consequence of sexual violence that women who have experienced one or more events are more likely to report a poorer overall health status than the general population (Golding 1994), and experience a range of chronic illnesses (Koss and Boeschen 2000). Additionally, it is common to experience somatic symptoms, medically explained or otherwise, in the aftermath of sexual violence, with many of the self-identified somatic responses detailed above, consistent with those noted in the literature (Kimerling and Calhoun 1994, Martin et al. 2007, Thompson et al. 2002, Waldinger et al. 2006, Boyd 2011, Golding 1994, Koss and Boeschen 2000). In relation to social costs and personal impact, the long term consequences of sexual violence, are 'alarming' (Koss and Boeschen 2000, 4). Chronic illnesses such as tension headaches, gastrointestinal problems, and severe and prolonged pain, are cited as not uncommon (Koss and Boeschen 2000). With specific regard to symptoms associated with Post Traumatic Stress Disorder, often interpreted as a psychological illness, it is important to remember that disturbed bodily states lie 'at the core' (Rothschild 2000, 6–7) of this complex condition.

Other conditions such as hypervigilance, hyper arousal, and an exaggerated, or heightened startle reflex, are also identified as impacts from, and expressions of sexual trauma, and linked to feelings of increased vulnerability (ACSSA 2006, Brison 2002, Campbell and Wasco 2005, Crome and McCabe 1995, Foa and Rothbaum 1998, Koss and Boeschen 2000). As I have noted, women do not need to have experienced rape to hold fear in relation to the possibility of being raped (Easteal 1992a, Yodanis 2004), with women fearing being raped more than any other crime (O'Donovan, Devilly, and Rapee 2007). However, for women who have experienced sexual violence, 'feelings of never being safe' (Cook, David, and Grant 2001, 29), manifested as hypervigilance, or heightened states of fear and vulnerability, are not uncommon (Boyd 2011, ACSSA 2006, Campbell and Wasco 2005, Crome and McCabe 1995, Foa and Rothbaum 1998).

While the information from the women regarding bodily responses to childhood rape did not reveal any insights not already established in the literature, the information does offer a portal into the self-identifying feature of their survey responses. These women were not directed to select relevant symptoms from a list. For those women who had not had access to therapeutic discourses nor had connections made for them through counselling (these will be discussed later), the women's answers came directly from the assumptions they had made themselves. The implication here is that, irrespective of available rape trauma discourses which make specific links between rape and aftermath somatic symptoms, these women were aware that their adult bodies were responding to their childhood rape experience. This was also my process, although once I began to immerse myself in the literature for this research, this became more apparent as I read of more symptoms which resonated with my own somatic aftermath experience.

Making connections between trauma and symptoms: The findings

The survey and interview information revealed that of the nine participants (Carol, Felicity, Kate, Monica, Nancy, Nina, Patricia, Philipa, Ros), three of the women (Carol, Nancy, Philipa,) had made connections themselves between their somatic symptoms and their rape/s, and two of the women (Monica, Patricia), made connections with the help of health professionals:

Carol didn't state how she arrived at this conclusion but was very clear about the somatic manifestations of her childhood trauma.

Nancy had not initially made any connections between her somatic symptoms and her trauma experience but had made them subsequently, citing links between her eating disorder and her trauma. Nancy did not indicate what initiated her making these connections.

Philipa said she had made connections and had talked to healthcare professionals when she was in her twenties and thirties but the professionals were unable to make similar connections. She noted that after many years of counselling and 'inner work', she 'became far more assertive & able to talk about the whys & wherefores' having made direct links between the majority of her health issues and her childhood trauma.

Monica and Patricia indicated that they had only begun to make connections in their thirties and as a result of counselling. Monica stated that she was 'not aware they [her illnesses] were related', but once she had sought help and the counsellor had suggested that her bodily symptoms could be associated with her trauma, she was able to acknowledge a connection.

The remaining four survey participants (Felicity, Kate, Nina, Ros,) gave a range of responses:

Felicity was unclear about whether her body had responded, but stated that she 'covered up' her body as much as possible and 'push [ed] thought to back of mind [sic]'.

Kate's response made it difficult to ascertain whether she had made a direct link between her physical health and her trauma but she stated that she had felt disconnected from her body when growing up, that she had felt 'parts of my body were revolting, dirty and shameful', and that she had treated her body 'quite badly, through smoking, drinking, and self-harm.'

Nina's response made it unclear whether any connections had been made.

Ros didn't believe her body has responded in a 'physical sense' but noted she had developed Post Traumatic Stress Disorder following a traumatic childbirth experience. She stated she had felt 'betrayed' by her body as a result of this, and by the miscarriages she had suffered. Ros said that these experiences 'remind' her of the rape because 'there is a similar emotional response: betrayal, fear, powerlessness, rejection and the physical pain'.

As I've already indicated in Chapter One, I had experienced a range of somatic symptoms since 1971, and more especially during the 1990s. I did not begin to make any serious links between these and my childhood trauma until the growth of a malignant cancer tumour in my thyroid gland in 1997 precipitated major surgery and a major shift in my thinking. The tumour sat just below the region where I often experienced a 'fleshy' barrier slamming shut whenever I attempted to verbalise deeply personal and troubling concerns. I had already begun to consider a link between this phenomenon and my rape experience and because of this I believed the location of the tumour was not a coincidence. Without the benefit of a framework to allow the

> *2 April, 1973*
>
> *I just weighed myself. I'm 7st 3lb!!! I'm SO fat!!! I HATE MY FAT BODY!!!*
>
> [This diary entry was written when I was thirteen years old, two years after my rape experiences]

location and explication of my symptoms to migrate from more generalised medical discourse to more specific embodied sexual trauma discourse, and without relevant literature to support me, or healthcare professionals to guide me, I began to reflect on my earlier somatic symptoms and the possibility they might be connected to my unresolved rape trauma. I also began to reflect on my past behavioural patterns, specifically in terms of how I perceived I had treated and viewed my body post-rape.

The eating disorder I developed is an example of one of these behaviours which took on new meaning for me. I began to deny myself food in the mid-1980s when I was in my early twenties and my marriage was in difficulty. I was suffering a sense of rejection, and I was feeling a loss of agency. I was deeply unhappy, though not because I was starving myself. I felt triumphant at every ounce of weight I lost; the smaller my body became, the larger my power over my body felt, concomitant with an increased sense of autonomy in my life.

During the early 1980s, eating disorders received a high profile in the popular press after the death of the singer, Karen Carpenter. Her death, from Anorexia Nervosa, spawned a flurry of magazine and newspaper articles. I clearly recall reading anecdotal stories about anorexia nervosa and bulimia in the popular press around that time. I read that a perfectionist personality, a negative body image, out-of-control dieting, being overweight, or the fear of becoming overweight, were major features and underlying causes of these conditions. I read, too, that low self-esteem and feelings of powerlessness were contributory factors. I am certain I did not read that the trauma of a rape experience predisposes girls and women to the development of an eating disorder, a view the current literature confirms (Thompson et al. 2001, Wonderlich et al. 2001, Smyth et al. 2008, Thompson and Wonderlich 2004, SECASA 2012b, Dansky et al. 1997).

Post thyroid cancer surgery, and almost two decades later, as I looked back on this period, I slowly began to perceive links between my past patterns of behaviour, my psychophysiological health, and my childhood rape. I suspected that the origins of the sense of loss of agency and poor self-esteem I harboured in my early twenties, and which probably helped fuel my eating disorder, reached much further back into my past. I suspected these were directly linked to the profound sense of helplessness

I experienced when I was raped and silenced as a child and the loss of autonomy and feelings of self-loathing this spawned. I retrospectively perceived that, in temporal terms, my starvation strategy in my twenties was twofold. I perceived it as an embodied means of wrenching back control in the face of the slide into marital instability in the present, and I saw it as a way of inflicting further punishment on my body for being raped in the past, with loss of agency and self-loathing at its strategic core. Reading my behaviours in these ways, my self-soothing through food withdrawal was comforting and punitive, with my body a place of struggle and a site of resistance.

Making connections between trauma and symptoms: The meaning-making

At this point, I return to the condition, hysteria, already mentioned in Chapter Three. When hysteria was first described, two of the primary features of its symptoms were that they were almost always somatic; and they presented almost exclusively in women (Johnson 2008, Showalter 1998, Trimble 2004, Hustvedt 2011). The earliest documented aetiology of hysteria's repertoire of symptoms variously attributed symptoms to a dysfunctional and 'wandering' uterus (Showalter 1998, Trimble 2004, Scull 2009), or as a manifestation of an underlying physiological disequilibrium (Scull 2009). Subsequent aetiologies deemed that hysteria could present in many forms, the most dominant being conversion hysteria (Wilson 2004b). Hysteria and conversion hysteria symptoms were thought to be precipitated by a physical illness due to defective heredity (Showalter 1998); 'a disorder of the nervous system' (Hustvedt 2011, 26); 'physical conversions of unconscious conflicts' (Hustvedt 2011, 303) or, unresolved psychological distress (Grosz 1994, Hunter 1983, Scull 2009, Showalter 1998, Trimble 2004). This latter was attributed by Freud to sexual trauma in childhood (Scull 2009, Showalter 1998).

The features symptomatic of hysteria and conversion hysteria included fitting; vomiting; fainting; eating disturbances; headaches; convulsions; pain; insomnia; paralysis; choking; crying; muteness; loss of hearing; and loss of sight (Johnson 2008, Showalter 1998, Trimble 2004, Scull 2009, Ussher 1989). Diagnoses of hysteria and the cataloguing of its symptoms peaked in France in the late 1800s, primarily as a result of the work of Charcot (Showalter 1998, Trimble 2004, Hunter 1983, Scull 2009, Hustvedt 2011). While Charcot's treatment of his female patients may have been controversial, not least his practice of theatrically presenting his 'star' hysteria patients almost as exhibits at a freak show during his weekly lectures at his clinic at the Salpetriere Hospital, Paris (Hustvedt 2011, Showalter 1998), he nonetheless treated hysteria symptoms as 'no less real than those produced by Parkinson's disease [...] For Charcot, "hysterical" did not mean "unreal"' (Hustvedt 2011, 308).

Although hysteria is no longer recognised as a medical condition (Scull 2009, Showalter 1998), it is considered to have re-surfaced in the guise of a range of current and psychiatrically recognised disorders. These include Post Traumatic Stress Disorder (Scull 2009), which has a higher incidence amongst rape victims than amongst war veterans (Esposito 2005), and somatoform disorders which include 'somatisation disorder, conversion disorder, or dissociative identity disorder' (Showalter 1998, 17). Somatoform disorders are characterised by 'the repeated presentation of physical symptoms, with repeated requests for medical examinations, in spite of reassurance that the symptoms have no physical basis' (Trimble 2004, 29). Diagnoses of somatoform disorders are highest amongst women (Trimble 2004).

A feminist discursive reading of the prolific number of cases of hysteria recorded in the late 1800s makes connections between the phallocentric, repressive, and oppressive cultural discourses and social conditions present during this era, and the limiting effect these had on the intellectual, spiritual, and corporeal lives of nineteenth-century women. The parameter of this book prevents a detailed analysis of this. Suffice to say, these strictures, and the psychological distress they inevitably created, are credited with producing the symptoms commonly displayed by hysterical women, with the symptoms interpreted as a bodily means of expression for the psyche when verbal protest was not possible (Micale 1995, Showalter 1998, Hunter

1983). Indeed, the view that hysteria was a bodily form of articulation, was taken up at the time by the surrealists, Louis Aragon and Andre Breton, who insisted that hysteria be viewed as 'a supreme means of expression' (Hunter 1983, 1). Within this framework of understanding, the psyche was the unwilling and distressed recipient of gendered cultural discourses and practices with the body pivotal in articulating responses to the distress created by those discourses and practices. This reading of the hysteric's body locates it as the site of profound disturbance in response to repressive cultural discourse; a conduit for the articulation of that disturbance; and therefore, a site of social protest and cultural resistance. Within a feminist paradigm, hysteria itself, the body of the hysteric, and the somatic symptoms manifested in it, are understood as ways for women of this era to subvert patriarchal and limiting discourse and as a means for women to articulate their psychological distress by speaking the unspeakable through their bodies. Just how the conversion of thought into bodily symptoms is accomplished has been of less significance for feminist commentators. Wilson (2004b, 8) argues that some investigations into hysteria which avoid examination of the biological basis for hysteria symptoms, and she cites Showalter as an example, position bodies as 'inert and politically barren, mere ciphers for a complexity that is located elsewhere'. In such discourse-centric and reductive-phobic accounts of hysteria, the neurophysiological body, according to Wilson, becomes 'soma non grata' (2004, 8).

In this context, one other highly significant feature of hysteria was the medically unexplained nature of the symptoms (Johnson 2008, Showalter 1998, Trimble 2004). I make this point, not because I read the somatic symptoms of the participants in my research as medically unexplained, nor because I necessarily impose the possibility of rape experience onto all women who were diagnosed with hysteria,[2] although there are some symptoms common to both. Rather, I want to again draw attention to the

2 It is of interest that in her book, *Medical Muses*, Asti Hustvedt (2011) focuses her attention on three of Charcot's more well-known female hysteria patients. Two of these women, Augustine and Blanche, were raped or sexually assaulted when they were thirteen years old.

embodied focus of this book. I consistently argue throughout these chapters that all rape begins with the body. What I additionally emphasise now, in the context of a discursive reading of hysteria, and using the medically-unexplained aspect of hysteria, is that responses to rape experience occur at the level of the body irrespective of whether or not discourse exists to appropriately frame or 'explain' those responses, and whether or not women, or healthcare professionals make connections between their rape experience and their aftermath symptoms. None of the women participants had access to the kinds of discourses that I have had access to during my research. Without the benefit of being able to draw on an appropriate discursive framework to help make links between rape trauma and bodily symptoms in the aftermath, the symptoms themselves can float unanchored in a sea of possibility. Indeed, the literature has identified that symptoms are not always understood to be connected to the trauma by victims themselves (Calhoun and Atkeson 1991, Goodwin and Attias 1999). However, even if, as the findings confirm, some women are not able to make connections between their somatic symptoms and their past rape experience because they have not had access to the sorts of discourses that I have had access to, their responses underscore the danger of healthcare professionals and others taking at face value the sorts of meaning-making rape victims themselves make. Two of the participants' observations (Kate, Ros) amplify the fact that the sorts of discourses I have engaged with (which make specific links between rape trauma and somatic symptoms), are discourses that consistently draw our attention back to the legitimacy and eloquence of the body's nuanced responses. Such observations reinforce my point that even if appropriate discourses are not available to help victims frame all possible impacts of rape experience, this does not mean that the bodily symptoms do not occur. This is a highly significant point. Even if a patient does not disclose her history of rape and even if she has not made connections between her rape and her symptoms, this does not mean that healthcare professionals should not be alert to both the range of symptoms likely and the possible sexual trauma basis for their manifestation. And it does

> *'I struggled at times with eating at times as a general result of the stress of childhood Abuse. I did not realise it at the time.'*
>
> — NANCY

not mean that patients' complaints should be swept aside by professionals with 'reassuring' comments that claim the symptoms have 'no physical basis' (Trimble 2004, 29). Although these sorts of comments may be intended to reassure (the patient? the professional?), my experience tells me that they only cause greater damage by inferring the symptoms are psychosomatic and therefore not 'real'.

I posit an interpretation of the bodily symptoms of raped women that is two-fold in meaning and gives an inner and an outer movement to understandings. Firstly, these symptoms can be understood as secondary and performative manifestations of the primary embodied, stored, and unresolved responses to an original rape experience. And secondly, they can also be interpreted as acts of defiance to the dominant social, cultural, historical, and therapeutic discursive constructions of sexual violence that consistently diminish or ignore the impact of trauma on the body. In addition to this point, if, as Dianne Hunter (1983, 22) suggests, 'Hysteria is a self-repudiating form of feminine discourse in which the body signifies what social conditions make it impossible to state linguistically', then the externally perceived bodily eruptions of raped women can also be understood as a form of feminine discourse through the use of bodily semiotics to signal psychophysiological, intrapersonal, and interpersonal distress. Indeed, Wilson (2004a, 78) suggests that hysteria symptoms can be interpreted as 'one particular mode of biological writing.' As I've indicated, the feminist discursive reading of the aetiology of hysteria identifies phallocentric discourse, which inevitably works to silence women's voices, as a primary force behind the development of hysteria symptoms. I am not suggesting, by focusing on the body in this discussion, that discourse has no influence in the context of rape trauma. Clearly this is not the case.

By weaving together the connection between the unexplained somatic symptoms of hysteria and the nineteenth-century discourse of repression, with the sometimes unexplained somatic symptoms of sexual trauma, identified by myself and the participants, and the silencing impact of contemporary sociocultural-therapeutic discourse, and by then taking a step back to cast a reflexive eye over the tapestry this creates, an interesting, but two-dimensional image emerges. The unexplained somatic eruptions of hysteric women and the eruptions of raped women appear to intersect with the sociocultural silencing impacts of dominant discourses giving the impression that silencing alone provokes these symptoms. However, I am taking up materialism's call here for a wider reading of phenomena (Alaimo and Hekman 2008b, Barad 2003, Kirby 1997, van der Tuin and Dolphijn 2010, Kirby 2008) to argue that somatic responses to rape trauma cannot simply be read as by-products of discourse. The biologically traumatised body must, therefore, be awarded the same level of epistemological gravitas as other cites of investigation.

Self-perceptions and attitudes towards the raped body: The findings

During the second information gathering phase, the interview material from the four women participants (Kate, Monica, Patricia, Philipa), revealed that one of the most common direct outcomes of their childhood rape experience/s is the manifestation of extreme negative attitudes towards their bodies. All of the women acknowledged they harboured negative attitudes towards their bodies at some point since their rape experience/s, with some women acknowledging a shift towards a more positive attitude only as they've grown older:

Kate said she felt disconnected from her body when growing up, and that 'it felt like a stranger's body.' Kate noted that she 'didn't have a sense of my body separate from how an abuser might view and value my body. It was something I blamed for what was done to me. [...] I didn't have a sense that I was here in the world. I treated my body quite badly, through smoking, drinking, and self-harm. I felt that parts of my body were revolting, dirty and shameful.' Kate did, however, note her relationship with her body has undergone a shift and she is 'much more positive now [...] I feel much more present and connected between myself and my body than I have at any other stage during my life. There are still parts of my body that bring up feelings of shame and embarrassment for me, but I am able to recognise now that those aren't feelings I deserve to be carrying around. [...]As I have been able to let go of various bits of shame about my past, I've felt less need to "punish" my body, in a sense. Letting go of shame, and learning to value myself as a worthy human being has allowed me to value my body also, as a worthy and important – VITAL – part of me.'

Monica said that after her childhood experience, she 'wanted to never have breasts so I bound them for a long time. I couldn't stand touching my own skin directly and after my son was born I found it really hard to wash him because of my own fear that I would somehow tarnish him with my own filth. It took me decades to be ok with my own skin.' Monica was told 'it's just skin' after she disclosed her rape/s as a child. Monica implied she blamed her body for her sexual assault experiences in childhood, and again, for her rape at eighteen years of age. She appears to still hold her body responsible for attracting unwanted attention stating that she realised 'quite a long time ago that I maintain an overweight body because I am afforded less male attention.' In terms of her attitude towards her body now, Monica noted she finds 'it difficult to comprehend the long-term effects of dangerous habits, like smoking or drinking too much. I firmly believe living with PTSD makes this even harder. It's difficult to worry too much about the health effects of things when you cannot grasp onto a concept of a future and those effects ever taking place.' Monica indicated she had current weight concerns and accepted that being overweight is 'not healthy mentally or physically.' She now, however, acknowledges a shift in her attitude towards her body. As already noted, after a history of not wanting to have breasts and not being able to touch her own skin, she said she is now 'amused by my body naked. I like the feel of my body now and I have way less angst.'

Patricia noted she 'truly hated my body with a passion and imagined that it was dirty – particularly my sexual parts and my backside. I actually felt sick if I contemplated it for too long.' Patricia implied she blamed her body for her rape/s saying that she once 'considered having a sexual body was disgusting or dangerous.' In terms of how she now feels about her body, Patricia noted, 'Well, it can be a real mixture […] I have been very cavalier about self-care […]. However, I am able to be more nurturing; for example after a hard day I give myself luxurious baths with lovely soaps.' Patricia stated that she was currently overweight and had 'recently stopped smoking after a 32 year habit.'

Philipa said that she 'always seemed to hurt, & wishing my body and me could be completely different. I thought if I & my body were different it would not happen again.' With regard to her relationship with her body now, Philipa noted that she didn't have 'what I would call a relationship with it [her body]!! I'm just stuck with it!! I try to ignore it as much as possible!!' She stated that she had a history of chronic gynaecological concerns which had led to her having an oophorectomy and a hysterectomy. She said that following the surgery, 'rather than feeling less of a woman, I felt that I was far more comfortable with my body.'

As I've noted in various chapters throughout this book, like all of the interview women, I held extreme negative attitudes towards my body for much of my life post-rape. Not until commencing the autoethnographic somatic inquiry phase of my research and the Body-Mind Centering work, did I begin to soften my attitude towards my body and view it in ways other than punitive ones. I still have periods when I revert to entrenched behavioural and attitudinal patterns and view my body harshly or experience detachment, but these occasions are less intense and less frequent now. Like some of the participants, shame and self-blame were major influences on my negative attitude.

Self-perceptions and attitudes towards the raped body: The meaning-making

There is an abundance of trauma research acknowledging the presence of negative self-perceptions and self-blame attitudes amongst victims in the aftermath of rape (Anderson and Doherty 2008, Freedman 2006, Lievore 2003, Littleton et al. 2006, Najdowski and Ullman 2009, Ullman et al. 2007, Vidal and Petrak 2007, Weiss 2010, Koss and Boeschen 2000). The sexual trauma literature is also clear that it is not uncommon for negative body attitudes to develop following rape (Armsworth, Stronck, and Carlson 1999, Astbury 2006a, Boyd 2011, Clarke and Griffin 2008, Morrison, Quadara, and Boyd 2007).

Negative self-perceptions, self-blame and negative body attitudes are present amongst all of the interview women. The women also talk about their bodies in disconnected terms. These perceptions, attitudes, and ways of relating to my body are also a major part of my own rape aftermath story. The women's stories echo the spectrum of difficulties I encountered and, in combination, amplify the trauma literature. I argue that the findings from the interview material, in particular, support my assertion that all rape begins with the body. If childhood rape trauma is viewed from this perspective, negative body attitudes seem a predictable response; if the body *is* the site of the violence, why wouldn't a child victim see her body as the cause of the violence? And if self-blame attitudes *are* in attendance, why wouldn't she develop feelings of body hatred and want to distance herself from it? It seems apparent from my own experience and from the interview material, that negative body attitudes are an inevitable outcome of rape. In the absence of any other satisfactory explanation for being raped, the progression through feeling, in the quest for understanding in the aftermath, clearly returns victims to their body again and again, placing blame squarely on its shoulders.

Bodywork and rape trauma: The findings

At the time of the survey, only four of the nine women (Carol, Kate, Monica, Philipa) had attended sessions of bodywork. These practices included: massage (Carol, Kate, Monica, Philipa); chakra massage, kinesiology, sound therapy, chiropractic (Carol); reiki (Kate); hypnotherapy (Monica); and reflexology, 'Touch for health' (Philipa). In terms of how the four women thought their bodies had responded following their participation in bodywork sessions, there was a range of answers:

Carol found chakra massage 'kind of bizarre', massage 'ranged from sadistic to pathetic' with one male massage therapist causing her pain and leaving her 'totally bruised [...] crying and crying'; the male kinesiology practitioner had made her feel angry and unsafe; the sound therapy was very helpful and gave her useful strategies for her 'daily functioning'; and the chiropractic treatment had been successful at relieving intense pain because 'I can be unable to walk or blinded by pain and have even been carried into a clinic clutching a bucket as I vomit from the pain and walk out feeling fully functioning thirty minutes later.'

Kate noted that after massage sessions her body feels 'relaxed, comforted and safe.'

Monica noted that although she loves massage, she is 'not good at trust so have found the chairs in shopping centres [massage chairs] to be the best alternative/compromise.'

Philipa said that for many years she 'wasn't able to have full body massage & even now my body still "reacts" more "sensitively".'

The remainder of the women indicated they had not attended sessions but did not provide their reasons.

Across the years, my experience of bodywork was mostly confined to therapeutic interventions for pain associated with musculoskeletal problems rather than for self-care and relaxation. Aside from my more recent research engagement with Body-Mind Centering, I had previously, periodically, attended osteopathy, physiotherapy, and chiropractic sessions, and had a brief flirtation with a yoga practice in my early twenties, and occasional massage sessions since my forties. Like Carol, I found that the bodywork sessions ranged from ineffectual to brutal. Some physiotherapy and chiropractic sessions left me bruised and in tears. It is significant to note however, that during these sessions I felt so disempowered that I was unable to ask the practitioners to stop what they were doing or even to cancel other appointments.

Bodywork and rape trauma: The meaning-making

Research that has emerged from the neurosciences and biomedical sciences now demonstrates that the chemicals associated with emotion flow throughout the entire body (Pert 1999, Young 2006, Rensberger 1996, Rothschild 2000) and are not, therefore, limited to the brain. This information supports the trauma literature which confirms that trauma is held as memory within the tissues and systems of the body (Levine 1997,

Rothschild 2000, Scaer 2001, Herman 1992). In terms of the therapeutic bodywork practice that was, I believe, crucial to the re-integration of my trauma memory, it is of interest that only four of the women had previously attended bodywork sessions.

Given the profound, deeply traumatising, and bodily invasive nature of rape, it is possible to predict the presence of caution surrounding voluntary attendance at therapeutic practices which are body and touch-based. It is not surprising then, that five of the women (Fiona, Nancy, Nina, Patricia, Ros) had chosen not to attend bodywork practices. It is also unsurprising that two of the women indicated they had experienced mixed results from bodywork with reactions ranging from painful (Carol) to relaxing and comforting (Kate). It would have been helpful to have discovered (and not asking is a limitation of my research) what specific factors dissuaded the women from attending bodywork practices. Although, with safety, trust, and hypersensitivity identified as concerns, it is possible to speculate that those may have been factors in decision-making for the women. Given that reactions to bodywork ranged from painful (Carol) to relaxing (Kate), attendance at any therapeutic bodywork practice is not without risk. Because my engagement with Alice and the work of Body-Mind Centering was overwhelmingly a positive and transformational one, it saddens me that other raped women will never be able to experience similar work given the negative associations they have between touch and their bodies.

The use of touch within a therapeutic context remains a contentious issue in the psychotherapies (Bonitz 2008, Phelan 2009, Stenzel and Rupert 2004, Toronto 2001). Rothschild (2000, xiv) for example, argues that therapy involving no bodily contact between client and therapist is 'the most appropriate for use with traumatized patients.' Rothschild advocates only the judicious use of touch in trauma therapy, and only if both client and therapist agree. She cites a number of reasons for caution including the effects of transference,[3] the need for respect for clients' boundaries

3 *Transference* is a term used in psychiatry and psychotherapy and refers to the client's unconscious transfer of feelings and attitudes from a person or event in the past onto the therapist in the present (Hughes and Kerr 2000).

(especially rape victims), and personal preference. For somatic practitioners however, particularly body-workers, touch is a critical element of therapeutic practice. Within a bodywork paradigm, touch helps facilitate access to sensation and feeling in the body, helping with the development of an embodied consciousness. Through embodied consciousness, re-patterning (Bainbridge Cohen 2008), and somatic re-organisation and refined integrative function can occur (Juhan 1987). I argue that these are all necessary for the facilitation of post-rape healing.

Disclosing rape experience: The findings

Six of the nine women (Carol, Felicity, Kate, Monica, Patricia, Philipa) had discussed their bodily responses with a range of healthcare professionals. Half of the women, some of the time, had not had satisfactory interactions:

Carol had often felt unsupported, patronised, condescended to, compartmentalised, and dismissed. She felt the workers were often young and unskilled and that she had 'to train them to respond'. She also felt they categorised her because 'As soon as "childhood sexual assault" enters the discussion out come[s] the blinkers and the professional (?) starts to dismiss me as an holistic person with incredible survival skills and amazing talents. Or they would treat me like I was dirty'. Carol sometimes felt severely unsafe 'but cannot explain why.' And she often found that 'Most GPs seem too busy to discuss anything other than immediate symptoms and are often rude, abrupt, dismissing and make me feel like they couldn't care less.' Carol did however, note that when the professionals listened to her and showed respect, she was able to feel safe and supported, but implied this was the exception.

Felicity acknowledged that she had talked to a healthcare professional/s, however she didn't indicate what the qualities of these interactions were.

Kate noted that, 'Given my past experiences of trying to talk to healthcare professionals about having been raped, I do not feel comfortable [talking about her bodily responses].' Kate did not indicate what the specific qualities of these past interactions with healthcare practitioners were but they have clearly had a significant impact on her ability to now discuss the full range of her rape trauma.

Philipa recalled telling a GP about her rape experience/s when she was a young woman but remembered 'being totally discounted, & told not to make up silly stories!' She also noted that 'medicos were totally unable to relate any of my health problems to what might have happened to me as a child.'

By contrast, two of the women (Monica, Patricia) had attended counselling and had benefitted. Monica had not made any connection between her health and her childhood experience prior to attending counselling but found that after a counsellor at a sexual assault centre 'questioned if I felt my illnesses were related to childhood sexual assault', she was more mindful of this. Patricia had seen a female counsellor and had found her 'most understanding.' She acknowledged that this positive response 'took a lot of fear out of the symptoms.' Patricia did point out, though, that she now chooses only to discuss her bodily responses with professionals she trusts, which, she said, 'excluded GP's.' Patricia did not elaborate on why this was the case.

Of the three remaining women (Nancy, Nina, Ros) who had chosen not to discuss their somatic symptoms with healthcare professionals, two had differing reasons for their choices:

Nina held anxiety surrounding the possible responses from healthcare professionals, fearing 'I'd be forced to report the abuse.'

Ros didn't believe the rape had manifested somatically so she had rarely discussed it. On one occasion though, at an antenatal booking appointment, Ros answered in the affirmative to a question on childhood rape. The staff member had given her a pamphlet on child sexual abuse and advised her to 'seek professional counselling.' Other than that, she noted, 'No personal interest was shown, I just answered yes to the question and got the stock response.'

As part of this specific focus on disclosure, I was also interested to know from the four women who volunteered to continue into the interview phase, if they had talked about their rape experience/s at the time they occurred, and if not, how much time had elapsed between the experience/s and their disclosure. I have included the approximate ages of the women in this section to give the reader a temporal context for the women's interview responses.

Kate (25–34) disclosed her childhood rape experience to a healthcare professional but not until sixteen years after the event.

Monica (45–54) had been sexually assaulted in childhood and again raped at eighteen years of age. She said her first disclosure as a young child was ignored, 'one little girl wasn't important.' After her rape at eighteen she went to a GP who referred her to a male social worker at a hospital. The social worker told her he didn't believe her story and that she 'didn't have her facts straight.' Monica went to another social worker when she was about nineteen years of age. At about thirty years of age she attended a sexual assault centre for assistance relating to intimacy and relationships.

Patricia (45–54) had been sexually violated and repeatedly raped orally at around four years of age, and again, at around eight years of age. She said she had told her mother some time after the first abusive episode ended, but she could 'remember my mother telling me she didn't want to hear it.' Patricia only spoke of her second period of abuse when she was twenty-three and had sought counselling, some fifteen years after the event.

Philipa (68), as noted in the previous section, had spoken of her childhood rape experience as a young woman but her story had been dismissed by the GP. She did not speak of her rape experience again until she was in her early thirties, but 'even then, I didn't really spell it out & just hoped it would be understood without my having to go into any details.' Philipa said she really only began to speak about her experience in her late forties, several decades after the original trauma experience.

In relation to my own story, as I have already revealed in Chapter One, I decided against disclosing to my family at the time of my rapes and chose instead to disclose to a school friend[4] during the year they occurred. After my story was dismissed as a lie, I did not risk disclosure for almost

4 It is not uncommon for victims of childhood rape to disclose to a trusted friend, often during adolescence, rather than risk disclosing to family members (Kogan 2004, Smith et al. 2000).

a decade, and then only briefly to a family member and without a great deal of satisfaction. It wasn't until almost twenty years later and in my late thirties, that I was driven to disclose to my GP after I became desperate for help. Unlike some of the participants, though, I was fortunate that my GP was moved by my disclosure, and responded with compassion, as well as with an apology for failing to identify the source of my accumulating health problems himself.

Disclosing rape experience: The meaning-making

The literature has clearly identified that crimes of a sexually violent nature are least likely to be reported to formal support providers (Ahrens and Campbell 2000, Clark and Quadara 2010, Easteal 1992a, Kong et al. 2003, Neame and Heenan 2003, Stanko 1985, Tarczon and Quadara 2012). The literature is also clear that women who have experienced sexual violence fear a suite of possible consequences resulting from the disclosure of their experience (Ahrens et al. 2007, Neame and Heenan 2003, Ullman et al. 2007), including fear associated with the anticipation of negative responses (Ullman and Filipas 2001). Non-empathic or negative responses to sexual violence disclosure are not uncommon, and equally as troubling, such responses from healthcare professionals are not unusual (Ahrens 2006, Starzynski et al. 2007). Negative responses can exacerbate feelings of shame (Feiring and Taska 2005, Seu 2006, 2008, Vidal and Petrak 2007, Weiss 2010), and can lead to self-silencing practices (Ahrens 2006, Ullman and Filipas 2001). The shame which functions to sustain the self-silencing can also function as a source of further stigmatisation for women (Kaukinen and DeMaris 2009, Starzynski et al. 2007, Klein 2004), and can lead to secondary victimisation (Ahrens 2006, Anderson and Doherty 2008, Campbell and Raja 1999). For children who have experienced sexual violence, the fear associated with the anticipation of negative responses can reinforce the stigma attached to violence of this nature (Feiring and Taska 2005). And finally, research is unequivocal that negative responses to disclosure of rape experience has an adverse effect on victims (Ahrens 2006, Ahrens et al. 2007, Anderson and Doherty 2008, Feiring and Taska 2005, Seu 2006, Ullman et al. 2007, Vidal and Petrak 2007, Cook, David, and Grant 2001), and their health (Pennebaker and Stone 2004, Seu 2006, Ullman and Filipas 2001, Ullman et al. 2007, Vidal and Petrak 2007, Weiss 2010).

With this in mind, I will now pull together the strands of the women's somatic and disclosure stories to reflect on, and make connections between, the impact of the responses they received to their disclosures, the considerable periods of time that elapsed between experience/s and disclosure/s, and the women's somatic symptoms that have already been revealed.

In terms of disclosure, only two of the nine survey women (Monica, Patricia) indicated they had disclosed to family members as well as healthcare professionals. The remaining seven women (Carol, Felicity, Kate, Monica, Patricia, Philipa, Ros) gave no indication they had disclosed as children but stated they had disclosed as adults to a healthcare professional/s. In terms of how their disclosures were met, not all had experienced positive responses.

More specifically, Monica and Patricia stated they had disclosed to family members as children but their stories were dismissed as fabrications. Monica also had her subsequent rape experience, at 18 years of age, dismissed as untrue by a healthcare professional. Carol indicated she had received many negative responses from a range of healthcare professionals, including being made to feel dirty, made to feel as though her concerns were being dismissed, especially by GPs, and as though she was being compartmentalised. Felicity had talked to a healthcare professional but now chose to avoid thoughts related to her childhood experience. Kate implied she had not received positive responses from healthcare professionals and consequently did not feel comfortable talking about her experience or related health concerns. Philipa disclosed to a healthcare professional as a young woman but was told not to make up silly stories. And Ros had disclosed to a healthcare practitioner but implied that the interaction was impersonal and therefore unsatisfactory because she felt she was given a stock response.

By contrast, only three of the women (Carol, Monica, Patricia) observed that they had, on occasion, experienced satisfactory interactions with healthcare professionals. Carol, who had not had a great deal of satisfactory interaction did acknowledge that she felt supported by professionals who showed her respect and listened to her without being patronising, but implied these were the exception. Monica's early interactions were mostly negative, however she had received empathic counselling at a sexual assault centre. Patricia now felt less fearful of her symptoms after counselling.

Of the three women (Nancy, Nina, Ros) who had chosen not to discuss their somatic symptoms with healthcare professionals, Nancy did not state why; Nina said she was too frightened to disclose in case she was forced to report the rape/s; and Ros had disclosed but did not believe the rape had impacted on her physically so generally chose not mention it.

In terms of the length of time that elapsed between the rape experience/s and disclosure to a healthcare professional, it is clear that some of the women waited extensive periods of time before disclosing their rape experience/s and before seeking help from healthcare workers. For example, Kate held onto her story for sixteen years before finally disclosing; Monica, having had her rape experiences as a young child, and again as a teenager, dismissed as fabrications, also waited a considerable period of time before again risking disclosure by seeking help; Patricia waited fifteen years before risking disclosure again after being ignored as a child; and Philipa, whose story was also dismissed as a young woman, waited until she was in her early thirties before she attempted to discuss it again but noted it wasn't until she was in her forties that she felt she could really talk about it.

As I have noted, negative responses from healthcare professionals to the disclosure of sexual violence, are not uncommon (Page and Wessely 2003, Ahrens 2006, Starzynski et al. 2007). This is particularly regrettable given that my research, along with other studies, indicates the reality that women may have waited a significant number of years before attempting disclosure (McKie, Fennell, and Mildorf 2002). This is certainly the case for some of the women who waited considerable periods of time prior to, and between disclosures.

With regard to feelings of being silenced, the literature discussed in Chapter Four has already established this is a common outcome in the aftermath of sexual violence (Ahrens 2006). It has also revealed that self-silencing practices are a consequence of the internalisation of culturally determined shame (Feiring and Taska 2005, Seu 2006, 2008, Vidal and Petrak 2007, Weiss 2010), and corresponding feelings of self-blame (Lievore 2003, 2005, Weiss 2010), and that each commonly manifest in the aftermath of sexual violence (Vidal and Petrak 2007, Lievore 2003, Weiss 2010).The literature is also clear that self-silencing practices can further disempower victims (Ahrens 2006, McAndrew and Warne 2005), although links have been made between self-silencing practices and an appreciation of concealment (Mahoney 1996). If viewed in this way, self-silencing practices can be interpreted as a form of self-protection, especially for children. In relation to this, findings from a large US study (Smith et al. 2000) determined that half of the childhood rape victims did not disclose to anyone for five years, and, in one quarter of the cases, the victims had not disclosed their rape experience at all until they participated in the study. These findings are consistent with other research which indicates that disclosure of sexual violence can take months, years, or in some cases, not occur at all (Easteal 1992a, Esposito 2005, Forbes et al. 2007, Mazza, Dennerstein, and Ryan 1996, Robohm and Buttenheim 1997, Ahrens 2006, Ahrens et al. 2007, Neame and Heenan 2003, Quadara 2008, Smith et al. 2000, Starzynski et al. 2007). The impact of externally imposed and self-imposed silencing, without doubt, has long term and detrimental health consequences (Pennebaker and Stone 2004, Seu 2006, 2008, Ullman and Filipas 2001, Ullman et al. 2007, Vidal and Petrak 2007, Weiss 2010).

As I have discussed previously, specialist post-trauma psychiatrist van der Kolk (2007) insists that healthcare professionals must make themselves aware of a patient's trauma history if they are to help facilitate appropriate treatment. This is a position held by others in the field of trauma (Ahrens et al. 2007, Havig 2008, Hurst et al. 2003). With regard to an individual's possible history of sexual trauma however, the literature has established that low rates of questioning by GPs persists (Lee et al. 2012), and is further compounded by low rates of voluntary disclosure by patients (Esposito 2005, Forbes et al. 2007, Mazza, Dennerstein, and Ryan 1996, Robohm and Buttenheim 1997, Lee et al. 2012).

For women like Kate, who held her story of rape violation in silence for sixteen years, the disconnection from her body this created and the accompanying feelings of self-disgust and shame, have had dire consequences. For women like Monica and Patricia, who, like me had their disclosure dismissed as children (and for Monica, again as a teenager), and whose symptoms were not linked to their trauma until well into adulthood, the multiple impacts have been devastating. The literature is clear that, for women like Nancy, who chooses not to discuss her trauma with healthcare professionals, and Nina, who is fearful of having to report the rape/s if she seeks help, the consequences of not speaking about their trauma experience can be highly damaging (Ahrens 2006, Ahrens, Stansell, and Jennings 2010, Ullman 1996).

For women like Philipa, who indicated she had disclosed to healthcare professionals in her twenties and thirties but her somatic symptoms were not considered to have any connection to her rape trauma, the repercussions have been long term and profound.

It is critical to note that, despite low rates of questioning by GPs and low rates of disclosure by patients, women who have experienced sexual trauma are not resistant to the possibility of being asked about whether they have a history of trauma. Research with patients who had attended gynaecological healthcare practices reveals that women acknowledge it would be appropriate for a healthcare practitioner to ask questions about a possible history of sexual trauma (Hurst et al. 2003). This is further supported by research which tells us that when women are asked by healthcare professionals about a possible history of sexual trauma, they feel relieved rather than offended (Lee et al. 2012).

Philipa's experience of 'hoping' for many years that healthcare professionals would understand her history without her having to spell it out, mirrors my own experience. I also sat in front of many healthcare practitioners over a number of years, and in two countries, hoping they would somehow recognise the origins of the health difficulties I was experiencing. I was repeatedly and frustratingly disappointed by their failure to detect this. Regrettably, this led to further self-castigation for my failure to communicate and further entrenched my feelings of low self-worth and isolation.

Personally, it's difficult to know precisely how I would have reacted if I had been asked by a healthcare practitioner about a possible history of sexual trauma. I can make an assumption, though, based on my considerable experience of disclosure avoidance in other, non-medical scenarios. I can assume that my likely and observable bodily responses to difficult interpersonal situations (flushed face, shallow breath, sweating, downcast eyes, my inability to speak) might have given me away if the practitioner had been empathic and observant, and I might then have been coaxed into disclosure. I can make another assumption too that, although it would have been terrifying to have been coaxed, like the participants in the Lee et al study, it would also have been a relief. I could then have had my story validated through externalisation and perhaps been guided and encouraged into accepting therapeutic help much earlier. It's possible that had this occurred, I would not have suffered so deeply, and for so long, from the multiple and complex psychophysiological manifestations of my prolonged secrecy and self-silencing practices.

In relation to this, the information gathered from the women, when held alongside my own story, identifies three significant areas of familial, social, and cultural influence which impact on disclosure and exacerbate the silencing of rape trauma. These include a lack of empathic engagement; inadequate professional understandings of sexual trauma and its multiple ramifications; and culturally-determined shame becoming internalised and serving to hold experience in silence. Clearly, silencing and self-silencing practices are significant features of the aftermath of childhood rape, not only for this group of women and for me, but also, as the literature has already illustrated, for a wider population of girls and women. This is unacceptable given the likely prevalence of rape in our culture.

I am unapologetic about my demand for changes to current understandings of the somatic aftermath of childhood rape; for more empathic responses to rape victims; and for greater vigilance within a healthcare setting to the possibility of underlying sexual trauma in patients and clients. It is my argument that familial and cultural silencing, as well as silencing due to a lack of empathic engagement in a healthcare setting can be as damaging as the violence inflicted on girls and women by the act of rape itself.

***

The focus of the following chapters now shifts from other women's somatic inquiry narratives to the details of my autoethnographic somatic inquiry. As the shift occurs, I take the reader from an examination of the macro presentation of post childhood rape symptoms manifested in the bodies of the participants to an examination of the micro, more cellular expression of rape trauma symptoms as they manifested in my own body.

CHAPTER SEVEN

Speaking of and with and through the raped body

> It is in writing, from woman and toward woman, and in accepting the challenge of the discourse controlled by the phallus, that woman will affirm woman somewhere other than in silence, the place reserved for her in and through the Symbolic. May she get out of the booby-trapped silence! And not have the margin or the harem foisted on her as her domain!
>
> — HÉLÈNE CIXOUS[1]

> The not-me dwells here in the me. We are one, and more-than-one. Our stories utter one another.
>
> — NANCY MAIRS[2]

When I set out 'on the edge of things, on the brink, on the foggy coast' (Le Guin 1989, 48) of my old and limited somatic world in pursuit of a new world through my research, I couldn't anticipate with any certainty what I would encounter along the way.

I had prepared myself as best I could for the labour of my explorations, fully expecting the project to be confronting. I bolstered myself in anticipation of competing feelings, emotions and responses to the autoethnographic component of the research. Through my somewhat restricted imagination (how can we ever truly prepare ourselves for an assignation with reality?), I readied myself for my exposure to the possible

1 From: Cixous, Hélène (1986). *Sorties*. In *A Newly Born Woman*. Minneapolis: University of Minnesota (93).
2 From: Mairs, Nancy (1994). *Voice lessons: On Becoming a (Woman) Writer*. Boston: Beacon Press (120).

unveiling of my dis-integrated and unresolved trauma memory. I tried to imagine how it might be to meet the bodily dissonance I harboured in ways other than punitive ones, how it might feel to be less punishing of my body. I wondered how I might respond should I be challenged to alter my habitual patterns of behaviour that had thus far held me safe as an adult but had limited my capacity to engage fully and openly in intrapersonal and interpersonal relationships.

These imaginings ran the gamut of my emotions. Some were ripe with a combination of adrenalin-charged nervous excitement and infinitely delicate hope. I rolled around in their possibilities. Other imaginings were full of apprehension and fear, rippling with feelings of vulnerability and uncertainty. Although I didn't dwell in their particular and difficult company for too long, I didn't fall into habitual numbing responses to them either; I simply put them, with awareness, to one side. When I took up the writing of this book, and as I began to run a retrospective eye across the terrain of my research, what I came to see was the vast range of responses I hadn't anticipated: the relentless and sometimes vertigo-inducing switchbacks in responses when dazzling, rich, and profound insights broke through the darkness, despair, and shrouded intimacy of my story; the occasional spontaneous eruptions of cellular memory that were distressing to re-experience but also brought shafts of revelation and new ways of co-habiting with my trauma; the reality of the depth of my grief at the loss of relationship with my body; the pure joy I experienced during moments of bodily connection; the love and respect that developed towards my somatic self over time; the wondrous if bewildering somatic paradoxes that presented themselves as I struggled for clarity and understanding; the emergent stirrings of a more tolerant and accepting relationship with my body that made my habitual patterns stand out in stark relief; and the growing frustration with and lack of confidence in language to adequately capture and convey all of these colliding and challenging states. The depth and range of feeling was vast. In terms of conveying this to readers, and in terms of holding the reader's attention, the prospect was daunting.

Laurel Richardson (2000, 924) ponders the question of how to engage and sustain the interest of readers of qualitative research by finding ways to turn them towards texts rather than away. She asks 'How do we create texts that are vital? That are attended to? That make a difference?' Echoing these questions but relating them specifically to autoethnographic texts and performance, Julie Salverston (2001) suggests the autoethnographic space in which personal testimony is laid bare to the reader/audience is a space of risk ostensibly holding the potential for empathy but troubled by the possibility of failing to hold the reader/audience in a critical engagement with the text or performance.

When I first began to shape the research, running alongside my speculations and anticipations were many questions that seemed like rhizomatic outgrowths of Richardson's and Salverston's observations. My questions revolved around sustaining a reader's attention as well as concerns surrounding the dissemination of my findings from the research. How would I write of embodied knowledge in the context of the raped body without inhibition? How would I deliver knowledge of this nature so as to engage the reader's attention without causing dis-ease? What sort of writing conventions would I need to disrupt/engage in order to reveal and illuminate the somatically experienced aftermath of childhood rape in the adult body? How would I navigate my way from the micro to the macro, the personal to the political, in order to signal the existence of, and place for my research in existing bodies of knowledge? Would my research be taken seriously? Would the struggle to speak with the body voice also be the struggle for that body voice to be heard? How would I facilitate this? How would I attempt to uphold the materialist call to redress the dichotomous privileging of brain intelligence over body intelligence without falling into a binary myself?

As I speculated I recalled the words of Brison (2002), and her *narrative of liberation*. And I recalled too the words of autoethnographer and performance artist Spry (1995). Spry writes of the difficulties inherent in understanding her experience of sexual violence 'from within [...] a phallocentric language' that inscribes the body as 'an object that things are done to, or erased from the experience completely' (1995, 1). These women's words tumbled and reverberated within the questions I was asking myself, shaking them, and me, about. And then I paused to breathe and allowed my questions to return slowly and turn to face me:

If I was to give written voice, through the body, to the somatically experienced aftermath of rape in the female body, were my questions relevant? If I was to cleave open the silence that continued to mute the raped female body, thereby contributing to Brison's *narrative of liberation* (2002), should I have been considering my questions at all?

The answer was yes.

And the answer was no.

To speak of the raped body is to speak with both a personal and a political voice. How can it be otherwise? Holding embodied knowledge of the raped body is personal; to speak this knowledge shifts it from the personal to the political. To speak of the embodied knowledge of the raped body in order to broaden existing sociocultural and theoretical understandings to help effect change is a political act. In order to allow the raped body to speak and thus facilitate the shift from the personal to the political it was necessary for me to consider my questions and simultaneously not consider them.

On the one hand it was essential that I paid heed to my questions because words that disengage the reader or repulse, or even bore them, are words that drift to the ground and are lost. On the other hand, if I were to coax my words into a more palatable shape, one that sanitised the unique embodied knowledge of the raped body, I would run the risk of censoring or silencing this knowledge and then falling into the body-object-erasure trap that Spry (1995) speaks of. Or, if I took this knowledge into a non-specific universal realm in order to avoid this censoring/silencing effect, the risk would become one of self-censorship, or worse still, self-silencing. Additionally, if I didn't challenge the phallocentric privileging of brain intelligence through the engagement of an active body voice, the risk would be one of colluding in the silencing of the body and the perpetuation of that privileging.

Together we wrestled, these many questions and I. I held them and turned them over; I flung them to the floor and scooped them up again. I stood alongside these questions vacillating between the desire to speak and engage, and the desire to retreat to the relative safety of the silent space. I grappled often with the issue of responsibility; was I, as the writer-researcher responsible for the response of the reader? I found myself resisting the urge to shout that it's NOT the responsibility of girls and women who've experienced rape to console those they disclose to, completely aware that this contributes to silencing as much as anything. And finally, I struggled with the risk inherent in placing my somatic narrative and experienced raped body together with the bodies and somatic narratives of the other women in my research, not merely as a shadowy peripheral silhouette, but overtly centre stage, in order for my body to take up an ontological and epistemological position, present and fully embodied.

Hélène Cixous stepped in to provide wise counsel. 'Censor the body' she reminded me 'and you censor breath and speech at the same time. Write yourself. Your body must be heard' (1976, 880).

I took Cixous' words seriously. I did so because I fully understood the myriad impacts of censorship and silencing, externally imposed and self-imposed. These had shaped my life, my patterns of behaviour, and my body from childhood. Fear of accidental disclosure had robbed me of the ability to fill my lungs to capacity, leaving me feeling as though I lived in a state of partial asphyxiation, my cells existing on a restricted and impoverished oxygen supply. Without sufficient air to allow cellular memory and speech to bob to the surface of my body, the weight of my trauma memory and the associated self-narrative sank into and remained trapped in the sediment of my tissues, mouth agape, eternally gasping for air.

I intuitively sensed this state of slow somatic suffocation impacting on my life, preventing me from participating fully in my familial and social world, preventing me from participating in my own physicality. I felt strongly that in order for my body to be heard, by my self and eventually by others, I must first attune my awareness to its delicate cellular whisperings and mutterings, its nuance, its infinitesimally subtle movements, its somatic ebb and flow. I understood that in order to attune my self, it would be critical to open my perception, sharpen my

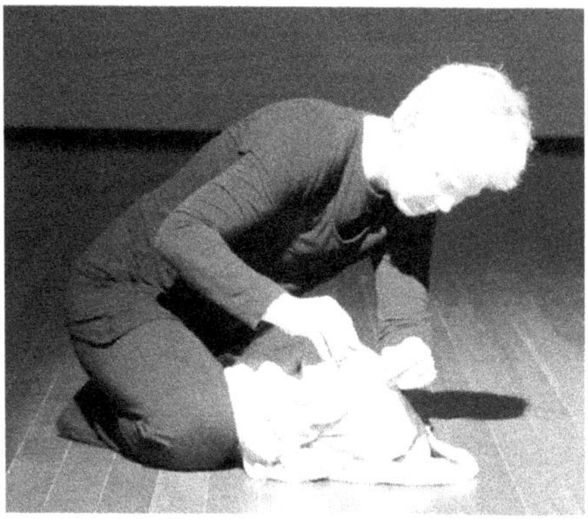

awareness, and give my self over fully to whatever sensations arose. I understood too that becoming familiar with the nuances of my body's language would require me to lift up a corner of my self, slide inside and remain there, listening with deep attention, with as much consciousness and compassion as I could muster. I knew this would take great courage and I approached the research with a complex combination of competing emotions. After all, the powerful hold I had maintained over my body thus far had served me well, intentionally creating a corporeal/cognitive separation. This conscious separation was engineered precisely to avoid confronting the unresolved trauma I feared and which I suspected remained trapped in my body. Now my research had initiated an energetic, if apprehensive, inquisitiveness regarding this and a desire to release my hold, move inside my self and greet whatever awaited me. I was also drawn to learn of the experiences of other women, something I had previously avoided in order to circumvent the exacerbation of my own pain. This added another layer of uncertainty and was a further test of my capacity to sit inside the difficulty and complexity of researching my own embodied responses to childhood rape.

In combination, these questions, anticipations and apprehensions felt a little like attempting a base jump with a parachute: would it open, or would it not?

***

5 June, 2010

I became acutely aware of my desire to remain in my body ... to remain well beyond symbolic representation.

7 March, 2011

I find now that language so easily shifts my attention away from my body. It's paradoxical that I must use language to describe somatic sensation or movement and yet it feels increasingly separate from my somatic experience.

Words were the primary medium I had at my disposal in the shaping of this book. I was reliant on language to mould the abstract and fragmented bodily/cellular moments of my experience in order to craft them into symbolic shape and transmit their meaning through writing. It was an ambivalent and, as Nancy Mairs (1994, 5) says, 'tangled relationship to words'. And because of this, a monumental task, this crafting and shaping of lived somatic experience and unfolding self-knowledge. Monumental in that this translation of bodily language with its unfamiliar, unspoken and slippery tongue anchored in the somatic mouth, concealed by lips that so often refused symbolic representation, was being forced into language, itself anchored in the masculine mouth.

Women writers who attempt to speak of personal experience face a double dilemma. On the one hand they face the constraints and limitations of a masculinist language; on the other hand they face censure. Almost one hundred years ago Virginia Woolf (2008) wrote of the difficulties encountered by women writers. The difficulties, as she perceived them, rested in the appropriateness or relevance of patriarchal language when writing from and about women's experience. Woolf identified the structure of language as masculinist and cited the dilemma and struggle this posed for women at that time when attempting to assume a writing position that spoke with the voice of the feminine constrained by the language of the masculine. She noted that 'the very form of the sentence does not fit her [the woman writer of fiction]'. In the struggle to find words to accurately capture what it is she, the woman writer, wishes to say, Woolf argues she must engage in the process of re-moulding the existent masculinist language, '[...] altering and adapting the current sentence until she writes one that takes the natural shape of her thought without crushing or distorting it' (136).

Woolf is not alone in speaking out about the constraints present for women writers struggling against the dominant tide of patriarchal culture and the limiting effect of entrenched and pervasive masculinist language. Some six decades after Woolf's essay, the academic and feminist author Caroline Heilbrun (1988) examined the difficulties and conflicts present for women writers when attempting to write truthfully of women's lives while avoiding the re-inscription of their subordinate position. In a culture dominated by phallocentric language and one which maintains particular beliefs about how women's lives should be lived, she asks: 'How can women create stories of women's lives if they have only male language with which to do it?' With specific regard to women engaging in autobiographical writing,

Jill Ker Conway (1999, 3) argues that Western language and literary forms of narrative such as autobiography, are constructed in ways that privilege the masculine and help facilitate the documentation and interpretation of the masculine life. 'How can a woman write an autobiography' she asks, 'when to do so requires using a language which denigrates the feminine [...]?'

Contemporary Australian writer Drusilla Modjeska (1995) writes too of the difficulties faced by women writers. In *The Orchard*, Modjeska explores Virginia Woolf's theme through a slightly different lens, one not of masculinist language per se but of the gendered historical and cultural positioning of writers. More specifically, Modjeska writes of the difficulties faced by women writers when writing, autobiographically or otherwise, on the topic of love affairs. She asks: 'How can she [a woman writer] write about a love affair when the world of criticism and opinion favours a man's facts or his myths, over a women's romance, her fantasies, her gossip?' (31). She notes that when a man writes of a love affair, he does so to simultaneously affirm his entitlement to sexual gratification and give narrative reality to his experience. For a woman to write of love, says Modjeska, 'it is a risky business, for her agency with the pen contradicts her prescribed destiny as a woman' (31). She continues:

> If a woman writes of love, and in doing so speaks her mind, breaks the restraints, the constraints of definitions and names that are ever-present to her – wife of, mistress of – if she bursts out into anger, or a shadowy ambivalence, or into grief, it's considered an unseemly act: embarrassing, slightly pitiful. Her critics, the critics, will accuse her, the woman who writes in this way, of confession. As if the 'I' on the page should have known better than to let slip a messy reminder of the body that holds the pen. As if there weren't in any case gaps and fissures between that 'I', that body, that pen. As if confession was a transparent term. (31)

Modjeska challenges the labelling of writing of this nature as 'confession' and admissions of guilt. Instead, she positions this type of writing as a reflexive process, as a woman's way of engaging with experience in order not to confess but to make sense of the experience itself and its impact on her voice as a woman and her sense of being. She suggests that perhaps the act of telling:

> can evoke confession in a woman; but where they, the critics, mean to imply that all she does is kneel in the dark and confess her sins, a list of failings she already knows, what she does in writing, in telling, is to search, sifting through the many versions and possibilities to find the shape and truth of her life, the story she doesn't yet know, the image and narrative she struggles to bring, like her self, into being. (32)

Like Woolf, Ker Conway, Heilbrun and Modjeska, I too have faced the difficulties of writing from personal experience while operating within a masculinist system of language. The autoethnographic 'I' on the page understands with full consciousness that the placement of this subjective personal pronoun acts precisely as *a messy reminder of the body that holds the pen*. That is my intention. My raped, female, and fleshed body holds that pen consciously and reflexively as I sift through the multiple and emerging layers of my story to *find the shape* of my life and the *stories I don't yet know*. I occupy the privileged position of both researcher and researched. My researcher-participant speaking body oscillates between these two locations in reflexive motion. The autoethnographic 'I' reminds the reader of the presence of the fleshed researcher behind the words and simultaneously problematises that presence. I cannot, but more importantly, will not, avoid filling the page with my speaking body. The hand that holds the pen cannot be separated from the body under investigation. Yet all the while the wrestling with language and the resistance to censure persists.

Nancy Mairs (1994) is familiar with the limitations of masculinist language:

> She [Mother] didn't hint that language, which seemed to be a tool – ordinary to the point of transparency – for representing my daily needs and demands and desires, could function as a giant india rubber for effacing the very subject of those needs and demands and desires. 'Phallogocentrism,' theorists have called this restriction on utterance: the erection of the Word to plug up the hole that holds 'the feminine.' [...] The language a woman who has planned to use to express her experience turns out, in this scheme, to depend for its very existence and efficacy on her repression. (5–6)

Rosie McLaren (2001a, 7) writes too of the ways in which words can confound attempts to describe un-languaged experience, of the difficulties inherent in finding ways to 'express the unsaid'. What McLaren is referring to here is what lies implicit in works of visual imagery and refers specifically to paintings and drawings that sit outside symbolic language. These works, produced by women participants in McLaren's doctoral research, were created as a means of artistic and non-verbal articulation of personal story and collectively become evocative representations of the women's experience of menopause to help shape new meaning through alternative forms of articulation. Additionally, McLaren understands that meaning arises not just through language but also from our bodily response to other forms of creative expression. She argues that a complex suite of responses is possible in any interaction with the articulation of story, image-based or otherwise. As the researcher, when trying to form language to articulate the women's experience of artistic creation, McLaren found herself 'groping for words that are at times hidden and unformed, to give voice to the intense immediacy of our sensory bodies' perceptions and feelings'. She grappled with 'incongruity in using already constituted language'. As an autoethnographic researcher exploring the somatic impact of rape, I too grappled with words that seemed perpetually and frustratingly inadequate to the task of representing the viscerality and immediacy of my somatic inquiry experience.

Cixous (1986) once again provides wise counsel in her reflections on phallogocentric cultural traditions that limit the voice of the feminine. She offers a strategy for opening up a new space for women to write with freedom and *jouissance*:[3]

> If woman has always functioned 'within' man's discourse ... now it is time for her to displace this 'within', explode it, overturn it, grab it, make it hers, take it in, take it into her women's mouth, bite its tongue with her women's teeth, make up her

3 Betsy Wing notes in the glossary of 'The Newly Born Woman' (Cixous and Clement 1986, 165), that the meaning of the French word *jouissance* is difficult to translate into English. She suggests that 'total sexual ecstasy is its most common connotation' however, 'in contemporary French philosophical, psychoanalytic, and political usage, it does not stop there, and to equate it with orgasm would be an oversimplification'. In the 'Introduction' to this text, Sandra M. Gilbert suggests *jouissance* 'implies a virtually metaphysical fulfilment of desire that goes far beyond any satisfaction that could be imagined ... [it becomes] a fusion of the erotic, the mystical, and the political ...' (xvii).

> own tongue to get inside of it. And you will see how easily she will well up, from this 'within' where she was hidden and dormant, to the lips where her foams will overflow. (95–96)

In the context of the earlier story of Philomela, Cixous could be responding here to the dilemma faced by the mythical Philomela when her tongue was removed. Philomela's loom replaced her own tongue, and the story she wove in cloth became her means of biting the tongue of the masculine power and phallocentric discourse that had silenced her.

My close engagement with the conceptual thinking of Cixous (1991a, 1976, 1990, 1991b, 1993, 1997, 1998, Cixous and Clement 1986) throughout my research process has helped support my research praxis and practice. Her writing has been a reassuring and encouraging presence, not least her perception of the shortcomings of language. By juxtaposing her writerly dependence on words as a medium of expression with, as she perceives it, a painter's less limiting dependence on the mix of colours from their palette, Cixous (1991a) says:

> I would like to write to what is living in life; I would like to be in the sea and render it in words. Which is impossible. I would like to write the rose-colored beach and the pearly ocean … Completely impossible. My words can't tell you the simultaneously infinite and yet finite beach rolled out like an immense carpet of rosy sands. My words are colorless. Barely sonorous? What I can tell you, a painter would show you […] I would like to break your heart with the magnificent calm of the beach safe from man. But I can't do it, I can only tell it. All I can do is tell the desire. But the painter can break your heart with the epiphany of a sea […] I don't paint. I need painting. I write in the direction of painting. I position myself toward the sun. Toward the light. Toward painting. (105–106)

Reflecting on the Dutch painter Vermeer, Cixous (1998) notes he was adept with light. 'The outside knocks on the windowpanes', she writes, and 'The exterior enters the interior' (6). Vermeer allows just enough light, invariably through a dim mullioned window, to angle onto the subjects of his paintings, invariably women in isolation. Just enough light to attract the eye and draw attention to their shape without blinding or distracting. His light-filled illuminations appear to lick the flesh of his subjects rather than the canvas on which they are held. He painted *toward the light*. The subtlety of his light is dazzling. For me, Vermeer creates story with that light, just enough story for his paintings to seduce with a gesture of embodied invitation. They tempt me to become a responsible viewer, step into the palette of my imagination and my lived experience, and take up the role of story-maker, the static scene on the canvas offering the entry point to my body and the inspiration for the movement of my creativity. This is my task in the writing of these chapters: to offer the reader an entry point into their own bodies, lived experience, and knowledges by writing *toward the light* and in the *direction of painting*. I write from the murky interior of rape trauma to cast light on the complexity of the somatic aftermath crouching there in order to illuminate what I found. But words cannot always see into the corners where the shadows are deepest.

Cixous (1991c) acknowledges she *writes in the direction of painting*. Although she deems language inadequate to the task of creating sufficient light, she attends to the task of its apprehension with every stroke of her pen just as diligently as the brush-holding Vermeer, and yet remains dissatisfied:

> There are mimosa in the garden. I want so much to give them to you to see [...] If I were a painter! I would give you each mimosa-cluster whole. I would give you my mimosa-soul, down to the most minute quivering of the yellow spheres [...] But I can't nourish your eyes with mimosa light [...] see the mimosas that I see. Imagine the mimosas. See what you don't see [...] I gather words to make a great straw-yellow fire, but if you don't put in your own flame, my fire won't take, my words won't burst into pale yellow sparks. My words will remain dead words. Without your breath on my words, there will be no mimosas [...] I write. But I need the painter to give a face to my words. First of all, I write; then you must paint what I've said to you. (106–108)

My words will remain dead words. My reflections on this passage emerge in the movement through layers of complexity. I am reminded that collections of written letters juxtaposed to form words are incapable of standing alone on a page and touching others with meaning without intervention. Words, in any symbolic language, are not inherently entitled to be understood simply because they have been inscribed on a page. There are intricate anatomical, physiological, and cultural processes involved in understanding inscriptions that sit beyond the markings themselves. To understand these processes, I engage my embodied imagination, sense an orientation away from the page, and step outside the parameters of my flesh in a sort of dissociative turn back towards my body. In this rotation I move through another layer. I'm prompted to imaginatively transform and take up the colour and shapes of letters and enter my body through the continually adjusting aperture of my eye. The light of my shapes is refracted and I float in a sea of neurotransmitters along the optic nerve to the language centre of my brain where these letters undergo reorganisation. Because my brain has been trained to read, these markings are interpreted as words, known and unknown. My imagination penetrates another layer of understanding. It would be too straightforward, and hierarchically privileging of the brain, to suggest that once these markings are interpreted as words they immediately take on meaning without other elements of influence.

***

'A word is the memory of its meaning' writes poet Anne Michaels (1997, 44), delicately but insistently scooping up the material body and implicating it directly in other ways of knowing. For Michaels, as for Cixous, experience and feeling originates in the body. Michaels takes us directly there through this poetic line. She guides us into the experienced subjectivity and material intelligence of the body where meaning gestates. Her words turn the gaze inward towards our non-verbal, cellular selves. Implicit in Michaels' words is the suggestion that it is in the feeling and sensorially responsive and material body that meaning begins, that bodily ways of knowing precede the application, intervention, and reinterpretation of experience through language. The body, for Michaels, is always necessarily present and meaning is already in process in the instant of experience as happenings are experienced, absorbed, and responded to by the cells. The body is constantly participating in the production of meaning; it is always in the act of making knowledge, always in movement, full of sensory signals and molecular exchanges. And then, in all this perpetual cellular activity and abundance, the brain responds. Words slide into consciousness to appropriate bodily experience and form the semantic conduit for the intellectually-situated and symbolic representation of these happenings.

It's at this point, at the intersection of bodily experience and the articulation of it, that *everything beats faster* for Cixous and her *entire body readies itself* for linguistic expression, for a surge of language with the force of these bodily processes behind it. When her words stream across the boundaries of her flesh and spill over and onto the page, Cixous accepts they have meaning and image in the intelligence of her own body and brain and her own embodied imagination, but none beyond. She acknowledges that once independent of her body, her writing must be engaging enough to become participatory in order for meaning to be transmitted. Her words become necessarily invitational and relational, reliant on the breath of the embodied imagination of another entity: the reader. If meaning is to be shared at all, as the worded text emerges from one body (Cixous') and enters another (the reader's), an intimate union must be forged between Cixous, the text, and the reader with the present and imaginatively and empathically engaged body binding all three. This of course is not a union unique to Cixous and her readers; it is the case for any writer whose reliance on words for the dissemination of meaning, feeling and knowledge necessarily invites the participation of another entity to light the touchpaper of the writer's own *mimosa* words. As that entity, the reader puts in *their own flame* through their bodily response, the writer's words *burst into pale yellow sparks* and they, the reader, have performed the transformation of received word into personal meaning and image through embodied imagination. This is the provocation intrinsic to the work of this book. Within the words must also lie the invitation for participation, the writing must be invitational and performative as it moves with collaborative gesture across the intersubjective space towards the reader.

***

Embedded in and emerging from the matrix that forms between Cixous' and Michaels' words, is the material and porous body, the cellular ground of feeling and experience, the maker and absorber of meaning. For each of these writers, whether in relation to the transmission of meaning to others or the unfolding of self-meaning, the body is intrinsic to the process of understanding, it is essential for experience; for the production of text; and, for meaning-making through embodied imagination. In this way, a more balanced somatic-cognitive understanding of the body and mind relationship begins to unfold.

The additional task for me in this written and enacted articulation of the somatic aftermath of childhood rape is to continue the challenge of maintaining this alignment of body and mind. In this book, itself a performance of sorts, the intelligent, knowing, and material body isn't situated in the program below the mind, as a less experienced performer might be, or even in opposition to the mind on a separate billing. In the list of performers the intelligence of the body is elevated and repositioned on the same line of the program, sitting alongside the intelligence of the mind, as a soloist and partner of equal merit sharing an equivalent status in this production of meaning and knowledge.

This is not an improvised production. I have consciously created a similarly choreographed arrangement of movements that mirror Cixous and Michaels in order to draw attention to the body. Historically and culturally, the mind has been given star billing and an abundance of centre stage exposure. In the score I have created for this dance of inquiry, the mind waits in the wings, side-of-stage for most of the performance, while centre stage is temporarily given to the somatic to allow the raped body to move freely around the stage of this book as an unencumbered soloist. The stage lighting will reflect Cixous' desire to *write towards painting* and will attempt to mirror Vermeer's 'just enough light'. The glare of full stage lighting will reveal the raped body's fleshed and exposed surfaces; more subtle lighting will deepen its shadowed folds. It is my intention to deliberately direct the gaze of the reader towards these surfaces and into these folds to invoke imaginative engagement with the stories they tell as well as the stories that remain in shadowy attendance. In this way, the raped body and the corporeally constituted aftermath stories claim space in the production of these chapters. This concentrated attention is not to eclipse the mind but to allow the reader the opportunity to view the raped body's capacity to articulate experience without the distraction of a shared stage and a more culturally, philosophically, and discursively dominant partner.

My intent in this methodology is not accidental. I want to draw the reader away from more masculinist and consciously disembodied methods of knowledge production and delivery modalities by insisting on the centrality of the body on these pages. Richardson (2000, 924) cautions that 'Qualitative work carries its meaning in its entire text' and that this type of research 'has to be read, not scanned; its meaning is in the reading'. She makes the point that research that fails to be read also fails to add to existing knowledges in ways that echo Cixous' concern about words being *dead words* unless they are given life by the reader. Drawing on Cixous and Michaels, I argue that text, or experience, is also carried in the body as cellular memory, and lingers not just in written and imaged form in the brain. It is the failure to read the language of this text, this body-as-text and this text-as-body, that overlooks and therefore denies other more materially cognisant ways of coming to knowing. I further argue that for the reader to engage dynamically and empathically with a rape trauma narrative, any reading of the text, be it fleshed or worded, must necessarily entail both an intellectual as well as a feeling and embodied engagement with the text. To resist the drop into a feeling embodied state risks only a partial reading.

The autoethnographical perspective of my research necessarily means that I must write in the first person. As a feminist researcher interested in bringing the rape aftermath stories of other women into the research, I am conscious of the importance of providing a welcoming subjective space for these other women to sit at the centre of their own story (Hopkins 2009) and 'to occupy and speak from the centre of their own lives' (Metta 2010, 292). As a feminist researcher interested in rape aftermath narratives which focus on the adult female body, I am already in a personally situated and embodied material space. These narratives, emerging as they do from raped bodies, inevitably speak with the embodied voice of the personal. The 'I' and 'me' and 'my' of these stories is what gives them authority, irrespective of gender. It is the use of these pronouns that provides the key to the door of entitlement. In this instance, the door swings open to reveal the sexual trauma stories within, and it is on women's subjective embodied experience that the door's hinges hang.

By focusing on the somatic aspects of rape trauma, I resist and disrupt modalities whose 'disavowal of materialist epistemologies' (Dolmage 2009, 4) deny the intelligent body the opportunity to participate in meaning-making practices and prevent it from contributing to alternative forms of knowledge delivery. By situating my research within arts-based inquiry, by offering an embodied and contemporary alternative, I implicitly discredit masculinist ways of knowledge-making and transmission which are still attached to ancient phallocentric philosophical traditions (themselves still attached to self-serving mythology). My work explicitly challenges the unbroken genealogy that continues to render the raped female body silent and invisible. It works in explicit rejection of the traditional masculinist methods that have 'limited our ability to recognize and communicate with and from our own real bodies' out of 'fear of the body and of bodily difference' (Dolmage 2009, 3). By placing the raped body centre stage, by revealing the somatic narratives from my own raped body along with the somatic narratives from the bodies of other raped women, this book attempts to uncover the potential the material body holds to communicate, through its own unique vocabulary, unresolved echoes of trauma. In doing so, my words aim to demonstrate the valuable contribution this type of knowledge can make to the field of sexual trauma and to sexual trauma healing.

CHAPTER EIGHT

Coming to knowing: A methodology of embodiment

> I like being in the present; am interested in what's in process: of passing by, of happening. The instant – the eternity of the instant.
>
> — HÉLÈNE CIXOUS[1]

The raped body and the embodiment of unresolved rape trauma memory lie at the heart of my investigation. The raped female body, my raped body, the raped bodies of nine other women, are not marginal to the shape of my methodology. They are the pulse for the methodological framework that supported this research. The research focus on the specific somatic expression of childhood rape trauma is a way of coming to knowing that upholds an ethics of embodiment and acknowledges a less well understood aspect of sexual violence.

In this chapter, I discuss the rationale behind the use of an embodied methodology for my research. Four different, but complementary, knowledge-making practices of inquiry made up the composite whole of my embodied methodological framework. These practices are: autoethnography; somatic inquiry; writing-as-inquiry; and performance-making-as-inquiry. There is no epistemological hierarchy at play here, sometimes these knowledge-making practices overlapped; sometimes I used them in tandem; rarely did they occur in a predictable sequence as discrete steps in a logical process of inquiry.

I have already established that within contemporary sexual trauma scholarship, psychological investigations dominate. Much attention

1 From: Cixous, Hélène (1998). *Stigmata*. Abingdon, Oxfordshire: Routledge (43).

has been given to the psychological expression and treatment of trauma following rape with links between the two firmly established (Anderson and Doherty 2008, Campbell and Wasco 2005, Feiring and Taska 2005, Rothschild 2000, Scaer 2001, Ullman et al. 2007, Vidal and Petrak 2007). Far less research has focused on the somatic expression of trauma following rape, although connections have been made between the experiencing of rape and the somatic manifestation and expression of that experience in the aftermath (Martin et al. 2007, Ogden and Minton 2001, Rothschild 2000, Thompson et al. 2002, Waldinger et al. 2006). In order to contribute to discussion surrounding the role of body-held trauma and to support the feminist materialist call for research that embraces the discursive and the corporeal (Barad 2003, Grosz 2010, Hekman 2010, van der Tuin and Dolphijn 2010, Kirby 1997, Wilson 1998), this research rejected neither, to maintain an embodied-discursive focus throughout its methodological structure, information gathering methods, and theorising.

***

The methodology emerged from the subjective embodied experience of rape in childhood. As a result of the sexual violation I was subjected to in 1971, the shame and misplaced guilt engendered by the experience destroyed my capacity to speak of this experience for decades. I argue that this quasi erasure of my experience grew out of a social, cultural, and philosophical deficiency that made no room for the articulation and disclosure of such an experience, making self-silencing and the concomitant loss of voice inevitable. Although silenced by and through this violation of my body, I was never free of the sound of its presence, incapable of moving through the world entirely independent of it. I had no alternative. I was forced to hold in my body the silenced and unresolved trauma memory and hold it with vigilance so as not to allow its presence to escape beyond the boundary of my flesh. This conscious repression had serious long-term ramifications for my overall health, my relationship with my body, and how I moved and interacted in the world. It also set the scene for my feminist ideology.

This is the experiential context from which my methodology grew and is grounded. Understandings of embodiment in the aftermath of childhood rape that were revealed during the research process are my means of responding to that social, cultural, and philosophical silencing and a way of drawing attention to the significant knowledge-holding and knowledge-making capacity of the raped female body. Consciously locating the raped female body central to my research, was both my methodological strategy and, in the information gathering somatic inquiry phase, my method of investigation. The raped body and embodied experience were the 'how', the 'what' and the 'why' of my research, both the means of investigation and the means of illumination facilitating the fusion of the 'research praxis and the process' (Metta 2010, 167). This methodology is in line with the feminist materialist demand for more inclusive modes of investigation that reflect the many facets of experience.

***

In order to plot the development of my methodological framework it was been necessary for me to wait for the movement that breath invites, listen carefully to the rhythm and pulse of the work, and walk my way backwards through the delicate cellular network that made up what could be called the connective tissue of my research. In the human body, connective tissue offers a structural framework and plays a vital role:

> It binds together, supports, and strengthens other body tissues; protects and insulates internal organs; compartmentalizes structures such as skeletal muscles; serves as a major transport system within the body (blood, a fluid connective tissue); is the primary location of stored energy reserves [...]; and is the main source of immune responses. (Tortora and Derrickson 2009, 38)

I was compelled to do this re-tracing through the micro layers of the methodological connective tissue to tease out the capillaries, veins and arteries that were the methods of inquiry and the blood-flow within the body of the research. This was necessary because the methods of embodied knowing and the coming to knowing in the primary autoethnographic component of the exploration often seemed to occur simultaneously. So closely entangled were they that at times it was difficult to detect the almost osmotic movement from one to the other. Indeed, to stop to consciously register the beginning of one and the start of another would have risked interrupting the process. For it was in the *process* of embodied inquiry, in the fecund space of the sometimes straight forward, sometimes slippery and oblique, sometimes opaque and barely detectable transition from knowing and coming to knowing that my embodied and theoretical understandings gestated and grew.

The use of the connective tissue metaphor imaginatively reminds me of the ways in which my experiential context, my feminist perspective, and my embodied approach to the research *binds together, supports, and strengthens* my inquiry. A close examination of the methodological framework through the connective tissue metaphor allows me to begin to clarify particular aspects of my research. The metaphor helps provide an evocative anatomical mapping of the ways in which the methodology facilities the transportation of these different epistemological and ontological elements throughout the body of my research. It offers a way to view the storage of these elements as energising and motivating forces that underpinned, sculpted and drove the various components of the project. It supports the articulation of the evolution of my methods and, finally, it reinforces the ways in which my embodied inquiry and my conceptual and theoretical understandings organically unfolded throughout the length of the research.

By centrally locating embodied rape trauma experience, the 'self-knowledge' (Peseta 2007, 16) of sexual violation, I attempt to subvert the dominant social, cultural and discursive silencing of embodied rape experience by facilitating the potential for the enablement of corporeally-located voice. This book makes room for the articulation of the messiness, rawness, grief, contradiction, and incoherence that brews in the body in the aftermath of rape. In this way, the raped female body and its evocative language is given currency in the economy of sexual trauma scholarship, challenging and problematising disembodied and discourse-centric constructions of the aftermath of rape that fail to take into account the profound and long term cellular impact of rape trauma, and fails to acknowledge the body as an ontologically rich reserve of experiential knowing.

I argue that for both the mind *and* the body to be recognised as legitimate holding grounds for trauma and trauma memory it is necessary to haul things around and view things from a different angle. If the experiential nature and knowledge-making capacity of the sexually traumatised body is to be fully recognised and acknowledged, if the material body is to be taken seriously as a legitimate site of ontological and epistemological meaning-making in rape trauma research and scholarly circles, then a re-positioning of the corporeal must take place.

I am aware that by insisting on the central location of the raped body in this research I may be seen to be walking into a minefield. The reader might be wary of a slide into the perpetuation of the mind and body oppositional trap or worse still, a stumbling into an 'essentialist' snare, as any move towards the material is wont to be termed (Alaimo 2008). As a feminist somatic researcher wishing to dismantle hierarchical and oppositional dichotomous thinking, I want to reassure the reader that my manoeuvre here is a reverse one intended to encourage and contribute to a more equitable eventual outcome. For the purpose of this research, unlike the disembodied Western masculinist and hierarchical elevation of the rational, linguistic and discursively-dependent mind which elides the non-rational, feeling body, I am claiming the *provisional* elevation of the body over the mind. In doing so, it is not my intention to elide the mind. Rather, I am temporarily turning the masculinist-privileging discourse/corporeal binary on its hierarchical head by privileging the material raped body in order for the body to be viewed as an equally significant source and site of knowing and coming to know. In doing so, I am not turning my back on the mind or discourse, or downplaying their significance. My intention in performing this manoeuvre is to locate the material reality of childhood sexual trauma *alongside* a discursive framework. This strategy will ultimately privilege neither the corporeal nor the discursive but rather, will integrate the two in a non-hierarchical embodied *and* discursive body-mind marriage to reflect the intelligence of the body and the embodiment of the mind. In a contemporary feminist world where the materiality of the body is being re-viewed by materialist scholars such as Vicki Kirby, Elizabeth A. Wilson, Stacy Alaimo, Susan Hekman, Karen Barad, Iris van Tuin, Claire Colebrook and others, it is timely to promote the ontological and epistemological attributes of the raped and material body. But what gave rise to the emergence of this new and exciting branch of feminism?

***

Postmodern and poststructural feminist thinking grew in strategic response to modernism's theoretical assumptions surrounding women's subordinate social position. One of these assumptions held that women's destiny was inextricably linked to their corporeality (Firestone 1970, Friedan 1963), and was 'the natural outcome of biological sexual difference' (Somerville 2004, 47). In the late 1980s and early 1990s, poststructural feminist theorists took arguments for women's oppression and identity into more linguistically-focused, plural, and non-biological territory, a change of direction for feminism termed the 'linguistic turn' (Lam 2012, Barad 2008). They also aimed to politically and theoretically distance themselves from modernism's essentialism with its biological basis for oppression (Somerville 2004). This stance made an 'underlying assumption that some aspects of "biology" are fixed' (Birke 1999, 44). By adopting the fixed category of 'woman', modernists were heavily criticised for universalising women's experience (Tong 1992) and for downplaying or ignoring important differences emerging from particular experiences of class, ethnicity, and sexuality (Lorde 2000, Spelman 1988, Assiter 1996). Poststructuralists, in particular, argued modernism failed to take into account the specificity of women's individuality and experience (Rogers 2005), as well as the powerful influence of discourse in shaping identity. Feminist poststructuralists, then, challenged modernist notions of biological stasis (Stacey 1997), to argue instead for discursive readings of the plurality of women's experience (Weedon 1992). Additionally, postmodern and poststructural feminist theorising actively challenged hierarchical, gendered, binary oppositional thinking, a system of thought that valorises the first in the binary pair while designating the second in the pair as deviant or 'other' (Tong 1992).

I had been immersed in postmodern and poststructuralist theory during my undergraduate studies. While poststructuralist theorising in particular, with its discursive reading of women's subordination and notions of fluid rather than fixed subjectivity, were new concepts for me, they were not ones that felt alien. As my degree progressed, I became increasingly aware of the pervasiveness and covert nature of hierarchical and gendered dichotomous thinking within Western philosophical traditions (Alaimo and Hekman 2008a, van der Tuin and Dolphijn 2010). I was introduced to the work of the French feminist theorists Hélène Cixous (1976, 1991b, Cixous and Clement 1986), Luce Irigaray (1985b, a, 1993), and Julia Kristeva (1982a, b) who, despite having 'distinctively different agendas', shared 'a common desire to think nonbinary, nonoppositional thoughts' (Tong 1992, 233). I came to understand subjectivity as 'linguistically mediated and constituted' (Fleckenstein 1999, 282), and how subjectivity is shaped by powerful and influential discursive and cultural practices that are unconsciously and uncritically absorbed and then taken up 'as one's own' (Davies 1992, 54). I came to perceive how language 'operates to produce very real, material, and damaging structures in the world' (St. Pierre 2000, 481), and that language does not represent or reflect experience but instead constructs it (Alaimo and Hekman 2008a). I learned of the ways postmodern and poststructural feminism problematises the concept of 'woman' (Rogers 2005) and 'the notion of any fixed identity category' by suggesting that 'woman' 'could be regarded as a constantly shifting signifier of multiple meanings' (Stacey 1997, 55). I learned that poststructural theory is underpinned by an interest in 'exploring shifting subjectivities and in the intersubjective and dialogical qualities of (women's) lived experience' (Gannon 2004, 108). I was made cognisant of the presence of powerful, competing, dominant and sometimes contradictory discourses which influence subjectivity through the formation, not of fixed identity, but of identity that is 'fluid, fractured and fragmented' (Stacey 1997, 55). I came to understand that poststructural theoretical positions worked in inclusive ways, with reciprocity, and across similarity and difference (Hopkins 2009).

While such feminist scholarship opened up new ways for me to perceive the world and offered 'complex analyses of the interconnections between power, knowledge, subjectivity, and language' (Alaimo and Hekman 2008a), by focusing on discourse and language, postmodern and poststructuralist feminist theorising had opened one window for me, but closed another. It had enabled me to see out and interpret the world through discourse, but I couldn't take my body with me. The focus on a purely discursive and linguistic construction of experience was problematic, as the following journal extract attests:

16 February, 2012

Last night I recalled an undergraduate lecture I attended some years earlier. During this lecture on poststructuralist theory, the notion that we are culturally and discursively constituted subjects was introduced. During my wakeful hours I remembered the strong feelings this concept evoked – I was devastated by the theoretical possibility that I was simply a composite of externally and linguistically imposed, dominant socioculturally constructed ideals and values, behaviours and attitudes. I was shocked at the suggestion that nothing of what constitutes me comes from me. I know that at the time I attended that lecture, I accepted the powerful influence of socially constructivist discourse on individuals, communities and cultures. I could see how these played out around me. What affected me so deeply was not that I couldn't give discourse credit for shaping me as an individual, but rather, that I couldn't give discourse FULL credit for shaping me. I was conscious that this intense difficulty was entirely connected to notions of erasure and loss of agency. I remembered wondering during the lecture, in a slightly frantic way that if these discourses were removed suddenly, if I were somehow discursively 'cleaned out', would I then be left with no structure, shape, or identity? Would I cease to exist?

I knew these questions emerged from my years of psychotherapy [which I had not long completed], years during which I had been exploring my feelings of translucence in an attempt to engender some sense of presence in the world, some sense of visibility, substance, wholeness, something to help me to feel as if I 'existed'. I had also been exploring ways to foster my limited sense of agency. After intensive cognitive behavioural work, I had reached a point in my progress where I finally felt I occupied space in the world, had developed a sense of place and self, albeit a somewhat fragile sense of each, and the beginnings of a greater sense of agency. So, when I recalled sitting and listening to that lecture and hearing that I was probably little more than a discursive construction, I was left wondering what point there was in continuing with life if what constituted me came entirely from beyond my self. I remembered the complete erasure of individuality this suggested, and the lack of autonomy implicit. I still felt in the night the feelings of hollowness and invisibility, and the lack of agency this precipitated at the time. And I also felt how it had compounded my precarious sense of self and place in the world, how it had pushed me further away from my raped body which, until then, had filled me so completely with a sense of (secret) identity, and how it had plunged me into a space of gravity-free drop, arms and legs flailing as I plummeted into darkness with nothing to hold onto.

In its bid to distance itself from women's bodies, and as a result of its relentless insistence on the promotion of discursive theoretical understandings and linguistic representations of women's existence, poststructural feminism has been critiqued by new materialist feminists as anti-essentialist (Bowden and Mummery 2009, van der Tuin and Dolphijn 2010), and anti-biologist (Wilson 2004b). It has been criticised for reducing the living, breathing, experiencing flesh of women's bodies to 'textual lacunae' (Fleckenstein 1999, 285). In a move perceived as corporeal tokenism, new materialists contend that poststructuralism makes only a gesture towards 'the material existence of the body' (Alaimo 2008, 237), through its often disembodied retreat into linguistics and discourse. While there has been an abundance of corporeal scholarship since the 1990s, much of this has been critiqued for its 'analysis of discourses *about* [author's own emphasis] the body' (Alaimo and Hekman 2008a, 3). By suggesting women's bodies are discursively 'constructed, filled, and colonized' (Fleckenstein 1999, 285), poststructuralists have also designated the body as passive (Alaimo 2008, Hekman 2008). Myra J. Hird (2004) unintentionally, or perhaps entirely intentionally, flings us back to ancient Greece and Plato's application of the term *chora* to the maternal body, when she argues that poststructural theory has transformed the material body into 'an inert container for outside forms' (Hird 2004, 227). And Fleckenstein (1999, 285) argues that although discursive positionings allow us to view 'how bodies are sculpted by discursive practices, bodies too easily become passive prisoners of those practices, contributing nothing to the discourse. A body is not an ideology, not solely a discourse.'

Kirby (1991, 4) argues that contemporary feminist thinking can be described as 'a discourse that negotiates corporeality, what a body is and what a body can do.' She suggests that 'the spectre of essentialism' (4) has driven the biological body from feminist investigations and created a somatophobic nervousness within postmodern and poststructural feminist scholarship which provides 'a remedial against essentialist reductionism' (151). Kirby poetically describes the current critiques of postmodernism as ones warning against 'the effects of presuming to dissolve matter in an acid bath of rhetoric' (1997, 102). She is curious however, 'about the motivations behind the sort of intellectual defensiveness that kicks in with the swiftness of a visceral reflex' (1) when she posits questions surrounding corporeality in feminist environments more comfortable with discussions surrounding discourse than those concerning the body. These views are consistently shared by those working within the materialist paradigm who caution against limiting discourse-centric theorising (Alaimo 2008, Alaimo and Hekman 2008a, Hekman 2008, Hird 2004, Kirby 1997, van der Tuin 2011, van der Tuin and Dolphijn 2010, Wilson 1998). Elizabeth A. Wilson (2008, 377) goes so far as to insist that the successful infiltration of social constructionism into the social sciences in the 1990s was largely dependent on 'an axiomatic anti-biologism.' Fleckenstein (1999, 283) eloquently argues that 'By eliding bodies and denying the language of blood and bone, a poststructuralist orientation amputates physiology from meaning, crippling its own transformative critique [...].' She further notes that 'In sacrificing bodies to some illusion of either transcendent truth or culturally-constituted textuality, we cut ourselves adrift from organic anchoring in the material reality of flesh' (1999, 281).

Not only does this position cut us *adrift* but it also, as Susan Hekman (2008) notes drawing on the work of Barad (2001), perpetuates the discourse/matter binary. This point is taken up by Claire Colebrook (2008, 52). She draws on the work of Moira Gatens (1996), who notes that 'The idea that the world is constructed through language merely repeats a centuries-old privilege of the formal and logical over the material.' Barad (2008, 137) reminds us that 'Discourse is not what is said; it is that which constrains and enables what can be said. Discursive practices define what counts as meaningful statements.' It is precisely for this reason, she argues, that the superior position held by linguistic and discursive practices must be challenged. She states unequivocally that 'Language has been granted too much power' (2008, 120) and that matter has been diminished as a result. Grosz (2008) points out that in order to better understand the impact of discourse, we need to have greater clarity surrounding the forces of enmeshment behind the biological-discursive inter-play. She states that 'If we *are* [author's own emphasis] our biologies, then we need a complex and subtle account of that biology if it is to be able to more adequately explain the rich variability of social, cultural, and political life.' Grosz (2010, 50) acknowledges that 'Feminist theory has allowed the body to enter discourse, but only, ironically, through its reduction to discourse' and argues that 'We need to return to the question of materiality one more time.'

Barad (2008) has no uncertainties about the potential materiality holds to contribute to new knowledges. She argues for a way for matter, the matter of the cellular body, to be involved 'as an active participant in the world's becoming' (122). She does this, not by isolating postmodern and social constructionist epistemologies from ontologies that dwell in the material, but by bringing the two together to create what she terms 'onto-epistem-ology' or, 'the study of practices of knowing in being' (2008, 147). When Barad combines these theories of knowing and coming to knowing in this way, she highlights the artificial separation of the two and shows instead that they are co-constitutive, working together in reciprocal arrangement.

Barad further argues for a shift into ways of reading and interpreting our relationship to the world and to others that embraces this reciprocity. She suggests a move away from 'the representationalist trap of geometrical optics [...] to physical optics, to questions of diffraction rather than reflection.' Barad explains: 'Geometrical optics of reflection is much like the infinite play of images between two facing mirrors, [where] the epistemological gets bounced back and forth but nothing more is seen.' Barad is not suggesting a rejection of poststructural linguistic and discursive understandings but rather, a 'diffractive reading' of theoretical insights. Barad (Dolphijn and van der Tuin 2012) states:

> Diffraction, understood using quantum physics, is not just a matter of interference, but of entanglement, an ethico-onto-epistemological matter. This difference is very important. It underlines the fact that knowing is a direct material engagement, a cutting together-apart, where cuts do violence but also open up and rework the agential conditions of possibility. (53)

In the context of my research, by embracing a materialist approach, I am acknowledging understandings which emerge from the embodied intellect *and* understandings that emerge from the intelligent body. This methodological *entanglement* supports other conceptions of intelligence that insist that intelligence is found everywhere in the body, not just in the brain (Bainbridge Cohen 2008, Damasio 1994, Hanna 1986, Johnson 2012, Merleau-Ponty 1962, Pert 1999). By adopting this approach, I am acknowledging conventional forms of knowing and articulation, which rely on symbolic representation, *and* bodily forms of articulation. I am acknowledging discursive understandings of rape trauma *and* experiential understandings. By taking up this multidimensional approach, I do not disallow a broader and more reflexive reading of the somatic aftermath of rape and I do not deny the co-constitutive power and reciprocal capacity of each to inform ways of knowing and ways of coming to knowing in rape trauma research.

CHAPTER NINE

Coming to knowing through embodied autoethnography

> Just at the moment of the instant, in what unfurls it, I touch down then let myself slip into the depth of the instant itself.
>
> — HÉLÈNE CIXOUS[1]

> Giving oneself entirely to rediscovery. [...] One can tell facts. One can invent some. It is more difficult to tell than to invent. Inventing is easy. But what is most difficult is fidelity to what one feels, there, at the extremity of life, at the nerve endings, around the heart. And for that, there are no words. For what one feels, there are no words.
>
> — HÉLÈNE CIXOUS[2]

16 September, 2007

It was meant to be a game, a school-holidays-we're-bored kind of game.

I knew that.

I'd even played this game myself as a child. I understood its harmless and playful intent.

But when those young, primary-school-aged sweaty hands lost their accuracy in their haste to play the game and covered my nose and mouth as well as my eyes, and when the heat of the voices shouting 'Boo!' in my ear arrived simultaneously, the game went wrong.

Horribly wrong.

And I was helpless to alter my response. I was at the mercy of my history. Time and space collapsed.

***

1 From: Cixous, Hélène (1991). 'The Last Painting or the Portrait of God.' In Deborah Jensen (ed.), *'Coming to Writing' and other Essays*. Cambridge, Mass: Harvard University Press (104).

2 From: Cixous, Hélène (1991). 'The Last Painting or the Portrait of God.' In Deborah Jensen (ed.), *'Coming to Writing' and other Essays*. Cambridge, Mass: Harvard University Press (127).

In the darkness and confusion, fear saturates my flesh. My body assumes control. Panic courses through my veins, floods my limbs. My hands lash out; tear frantically at the ones suffocating me, trying to wrench their clammy weight from my face. I can't breathe. My head shakes desperately from side to side trying to rid my ears of the hot, deafening breath. In the struggle, a voice arrives in my chest and rises. It's insistent and possessive, takes up all the room, swells to fill the tunnel of my throat. It competes with my lungs for life.

***

My lungs bloomed with life again as air rushed in.

A sound erupted, filled my eardrums. It spiralled in strength and height then roughly elbowed aside the primary-school-aged giggles. It was a voice-sound, one I didn't recognise, yet one that I knew in every cell of my body. It was guttural and wild, primitive in its force and origin. The voice-sound quickly ran out of energy, settled exhausted on us all, blanketing our bodies with a sickly, cloying silence.

The small hands that had been torn away had left a residual heavy presence on my skin, a damp shadow-slick of misplaced fear.

My body heaved with sobs. Time and space slowly unfolded and reorganised itself. I looked around at my primary-school-aged children. They stared back, their faces pale stricken moons.

This substantial chapter reflects the primary autoethnographic and embodied focus of my research as I discuss the intensive and embodied exploration of the somatically-held and unresolved memories of my childhood rape experience. The chapter locates the research within a feminist paradigm and situates me as a researcher and research participant operating within the field of rape trauma scholarship and interested in autoethnographic and embodied ways of knowing and coming to knowing. Consequently, the chapter has a corporeal, experiential, and autoethnographic methodological focus. The chapter also integrates ontology and epistemology. It is a place where my research occurs and where, consequently, meaning is made. The opening discussion lays the foundations for the experiential methodological ground of the work. The chapter is then divided into three sections: *Autoethnography*, which positions me as a feminist researcher and discusses the autoethnographic focus of the work; *Autoethnographic somatic inquiry*, which introduces my understandings and the particularity of the method of somatic inquiry I engaged in during the autoethnographic phase of the research; and, *Feeling the fleshed body*, which draws heavily on journal material to examine my shifting relationship to my body prior to, and beyond, the commencement of my participation in Body-Mind Centering workshops, residential programs, and private session work.

***

This is my methodology. My body is significant. My body carries my life in its cells. My body records and performs the many happenings of Cixous' *instant*[s], and archives the myriad 'present absolute[s]' (1991c, 104) found in lived experience. It is through my body, through my subjective embodied experience, that I now give narrative shape to the ontological while simultaneously participating in the epistemological. No other body can experience and carry this life. No other body can narrate and perform this life story. It is mine to carry and mine to bring into the languages of performative word and embodied performance, in order to respond to other research and literature, deepen existing knowledges, open up new conversations, make way for new meaning, and contribute to new ways of communicating with and through the raped body. It is my uniquely experienced body with its many *present absolute*[*s*] and its multiple texts, known and as yet unknown, which propel this research.

***

Coming to knowing through embodied, autoethnographic, and performative modes of inquiry necessarily involved a continuous flow of information from inner to outer to inner, from body to mind to body. Grosz (1994) describes the ways in which the body and mind hold the capacity to twist and bleed through each other. While it has been noted earlier that Cheever (2000) appropriates the Mobius Strip to illustrate Feldenkrais' *new ensemble*, Grosz uses it as a metaphor and visual model for understanding the interconnectivity of mind and body. She writes:

> The Mobius Strip has the advantage of showing the inflection of mind into body and body into mind, the ways in which, through a kind of twisting or inversion, one side becomes another. This model also provides a way of problematizing and rethinking the relations between the inside and the outside of the subject, its psychical interior and its corporeal exterior, by showing not their fundamental identity or reducibility but the torsion of the one into the other, the passage, vector, or uncontrollable drift of the inside into the outside and the outside into the inside. (xii)

The autoethnographic methodological process of my research and the product of that process sit comfortably with Grosz's metaphor. The often seamless interdependence of the ontological 'being' of experiential knowledge and the epistemological 'doing' of discovering this knowledge mirrored *the torsion of one into the other* as my active and bodily engagement in the research, my reflexive analysis, and my theorising merged to establish the ideological and philosophical views that have shaped this research and out of which my autoethnographic methodology emerged.

23 August, 2011

It's the process that teaches me so much, the slowing down to a listening state, the easing into stillness in order to experience the movement of feeling. It's not simply taking off from one point and arriving at another, leaving one state of being for another, without anything happening in between, without any consciousness of change. It's in the process of doing and becoming, in the liminality of these crossings, that the learning takes place, where discoveries are made.

***

To situate myself as a feminist autoethnographer, I begin with a brief explication of the feminism which grounds my research. This feminist position locates me as a researcher who values experiential knowledge and embodied ways of being and becoming, qualities, I argue, that contribute to the positioning of women at the heart of their own knowing and coming to know practices.

A feminist grounding

Feminist research has at its core the understanding that girls and women are the focus of inquiry and is driven by the desire, through female-centred knowledge-making practices, to advocate for societal change for girls and women (Reinharz 1992). Feminist research then is grounded in the underlying assumption that 'women's lives are important' (Reinharz 1992, 241) and is characterised by a valuing of the uniqueness of women's experience (Letherby 2003).

Despite the difficulties of challenging traditional male-defined research practices, feminist researchers have continued to 'construct new positions from which to speak' (Gunew 1992, 27). Through the use of new frameworks of understanding and alternative knowledge-making practices, feminist research has made a significant contribution towards altering the societal position of girls and women (Sarantakos 1998). This has been achieved by engaging in research practices that place an emphasis on the validity and significance of women's subjective embodied experience in relation to knowledge production (Sarantakos 2005). While mainstream epistemologies traditionally 'deny the importance of the experiential, the private and the personal' (Letherby 2003, 42), feminist epistemologies by contrast, acknowledge that it is through the experiential that valuable insights can be gained into the ways in which women interpret their own lived experience. Importantly, by placing experience central to knowledge production, feminist research has allowed women a voice with which to speak that experience (Fonow and Cook 2005).

In relation to sexual trauma, and in terms of disclosure, voice and silence are major concerns. Two decades ago, Shulamit Reinharz (1994, 188) observed that 'silent people cannot be understood'. If 'silence is emblematic of powerlessness' as Courtney Ahrens (2006, 263) argues, to be victims of sexual violence and left without a voice is to be both powerless and denied the opportunity to be understood. To be silenced then, is to be incapable of expressing a subjective embodied experience in meaningful ways. Rape, like other forms of traumatic experience, undoubtedly has a disempowering effect on victims (Herman 1992, ACSSA 2005, Ahrens 2006, Brison 2002, Easteal 1992a, Nijenhuis and van der Hart 1999). It is possible to speculate, then, that victims of sexual violence who are denied a voice are at risk of suffering a double disempowerment, not only through the rape itself but additionally, through the loss of voice in the aftermath. My experiential understandings support this, although I argue that I suffered a form of triple disempowerment: the disempowerment of the rape experiences themselves; the disempowerment of the silencing that accompanied these experiences; and the disempowerment of experiencing rape in childhood before I had established any real sense of self and place in the world. In support of Reinharz' (1994) observation, voice then, in the guise of disclosure, is a critical element of healing in the aftermath sexual violence (Ahrens 2006, Ahrens et al. 2007). It is also essential for meaning making.

I stepped into this research with a strong feminist commitment to the valuing of subjective embodied experience as well as the certainty of the contribution it can make to knowledge-making practices within sexual trauma scholarship. My immersion in contemporary feminist and materialist thinking supports and propels me to position experiential knowing where it cannot be ignored or overlooked. It also propels me towards an autoethnographic mode of inquiry which conflates knowing and coming to knowing. At this point, in the context of voice and silencing, I include a journal extract which illustrates the interwoven nature of my research praxis and process as I began to make new knowledge out of personal experience. The extract focuses on a deeply embodied experience that spontaneously occurred as I sat at my computer on a day in 2010 when I was exploring the silencing impact of my rape experience through journal writing.[3] The extract gives an embodied account of the long-term ramifications of silenced trauma and amplifies the value I place on the location of experiential understandings within autoethnographic rape trauma research.

3 Some of this early explorative writing sits in Chapter One, *Philomela and me*.

28 October, 2010

I found my hands returning again and again to my face, hovering over it and moving in circular patterns around my face as if slowly erasing it while at the same moment, obscuring it from view. My hands also hovered over and covered my mouth particularly my right hand in a horizontal position, occasionally opening like a louvered window, to reveal my lips and then closing again. This happened several times and then I found my hands stroking upwards from my throat, in and away, encouraging energy to rise into and leave my mouth through my lips. As I did this, I began to sob, tears streamed down my face, I couldn't stop, I kept stroking upwards, giving freedom to my emotion through my gesture. I stopped when this became unbearable. This silencing has been too much to bear. [...]it was a profound and shocking experience for me and took me completely by surprise. It seems my body, despite the pain it's been going through, or perhaps because of it, is forcing its voice on me and forcing me to listen.

Autoethnography

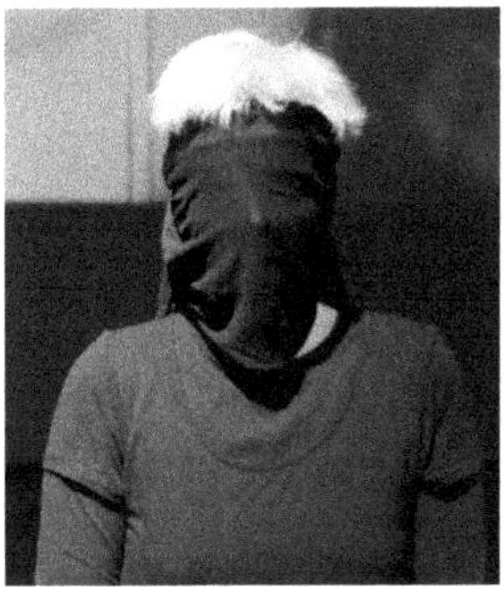

Autoethnography is an established method of knowledge production which values personal experience and situates the self and self-inquiry at the heart of the exploration while also locating it within broader contexts (Ellis and Bochner 2000, Reed-Danahay 1997, Richardson 2000, Spry 2010). It is an evocative method of inquiry and form of knowledge production (Richardson 2000). Carolyn Ellis and Arthur Bochner (2000, 739) recognise autoethnography as a process that intertwines memory with sociocultural interpretations to create 'multiple layers of consciousness, connecting the personal to the cultural'. Autoethnography is also 'a form of self-narrative inquiry that places the self within a social context. It is both a method and a text' (Reed-Danahay 1997, 9). Norman Denzin (1997) understands autoethnography as a form of inquiry that enables introspection whilst also allowing room for personal context to move within broader sociocultural settings.

Stacy Holman Jones (2008) takes up Denzin's point, elaborating further on the movement inherent in this form of inquiry by introducing the relational and fluid nature of autoethnography as it works to make sense of personal experience within shifting sociocultural contexts. She notes:

> Autoethnography works to hold self and culture together, albeit not in equilibrium or stasis. Autoethnography writes a world in a state of flux and movement – between story and context, writer and reader, crisis and denouement. It creates charged moments of clarity, connection, and change. (207)

The work of Jackson and Mazzei (2008) differs from that of Jones and challenges her claim that autoethnographic writing creates greater *clarity* as well as the notion that a personal account has increased potential for the facilitation of change. I argue that autoethnography does hold the potential to bring about change by slicing through the blur of the universal to create, in sharp relief, a portrait of one life and one life's experience whilst also reflexively placing that experience in a wider context. In this way, autoethnographic accounts offer a contrast, a moment of stillness perhaps in the rush of the impersonal. I suggest that juxtaposing one life against the lives of many helps bring clarity, particularly when the reader also brings their own context, their own subjectivity, to the interpretation of the account. In this way, refined and reflexive autoethnographic accounts of personal experience can enable a point of connection to the material under focus with the potential to lead to increased possibility for change.

The autobiographical nature and introspective style of this autoethnographic inquiry then, allows for the creation of an intimate space through which the unique insight of my personal experience can resonate. The reflexivity and critical reflection autoethnography invites (Spry 2011), creates a dance with different partners. Its choreography takes me in multiple directions as I move with my own story, the stories of other women, and the broader sociocultural storying of sexual violence. It is the movement of my own story through other stories and contexts that gives autoethnography its richness and porosity. To simply give an autobiographical account of my own somatic aftermath of childhood rape would take the reader into one story only. By contrast however, by reflexively drawing in other stories, other texts, other contexts, to invite an exchange with a range of conceptual and theoretical frameworks, I enable, with the sweep of this movement, the possibility of taking the reader into other realms of experience and understanding. As Jones (2008) suggests, autoethnography is:

> Setting a scene, telling a story, weaving intricate connections among life and art, experience and theory, evocation and explanation … and then letting go, hoping for readers who will bring the same careful attention to your words in the context of their own lives. (208)

As a potentially evocative form of knowledge dissemination, I argue that autoethnography has the capacity to reach out, through the *letting go*, to touch others by inviting the engagement of the reader's imagination in ways that more traditional forms of data presentation are less well equipped to do. Gwyther and Possamai-Inesedy (2009, 108) argue autoethnography asks more of readers than more objective and rational 'findings' and 'conclusions'-based research as it 'requires the reader to 'feel' the research and to be actively engaged in the production of knowledge through responding to, critiquing and interpreting the autoethnographic data.' Spry (2011) writes of the ways reading autoethnography is necessarily participatory and therefore collaborative. And bell hooks (1991) reminds us that it is the presence of imagination that enables us to develop empathy for others which in turn, allows us to respond more fully to other people's circumstances and subjective experiences. However, in the context of the enablement of change through personal testimony, Brison (2002) cautions that any words of disclosure offered by rape victims which are not engaged with fully by others cannot hope to contribute to change for victims. She notes:

> In order to construct self-narratives we need not only the words with which to tell our stories, but also an audience able and willing to hear us and to understand our words as we intend them. This aspect of remaking a self […] highlights the dependency of the self on others and helps to explain why it is so difficult for survivors to recover when others are unwilling to listen to what they endured. (51)

With regard to the critical role witnessing holds in relation to the *remaking of self*, I'm reminded at this point of the parallels between Brison's observations, the 'interdependent process' of performative autoethnography outlined in Spry's (2011) *Body, Paper, Stage* text, and my own autoethnographic work. Spry writes of the ways in which 'our bodies are inherently part of the meaning making process, how the meaning making process is inherently tied to language and writing, and how performance operates as the dialogic process within and between body and language' (27). My own autoethnographic process mirrored Spry's methodology as I journeyed into my experienced and experiencing body, acknowledged the necessity of language (although often struggled in my search for a vocabulary adequate to the task), wrote from this position, and then performed my somatically dialogic engagement with my bodily experience through a predominately non-verbal articulation in the performance work, *aperture*. In this way, my own autoethnographic methodological process moved from *body* to *paper* to *stage*, not only developing my understandings reflectively and reflexively in the movement between these, but also creating ways of sharing these understandings through embodied and performative ways of knowing. When written and performed in evocative ways that engage rather than dis-engage the embodied imagination of the reader-audience, an autoethnographic account can have multi-dimensioned, powerful and transformative qualities (Minge 2007, Inckle 2007). Autoethnographic accounts, then, have the potential for the enablement of empathic witnessing through active collaboration. They work in ways which are both intrapersonal and interpersonal, to fashion the *self-narratives* Brison talks of, but also to carry the potential to bring about attitudinal change through the presence and engagement of witnessing others. It is my hope that by exploring my own self-narrative of the aftermath of childhood rape through these pages, I can contribute to the unfolding of other women's self-narratives.

Autoethnographic somatic inquiry

> All these feelings and sensations existed in her at once, not jumbled, not in sequence, but layered, like a scroll of possibilities that exist only in the configuration of the moment, though had she been asked to name them she would have said that they passed too quickly for her to grasp.
>
> — DRUSILLA MODJESKA[4]

4 From: Modjeska, Drusilla (1995). *The Orchard*. Sydney: Picador (89).

I feel alone as I begin to gather together the qualities of this method of inquiry. To date, I have been unable to trace other autoethnographic sexual trauma research with a similar methodology to my own. While I am able to draw on the methodologies of large and well-established bodies of sexual trauma research, these are generally viewed through other lenses, those of psychology for example, or trauma studies. I have not yet discovered autoethnographic accounts of inquiry with a specific focus on cellular memory in the somatic aftermath of childhood rape. Nor have I been able to trace ones that combine an embodied praxis with an embodied process in a rape trauma context. My autoethnographic somatic inquiry method then, has taken on a somewhat unprecedented quality, emerging experientially and growing organically. Its shape holds the shape of my experience.

The particularity of embodied exploration

Cixous (1991c) is drawn to the particularity of the moment, to the immediacy of experience. Her essay, 'The Last Painting or the Portrait of God', reflects on the capacity of painters who, through the creation of image, are able to capture on canvas the instant of experience. She talks of wanting to live, of sometimes living, '[...] in the present absolute. In the happening of the instant' (104). Cixous says she would like to 'write like a painter [...] to write like painting'. A painter, she says, is 'a bird-catcher of instants' (104).

Cixous' desire to live in the present absolute while also being attentive to the happening of the instant is what makes her writing so embodied and so thrilling to read. 'I do not write to keep. I write to feel. I write to touch the body of the instant with the tips of the words' (1998, 195). She is present to her feeling and to every nuance of experience. She is able to gather up and absorb subtlety. She devours detail. By her own admission, she is myopic, and gratefully so. 'Details are my kingdoms' she says. 'Some people survey. Some people who are far-seeing don't see what is very near. I am someone who sees the smallest letters of the earth. Flat on my stomach in the garden, I see the ants, I see each of the ants' feet [...] such are the benefits of my near-sightedness' (1991c, 109).

Near-sightedness, myopia, has been appropriated from the ophthalmic world and used more broadly, culturally, in a pejorative sense to infer a lack, a certain limiting narrow-mindedness that restricts vision and the capacity to philosophically see beyond the self. In contrast to this, Cixous' 'myopic' view of the world is not limited or limiting. Indeed, it is her ability to rest in detail and the happenings of the moment, and to then touch the body of the instant with the tips of the words, that allows me, as the reader of those words, to be transported and transformed. Her capacity to scoop me up and plunge me into her delicate, eloquent, and evocative engagement with particularity facilitates my own focal, temporal, and bodily adjustment. The magnetism of her embodied writing holds me in the instant so I too can rest in feeling and detail; my attention to the happenings beyond me and around me are suspended momentarily in the interstitial space of possibility, in the fecund fissures between what I know, what I don't know, and what I could know. This point of suspension is exhilarating. Its height and trajectory, born of her words and the possibilities they convey, allows me to pause momentarily in time and motion. This pause is a place of resuscitation as I suck in breath through her words. As my lungs fill with new meaning I am moved, transported through histories of knowledge and across all my accrued understandings. I am carried along, through all the instants of that pause, by the oxygen of new insight, swept up and re-oriented, my perspective altered, my perception widened. The change of perspective may be minute, but even this can bring about a seismic shift in feeling. As I hover suspended over new potential, I can see out and beyond the parameters of my body and my subjective experience but, critically, I

remain all the while anchored in my corporeality, as Cixous does in hers. This re-orientation often relocates me within a larger sphere of organisation while never wrenching me away from myself or limiting me. This is vital. I have agency grounded in my body. I can linger in the specificity of detail or plunge into the broader generic space of overview. I am not limited by this but empowered and enlightened through it. I don't have to choose one over the other, forced to act within a binary, to exclude what one or the other has to offer. I can be both near-sighted and far-sighted but always moored to the certainty of my own embodied knowledge and experience. Cixous reminds me of this again and again in her writing: 'There comes the time of immanence. A desire to write rises in my body and comes to occupy my heart. Everything beats faster. The entire body readies itself' (1998, 192). Cixous is always moored to her body. She is always writing from a location of particularity and always with and through her body.

I bring Cixous in at this point because her close and evocative attention to detail mirrors the attention to detail that was necessary during my autoethnographic somatic inquiry. Her simultaneous sweep into broader realms of consideration echoes the reflexivity present at every level in my research, particularly this autoethnographic component. In order to first uncover the subtlety and nuance of my autoethnographic somatic inquiry and then illuminate this through evocative language, with as much exactitude as possible and with reflexivity, it was essential that I maintain a myopic or forensic awareness of my body at a cellular level while simultaneously holding my experience within a wider cultural context, filtering this through an aesthetic lens.

To help facilitate this somatic awareness, I undertook an extensive and intensive engagement with the body-based therapeutic and educative practice of Body-Mind Centering.[5] I commenced this work in June, 2010 by attending a workshop facilitated by Alice Cummins. I then moved to doing additional work as a private client with Alice later that year. Across the following three and a half years, I attended regular workshops as well

5 See Appendix 1 for an overview of this practice.

as engaging with Alice in private work in both Perth and Melbourne. In the following section, I give an outline of what these engagements entailed.

Body-Mind Centering workshop participation

Throughout my autoethnographic somatic inquiry, I attended ten Body-Mind Centering group workshops in Perth and Melbourne as well as six residential programs at Alice's country studio in Riddells Creek, Victoria. All were designed and facilitated by Alice. Each workshop had a specific focus and ran for three days and each residential program, also with a specific focus, for five days. Under Alice's guidance, and in a group situation, I creatively engaged with my somatic self throughout the duration of my participation in this extensive and intensive somatic exploration.

The foundations of the workshops and residential programs rested in the Body-Mind Centering philosophy which values experiential learning and enables exploration and integration of the work through a combination of somatisation; experiential anatomy; hands-on;[6] cellular listening; Authentic Movement; and self-reflection. As Alice suggests, the facilitation of inquiry through these means allows for 'intelligence to emerge from multiple sources in the bodymind and is not reliant or insistent on a dominant rational knowing. It requires a listening to the whole body that does not exclude intuition and feeling but employs them to deepen and enrich understanding' (Cummins 2012).

When I began my participation in mid-2010, I welcomed the opportunity to work from the ground of intuition and feeling and to learn through multiple and creative means of exploration. And I welcomed the opportunity to explore as both researcher and researched. However, there was a tension present. Although the researcher-I was ready, keen and full of curiosity, the participant-I, while eager to explore and ready for change,

6 See Appendix 1 for an explanation of 'somatisation' and the practice of 'hands-on'.

was deeply anxious and full of questions. I navigated my way 'into this maze of questioning' by 'hold [ing] fast to several threads' (Kirby 2012, 203). Would the participant-I be able to manage three days of moving and embodied inquiry? Would the researcher-I encourage the participant-I if things got difficult? Would the researcher-I bully the participant-I if resistance emerged? What if the participant-I didn't want to feel or move my way into my body? What if the participant-I tried but couldn't feel anything? Would that be the end of the research? What if the participant-I listened attentively but heard nothing? Could the participant-I back out? Would the researcher-I allow this? Would this be the end of the research or merely a disappointing finding?

The following journal extracts, selected from reflections on the Body-Mind Centering work written during the period 2010–2013, are an introduction, and offer insight to, the range of feeling I moved in and out of during this autoethnographic somatic inquiry engagement.

5 June, 2010

'Navel Radiation' workshop

The weekend workshop has finally arrived and I'm filled with a mixture of nervousness and excitement.

Alice: 'The work will raise questions, provide you with rich intelligence.'

Hands-on: This was the most extraordinary experience. I have never stayed 'in my body' for such a long period of time. Whenever my mind began to stray, the touch, warmth and presence of the toucher brought me back to my self.

[During this somatic exploration I worked with two other workshop participants; two people gave hands-on to the third person lying on the floor. Working with the radial pattern of the body, one person placed a hand lightly on the navel area of the body while the other person placed a hand lightly on one of the limbs. For the person receiving, this helped bring awareness to the centre and the periphery of the body simultaneously.]

26 September, 2010

'Organ vitality' workshop

It seems that every time I enter into a movement exploration of my internal landscape, I'm filled with a sense of despair and a profound and unresolved sadness. It's fascinating how such powerful emotions can reside so close to the surface and yet still remain so contained. Or do they reside close to the surface? Perhaps Alice's work takes me much further into my body than I could ever have imagined. It might be possible that I really have cast my sensory experiences into the darkest trenches of my body. It might be that the depth of their location allows them to remain, for the most part, undisturbed. Does this BMC work reach down, down to the bottom of those trenches, scoop up what lies as thick sediment, and carry it aloft?

6 March, 2011

'Membranes and the layered body: Navigating the interface' workshop

During this somatisation work, I also felt the whispered murmurings of a new and unfamiliar dialogue with my body ... a dialogue of trust. I'm beginning to feel that it's time I trusted my body. These are only murmurings and I can only hear them in moments of somatic spaciousness and stillness, or in gentle moving, but I'm beginning to feel it's time I had more faith in my body's capacity to function well and carry me through my life without the need for corset-like control and direction.

Alice encouraging us to 'let go of the idea of our selves' (during a movement exploration) doesn't now leave me with a feeling of despair and loss. I don't feel I will be left free-falling into a dark place if I let go of the layers of identity I've plastered one over the other upon myself. I don't feel there'd be nothing left to hold onto if I slowly shed these layers of protection I've grown. I'm beginning to see that I can hold onto my body and its knowledge because it's always been there, it will always be there, and it can be relied on. It's possible to strip away those superficial layers and still be whole because I would still be embodied. Perhaps I'm edging towards the realisation of what Mary Beth Cancienne and Celeste Snowber mean when they talk of not just having a body, but being a body (2003, 239). This signals a profound shift for me.

3 March, 2012
'The Fluids' workshop

Somatisation from the mind of cerebro-spinal fluid:

I am struggling today, couldn't enter this, couldn't take myself there,
fragile, resistant, tearful, bereft,
difficulty everywhere, can't locate the source of the grief,
it feels generic, but specific, present, complex,
and incredibly painful.

14 January 2013
'Perceptions, Planes, and the Vestibular System' residential program

Somatisation, moving from the sense organs:

I threw myself into a wild spiralling multidimensional movement, my mouth, nose and ears leading the movement. Up and down, forwards and backwards, spiralling, rocking, travelling through space, temporality dissolved into movement. It was exhilarating to let go, to give over to my body and feel the pleasure, freedom and vitality of this.

Cancienne and Snowber (2003, 238) argue that 'How we conceptualise the body intellectually is different from how we experience through dance the living, breathing, pulsing body from the inside out'. I would argue that it is possible to extend this concept beyond the 'dancing' body, to include the more generic 'moving' body to encompass a broader cross-disciplinary range of somatic practices which include dance but also include bodywork and somatic therapies, and other experiential and educative ways of learning such as the practice of Body-Mind Centering. The researchers go on to note that 'dance is a corporeal way of knowing, a different way of seeing, questioning, and challenging, […] the body becomes an articulate surface for exploration' (Cancienne and Snowber 2003, 243). Again, if 'moving' replaces dance, when attention is given to the cellular stimulus behind the moving, then it is possible to see how the feeling body can find creative expression through movement and can then enter into onto-epistemological methodologies and aid self-discovery. Merleau-Ponty (1968, 8–9) called his body 'the stage director of my perception', noting insight develops in the body, 'through its whole internal arrangement, its sensory-motor circuits, the return ways that control and release movements, it is, as it were, prepared for a self-perception [...]'. He further notes 'the experience of my flesh as the gangue of my perception has taught me that perception does not come to birth just anywhere, that it emerges in the recess of a body.' Bainbridge Cohen (2008, 115) argues the moving body is a perceiving body and that movement is the 'first perception of learning' while Alice maintains that 'we move to find out who we are' (A. Cummins, personal communication, December 26, 2013). I suggest that movement, combined with the capacity that touch and hands-on work have to hold and direct attention to the inner life of our bodies, expands the scope of corporeality to 'not just a recording of knowledge but a process by which we are awakened to new insights' (Cancienne and Snowber 2003, 248).

My journal extracts in this section sit as examples of the ways in which the workshop participation allowed me to enter into an embodied methodology. They evoke the ways I was able to uncover new understandings through the process of exploring my body from the inside out, not only via movement, but also through touch and other forms of experiential access and somatic expression.

Body-Mind Centering workshop reflective writing

During Body-Mind Centering workshops, pauses were given between somatic explorations in which Alice invited us to reflect and record. It was my practice during these intervals to record only what arrived spontaneously, particulars such as short notes, single words, longer notes, poetic writing, drawings. Immediately following each workshop, these notes became my guide when I fleshed them out more fully from memory and wrote them in my research journal. Although I was purposeful and diligent in recording during the workshops themselves, this practice was shaped by my intent to maintain spontaneity in my note-taking. I felt, even at the earliest stages of my autoethnographic somatic inquiry, that if I could write extemporaneously, I could also be held more authentically in sensing and feeling, in my bodymind, in Cixous' instant, without the distracting imperative of copious record-making.

My awareness that the final journal notes would become the source of information for the autoethnographic component of the research influenced the shape of my writing practice, but not in terms of generating volume. What was of most interest to me was my ability to capture the sensory and sensuous elements of my embodied experience, the colours and textures, the immediacy and intensity, the subtlety and nuance. I wanted the writings to stand as somatically acoustical fragments and repetitions of sensory experience and cellular memory, the more poetic writings, as lyrical concentrations of feeling when escape into free form seemed the only means of articulation. Although written a little over a hundred and fifty years ago, Emily Dickinson's (Gordon 2010, 94) evocative line, 'I felt my life with both my hands', became a metaphorical and corporeal mantra and prompt for my contemporary research. Her line reminded me of the tangibility, the materiality of human existence, of our capacity as sentient beings to hold experience, to hold feeling, to carry its weight in our flesh. In the context of my autoethnographic research, her words, like those of Cixous, reminded me again of the presence of my material body in the work of autoethnography and the vital role it plays in coming to knowing. They held me to authenticity (what *was* it I felt with both my hands?) and prevented me from straying too far into dis-embodied modes of documentation. While the information gathering for the research was of course critical to the project, I wasn't prepared to sacrifice the spontaneous quality of my somatic inquiry reflections in favour of producing a larger volume of notes.

In the post-workshop fleshing-out of all my somatic explorations, as much as was possible, I sought to maintain the relational thread between my experiencing body, my spontaneous feeling, and my reflective responses recorded during the intervals. My concern at the commencement of this component of this research, was to avoid entering a more masculinist, rational, and immediately analytical mode of recording, a mode I believed would steer me into my intellectual self and away from my experiencing self. In other words, I was concerned to avoid distancing myself from my embodied experience by rushing into a bid for linguistic coherence and analysis. For this reason, I never inflicted pressure on myself to wring out long and copious notes during the workshop reflection intervals. Indeed, Alice encouraged workshop participants to record only when they felt able to and to record only what arrived. This included images. On many occasions, I wanted to remain in a deeply non-verbal but still expressive state and the desire to draw emerged. I didn't stifle this form of expression, viewing it simply as an equally valid representation of my feeling state, and an alternative form of expression. If scant words arrived on the page then I would let this rest as an example of my authentic response without becoming unnerved by the possibility that later, I might have minimal or unconventional 'data' to draw on.

The Body-Mind Centering philosophy argues that in order for individuals to create change, reach their potential, and move effectively in the world, there cannot be a reach outwards without a corresponding yield underneath.[7] I drew on this philosophy to help locate my writing-as-inquiry practice within an embodied framework and as a way of describing the different writing processes I underwent. For example, when my note-taking or writing felt 'forced' or 'blocked', I re-framed this in terms of it being an action of unsupported over-reaching. When there was tension present in the writing and the words felt forced and extracted rather than fluid and flowing, I identified this as an over-stretched reach into my intellect. I viscerally experienced this as spatial disorientation, a sense of falling, flailing around, feeling unanchored. I understood this later, in Body-Mind Centering terms, as a reach towards intellectual knowing without the support of an underlying yield into a fully integrated embodied understanding grounded in experiential knowing and feeling. I also understood this later within the context of legitimacy; how was it possible for me to yield into bodily ways of knowing if I harboured reservations about the legitimacy of bodily ways of knowing?

7 According to the Body-Mind Centering philosophy 'yielding' underlies all the developmental movement patterns. See Bainbridge Cohen, Bonnie (2008). *Sensing, Feeling, and Action: The Experiential Anatomy of Body-Mind Centering*. Northampton, MA: Contact Editions.

This was neither a desirable nor a fertile place to occupy. To help overcome this uncertainty, in my reflective writing practice, I slowly developed the capacity to place trust in my body to offer up understanding as well as developing trust in the process of coming to knowing within my writing practice, quite apart from the trust that held me to my body in other ways.

Body-Mind Centering private sessions

Following participation in two Body-Mind Centering workshops, with my imagination and intellect ignited and already experiencing the therapeutic benefits of this work in my shifting relationship with my body, I was keen to explore my trauma memory on a deeper and more individualised somatic level alongside ongoing group attendance at workshops. I felt I could enable this deeper level of inquiry through a one-on-one therapeutic engagement and hands-on work. As a result, I moved to doing private Body-Mind Centering sessions with Alice in November, 2010. I continued to have regular private sessions with her in Perth and Melbourne throughout the duration of my research.

It troubles me to write of the private work I did with Alice. While it forms the basis of my autoethnographic somatic inquiry and is the primary mode of my information gathering for this component of the research, I feel a reluctance surfacing in the requirement to write of this as a method and then to write of the work itself. This work of somatic inquiry was deeply personal, touching on the most intimate and troubled areas of my life. And of course, my body was there, my raped body, exposed, inevitably central, conspicuously at the heart of this method of inquiry. I cannot write of the autoethnographically somatic without the presence of my body. Without my body there is no autoethnographic somatic inquiry. My body and this work must be present, here, on this page.

Yet it feels somehow mercenary to be tearing apart the details and the intimacy of this therapeutic engagement with the work of somatic inquiry and the shifting relationship with my body. In some ways I feel I'm dishonouring the process of somatic inquiry itself by deconstructing and writing it. What is it that causes me to think in these ways? Is it because, at this moment, I feel as though I'm being separated from the work itself as I step into the shoes of the researcher? But why should I be experiencing keenly the demand to write of this personal inquiry as emotionally challenging and ethically unprincipled?

Is it because as I navigate this transition I feel as though I'm treating the knowledge that has unfolded, simply as 'data'? Does this feel like a breach of the therapeutic relationship? Could it be that, although I willingly entered this relationship and offered my own body as a primary site of inquiry, the work and my body now feel like 'instruments of investigation'? Is it the perceived separation from personal experience and the move into 'writing up' as 'method' and 'research findings' that disturbs me? Is this what Karen Barad (Dolphijn and van der Tuin 2012, 53) calls 'an entanglement of subject and object, which is called the "phenomenon"'? Am I subjecting my body to just another form of objectification and therefore feeding it to the lion of the gaze? Does this feel masculinist in its shape and intention? Is the tension I perceive throughout my body as I contemplate the writing, emerging from the intersection of my resistance to masculinist modes of knowledge sharing and the work itself which felt so deeply embodied and so deeply aligned with the feminine? Is it also the frustration I feel in my attempts to find language for such an embodied and feminine process, a process that is not discursive in origin, and when so much of the language of methodology feels innately masculine?

The ontological roots of these questions and the reflexivity I bring to them helps me find traces of answers but this relentless lifting up, peeling back, shuffling, and probing in order to extend my exploration further, simply yields up more ground for contemplation and yet more struggle.

For example, I find myself sliding into a child-like state in which I feel as though I'm gripping onto something. I have a sense of temporal distortion, a kind of muddled déjà vu. It centres on questions of legitimacy, revolves around the uncovering of personal story, and spins on disclosure. If I share the details of this method of inquiry, gathered specifically for this component of the research and so deeply profound in its impact, will it be held and absorbed by the reader and given careful and serious consideration as a rigorous and scholarly piece of research or will it be misunderstood and casually dismissed as 'new age' or 'alternative' mumbo jumbo?

I feel the acidity of my uncertainty surrounding these concerns rising from my gut.

I feel something in shadow stir.

Bainbridge Cohen (2008, 114) understands the difficulties surrounding questions of legitimacy. In relation to a specific anatomical function, she cites her frustration at the ongoing exclusion from the sciences of 'the sensations of movement and visceral activity' from understandings of the major sensory-motor loops of the body. She argues their dismissal within the sciences is due to their connection with intangible bodily sensation and subjectivity and the impossibility of scientifically 'measuring' such phenomena in order to claim the data as 'objective scientific fact'. Within the competitive neuroscience community, Pert (1999) was frustrated by similar concerns in the 1970s. Her ground-breaking discovery of the opiate receptor in the human body, clearly present in laboratory experiments, could not be legitimated until she 'found a way to measure it and thereby prove its existence'. The frustrations of Bainbridge Cohen and Pert amplify my own concerns about questions of legitimacy with regard to somatic knowledge-making practices. How can something as intangible, as linguistically elusive, as experientially fleeting as sensation and feeling, hold up as legitimate knowledge?

When I began the somatic inquiry phase, I had a sense that my body was pregnant with another body, the body of the girl who felt the full force of the terror of sexual violation and contained this inside her child body, alone and unsupported after her sole disclosure was rejected as a lie. It was this child body that hid inside my maturing body, moved through adolescence and into adulthood still clutching the unresolved memory of that violation tightly to her breast. This long-term occupancy, I believe, perpetuated my sense of bodily fragmentation and disconnection. At the end of this research project and after several years of therapeutic engagement with the work of Body-Mind Centering, I now, for the most part, have a much healthier relationship with my body and feel more connected. And I have a sense of integration of the violated child and the memory of my trauma into my life story and my daily life. I no longer feel like a Russian matryoshka doll, one body within another, a story within a story. I am somehow more whole.

This new state of being feels miraculous and I suspect it's also because of this shift in relationship that I feel uncertain about the sharing of the embodied process that led to it. At some level I worry that the disclosure of the details of this process will be found in-credible, unreliable, unsound. I worry that should this occur, the work of the past three and a half years will slowly unravel and that healthy relationship dissolve into fragmentation again.

I am feeling exposed and vulnerable to the subjectivity of others.

As I was as a child.

Of course, I know it's not rational or adult-like to be thinking in these ways. But this research has never pretended to be based on rationality. The project arose from and is deeply fed by intuition; it sits and is grounded in feeling responses. What I acknowledge here is my feeling response to the writing of the methodological details of the private sessions I engaged in for my autoethnographic somatic inquiry. Through acknowledgment, I am honouring this response in the same ways that I am also honouring my somatic responses to childhood rape, for they too emerge not from rational thought, but from the complexity of the ground of feeling.

***

On the strength of this, I now offer an exploration of the private work I did with Alice. Again, I have included journal extracts to illustrate the process of somatic inquiry I undertook and the ways the work raised speculative questions.

***

> *13 August, 2011*
>
> *I feel the presence of my trauma most keenly in the centre of my physical self although at times, when we do hands-on, my whole body bleeds with the darkness of its history.*

Each of the Body-Mind Centering private sessions with Alice normally ran for an hour. Sometimes the sessions began with touch through hands-on work; other sessions began with Authentic Movement.[8] When we commenced

8 It is important to note that both hands-on work and Authentic Movement are used by Alice Cummins in her Body-Mind Centering workshops and private practice to encourage and cultivate cellular awareness, re-patterning, and re-integration.

with hands-on, we worked on the floor. This involved me lying, fully clothed, usually on my back on a blanket, my head and knees supported by cushions for comfort. Alice often began by holding one of my hands in her hand and by sometimes placing her other hand on my elbow or shoulder before moving to other areas of my body. As she worked, Alice would invite me to focus my awareness on the area she was touching, as she brought her awareness to this area of her own body. Sometimes she would invite me to engage imaginatively with my body to help visualise my body at a cellular level. The following journal extracts offer an insight into the hands-on work itself as well as the questions it raised in terms of its impact.

15 November, 2010
Melbourne. My first private session

I lay down on the white blanket spread out on the floor of her room. Alice covered my legs with another blanket and we began hands-on. Alice held my right wrist and hand lightly. She asked me questions –Did I feel safe? Was it okay to be touched? How had it been for me to carry my story? These questions never felt interrogative, merely asked in order to fill in the gaps and spaces in my story, to help her understand my story more fully, and ultimately to help me understand. All the while, Alice's hands rested lightly, surprisingly lightly, on different parts of my body. Although I felt incredibly nervous about doing this private work, the warmth from her hands was a comforting and reassuring presence. I felt very safe and very connected to what was going on in the work between us. I wasn't sure though, apart from the warmth, whether I was feeling anything else at a deeper level.

16 November, 2010
Melbourne, private session

Today, Alice encouraged me to enter my body through my imagination. With an existing love of human anatomy and a little knowledge, the imaginative visualisation of my organs, muscles, bones, the movement of fluids, the micro movement of my cellular environment, has allowed an alternative, and graphic, point of access for me. This has been particularly helpful given I'm not very attuned to my body and often find it difficult to find any sense of connection with it.

17 November, 2010
Melbourne, private session

Today, as we did hands-on, I felt a sense of inner expansion and, simultaneously, an emotional release. I felt a shift. I'm not sure how to describe this other than as a sense of inner movement, an opening of some sort (cellular?), an unclenching, a softening, an entry into and an exit out of my body.

18 November, 2010
Melbourne, private session

It occurred to me today to wonder whether Alice's hands-on work involves a kind of kinaesthetic empathy. I wondered if Alice is so attuned to the inner life of the body that she's able to detect micro cellular movement and so is moved herself, kinaesthetically. If, through kinaesthetic empathy Alice is moved and I am made somatically aware and moved also via her touch, then the reciprocity and dance of this is intriguing.

Just now, today, I have no idea if this is how BMC works. When I get an opportunity, I shall ask Alice, or try to find out through my own reading, but for now, it makes for exciting speculation.

19 November, 2010
Melbourne, private session

In the night I began to think about the power and nature of her [Alice's] touch and how it can induce the release of feeling and memory within me, a letting go of experience of sorts, which can be full of fear and sadness, while also being capable of encouraging a state of deep easefulness. It's almost my paradox again – taking myself into my body can be fearful while moving my body is joyful and a release, the two residing side-by-side. In similar ways, with the hands-on work, my body remains the focus and yet Alice's touch can prompt such different responses. I marvel at how disturbing somatic and sensory memories sit alongside deep relaxation with nothing but a gossamer-thin membrane between them.

I'm wondering if it's the non-sexual nature of this hands-on work that makes it so liberating and able to induce deep easefulness and with this comes trust and release. The touch allows me to feel 'held', supported enough to be able to allow my body memories to emerge even when they're distressing. When I had psychotherapy, I never felt physically connected enough to be able to release my hold for fear of what might happen, but with Alice, I trust her implicitly and trust her ability to help me remain somatically connected and guide me through it, safely and with compassion and respect. That must be it. Because her touch feels safe, I don't feel the need to struggle against, or control my somatic memories quite so much. I feel safely held in this private work. It occurs to me that this is the most basic of human needs, feeling safe enough to explore deep feeling, and that perhaps I've been severely deficient in this for a very long time. I suppose this is similar in many ways to how I felt psychologically 'held' by D. and by C. during my years of psychotherapy. Somehow though, my work with Alice seems more intense and profound.

28 November, 2010

Could it be that touch during hands-on work has a kind of Mobius effect, twisting deeply held somatic memory up through layers of awareness until it becomes both internally and externally conscious and able to be read/felt on a continuum at multiple somatic and intellectual levels? Could it be that this movement invites an opportunity for integration? Could the consciousness of this fluid action allow memory to travel through the cellular membranes and back again in a continuous sweeping movement without it catching and becoming lodged in the tissues and fibres of my internal landscape?

During this early work I did with Alice, I clearly had little understanding of how the hands-on practice served to both hold me to my somatic self and allow me to access feeling. As is apparent, my intense curiosity surrounding this led to lengthy speculation in my journal writing. I knew through the experiencing of hands-on however, that Alice's touch helped me simultaneously maintain a sense of connection with my body and a sense of connection to the external world.

During the hands-on work, wherever her hands were placed on my body, Alice often encouraged me to 'meet me [her] in the mind of that tissue' (A. Cummins, personal communication, June 2, 2011). I offer an explanation of what Alice meant by this by referring to the dynamic role touch plays in communication via the work of Bainbridge Cohen and the philosopher and phenomenologist Maurice Merleau-Ponty. In his working notes for The Visible and the Invisible, Merleau-Ponty (1968, 255) wrote that 'To touch is to touch oneself [...] The touching oneself and the touching have to be understood as each the reverse of the other [...]'. Bainbridge

Cohen (2008, 6), speaking from within a Body-Mind Centering context, argues that touch is not unidirectional but reciprocal and when we connect with someone through touch, 'they touch us equally'.

What Alice was asking during these hands-on sessions then, was for both of us to arrive in that tissue with conscious awareness in order to begin a reciprocal cellular conversation, with touch acting as the facilitator of that dialogue. As Alice touches she also accesses that area in her own body by bringing her awareness to the mind of that tissue and thus into consciousness (A. Cummins, personal communication, December 26, 2013). When I am her client, Alice's touch allows me to begin to also bring my attention to that area. Her external touch allows me to touch inner feeling held at a cellular level.

Early on in my work with Alice, I intuitively understood that touch was critical to the possibility of re-integration of my trauma memory. With the benefit now of the accumulation of many hours of private work together, I believe it was through touch that Alice was able to encourage me to go beyond superficiality, to move deeper into my somatic consciousness and feel, not simply feel my skin beneath her hands but rather, feel a sense of movement through my skin and into my body, to experience conscious awareness of my body in that area, and thus meet her there. Through discussions with Alice, my understanding of the therapeutic role this technique plays in relation to trauma is that, through her years of training and experience, Alice is able to detect changes and movement in her own cellular environment, in the mind of the tissue in her body and, via touch, in the bodies of her clients. Alice maintains it is through this ability to detect and affirm cellular change and movement via touch that feeling states can be authenticated: 'The work validates feeling because I perceive feeling in the body' (A. Cummins, personal communication, June 2, 2011).

Several critical points arise from Alice's statement. Firstly, I feel certain that I could not have achieved the level of bodily awareness that I currently have without the skill of an experienced somatic practitioner and without the trust that developed within the therapeutic one-on-one relationship. Secondly, I argue that the use of sensitive and non-sexual touch during the hands-on work was critical for the depth of cellular memory and feeling I was able to access. And finally, I consider the presence required by a skilled practitioner, such as Alice, to witness this process. The depth of perception she brought to each encounter was both affirming and necessary for the validation and re-integration of my trauma story. I argue that each of these points plays a critical role in post-rape healing. I would further add, that given a rape experience has the capacity to shatter a victim's sense of trust (Resnick and Schnicke 1996), as was my experience, without the initial establishment of a trusting therapeutic relationship, the path I travelled towards the re-integration of my trauma story, and the development of a greater sense of connection between my mind and my body, would not have been possible. Over time, the therapeutic relationship with Alice and the hands-on work we engaged in ultimately contributed to the cultivation and perpetuation of the trust I felt. This, in turn, eventually helped facilitate a progression to a greater sense of cohesion and integration between my mind and my body, between the silenced narrative I held close to me and the censored narrative I gave to others. The work supported a sense of honesty between my inner and my outer worlds grounded in trust and the affirmation of feeling and cellular memory. I suggest that empathy, both somatic and intellectual, was also key to the development of such a relationship and to the progression of the re-integration I experienced.

My journal extracts reveal that in the early months of my autoethnographic somatic inquiry work I used the term kinaesthetic empathy to help me understand the embodied and multi-dimensional therapeutic impacts of the hands-on technique. Cheever (2000, 18), more properly perhaps, uses the term 'somatic empathy' to describe what is necessarily present in the intersubjective space during bodywork when the flow of sensory information from one person to another helps facilitate somatic connection. My theoretical and experiential understandings tell me this intra and interpersonal somatically dialogic process is only possible through

> *18 November, 2010*
>
> *Alice talked of how she felt it was really important for us to engage in some deep re-integration work. She said she felt it was essential for me to experience touch as part of this re-integration work.*

conscious awareness and the presence that flows from attending at a deep level.

As mentioned elsewhere, critical to the enablement of my somatic exploration, I believe, was the totally focused presence of Alice as she worked with me during hands-on. Her deep attention helped me remain present to my body's responses. Additionally, through what is created in the intersubjective space, I developed a sense of being held and witnessed in those responses. With regard to presence, Alice notes, 'I meet you in the mind of the tissue … with everything I have … perceiving from every part of myself' (A. Cummins, personal communication, June 2, 2011). Experientially, I knew that the destructive force of social, and subsequent, personal abandonment caused through rape trauma and its silencing impact had far-reaching and profound implications. When everything I once knew about myself was shattered and certainty seemed a fragile concept, when my voice and agency were disabled, an attendant sense of invisibility developed. The presence of another person as witness to my story and to my feeling was profoundly moving and deeply affirming.

> *1 June, 2011*
>
> *I was held in the space, in my flesh, to my rape history, through Alice's touch. 'I felt my life' through her hands. It was extraordinary.*

Through presence and Alice's touch I was held to myself and this helped me remain inside a feeling of connection with my body, and with my trauma story. This inner anchoring, through the validation of feeling, further allowed me to venture out, and move deeper into the wider cultural and gendered story of rape. I argue that it was also through this embodied anchoring and the validation of my somatic narrative that I developed a voice with which to speak my rape trauma story and articulate my growing and attendant sense of identity and place in the world.

Hands-on work was not the only means of gaining affirmation. This also came during private sessions through the practice of Authentic Movement and the presence intrinsic to this practice. We sometimes began the private sessions with me moving in the space and Alice witnessing me in that movement. When engaging in Authentic Movement, witnessing is critical, providing the containment necessary for the moving (Stromsted 2009). Presence is essential for the witness in order to hold that place of containment. If the witness is not fully present 'it is limiting' for the mover (A. Cummins, personal communication, December 26, 2013). Presence is also a desirable state for the mover to help facilitate access to embodied experience and to open up the possibility of greater personal understanding through a 'movement into the unknown' (A. Cummins, personal communication, December 26, 2013) and thus to the embodied expression of that experience through the moving and feeling body.

5 March, 2011

The Authentic Movement felt different to any other that I've done to date. I felt so centred, so embodied, so grounded. I became absorbed in very deep listening unlike anything else I've experienced. My listening seemed to penetrate well beyond the superficial and through into the multiple delicate layers of my membranous tissue. I felt as if I was really inside my body exploring my interior world, my movement propelled by what I found there and felt there. I truly felt the 'The Wisdom of the Body Moving' (Hartley, 1995). It was wonderful to be able to pay close attention to this inner world, and to, as Alice says, 'let the movement make meaning'. I could feel the strength and knowledge within my cells and my curiosity drove me to listen with my full attention fuelled by the respect for my body building in me.

6 March, 2011

The moments of somatic connection through Authentic Movement can be completely transporting and thoroughly sublime.

2 June, 2011

I really love having the opportunity and time to move very, very slowly, to allow my body to move incrementally, to really listen to it as it moves and feel the beauty of the movement, the inner spaciousness and sensuousness of the exploration. And to be held in the exploration by the witnessing of that moving, it's so deeply affirming.

Body-Mind Centering private session reflective writing practice

As I recorded the private sessions with Alice and accumulated more notes in my research journal, I slowly grew to see how adept I was at recalling micro detail. This hadn't been especially apparent to me early on. As previously discussed, as a sexual trauma researcher also doing autoethnographic somatic research, I was working with a mode of inquiry that seemed to have no methodological precedent; I had no other literature to draw on to steer me in terms of documentation or to compare notes with. As a result, I was again guided by my intuition, which told me that whatever arrived in me following the sessions was worth recording as long as it felt spontaneous.

Unlike the workshops, I very rarely took notes during private hands-on sessions with Alice. I became reliant instead on my body's capacity to integrate and hold the work well enough for me to be able to retrospectively record the work in my research journal. I became skilled at this, able to retrace entire sessions and track practical as well as somatic detail. For example, I was able to hold the sequence of touch Alice used as she moved around my body, the lightness or weight of her hands, and most importantly for the research, the ways in which my body responded to her touch.

Early on, in the workshop participation, I was concerned that my sense of detachment from my body would lead to very few observations. The notes I did make during workshops, spontaneous and occasionally detailed, I attributed to the close proximity of the experiencing/recollection and the recording of these observations during the regular reflection intervals. I began to reconceptualise this assumption when the micro detail of my recollections became retrospectively apparent following private sessions, when I had taken no notes, and when others, including Alice, began to comment on my ability to call up detail. Prompted by this, I began to explore my post-rape sense of disconnection from my body by juxtaposing it with my history of hypervigilance. Since childhood, my need to maintain secrecy about my trauma story constantly alerted me to situations that held the potential for the escape of that story. While I experienced the hypervigilance required to maintain control as a feeling of disconnection or detachment from my body, I began to re-vision the hypervigilance as a strategy that held me to my body rather than distanced me from it. This point will be examined further in Chapter Eleven. I mention it here to illustrate the ways in which hypervigilance post childhood rape had quite possibly inadvertently prepared me for this somatic inquiry work. The level of attention I now suspect I must have been giving to my body since the rapes was attention that probably helped me track the hands-on work during the private sessions with Alice and retrospectively recall and record their detail as a result.

What follows are journal extracts written following my private sessions with Alice in Melbourne in late 2010. They serve as examples of our early work and the level of somatic awareness I was experiencing and recording at that time.

18 November, 2010

I told Alice that I was now aware of my belly region, how it felt absent and yet heavy, but not really heavy, that how I perceived it in my imagination was as a round black stone, present but absent in some way. [The word I was searching for was 'concave' but it didn't arrive in my mouth until later. My belly felt heavy and round but concave, present but absent, its absence heavy, and its presence empty.]

As Alice moved to my right foot and knee and hip, my eyes closed. She then took both of my heels in her hands, cupped them, and slowly raised them a little before returning them to the floor. This had felt disconcerting; the fleeting sense of immobilisation created by the elevation worried me. Alice moved to my left foot and knee. I opened my eyes. The heat from her hands was intense, and yet she wasn't applying a great deal of pressure, certainly no more than before, a light touch only, but my entire body responded by flushing with a rush of blood and my skin enlivened with a prickling sensation. I could feel my breathing become shallow again and faster. My gut clenched into a solid mass. The muscles of my thigh began to tense up. Alice placed one hand just above my knee and the other on my hip and I began to feel very anxious. The sensation of being pinned down that I had experienced earlier was very real and intense now and I was becoming quite agitated. She sensed this and stopped, then we talked.

19 November, 2010

Alice began today on my left side, gently holding my left hand in her left hand and my elbow and then shoulder with her right. She took a long time over this today and invited me to join her in imagining the inner and outer membranes of a cell, the semi-permeable membranes. She asked me to imagine how these might feel to me as she worked, with information coming in and out. To help me in this, I thought of Elizabeth Grosz's Mobius Strip. But I felt clear resistance in the membranes of my cells.

21 November, 2010

Today I feel somehow lighter.
More embodied.
As if I have an over-abundance of oxygen in my cells.
My body feels as though it's fizzing.
I can feel my body breathing again.
It's been holding its breath for so long.
How can I keep the somatic memory of Alice's hands-on work alive
in order to sustain this embodied state?
I don't yet trust myself to be able to do this alone.

26 November, 2010

I'm so much more aware of my left leg and lower body now and I feel there's been some kind of an emotional shift, a repugnance creeping in, a sensation of nausea and revulsion associated with the somatic memory of the weight of the perpetrator's body. I don't want to feel further alienation from my body but in this new experiencing of it, there's a new response emerging. Perhaps this repugnance and revulsion is anger? If so, it's confusing. If it is anger, it's new for me and it still feels like it's directed towards my self, towards my body. It feels like I want to detach further from the flesh that's producing memory sensation and yet I know, now, that to engage is to understand. How can I redirect this sensation so as not to ignore it, but work with it instead, without bile rising from my gut?

With even the deepest level of attention, it was often difficult to make sense of what I was somatically experiencing in the private sessions, let alone begin to hold it in coherence through language. My bodily experiences often felt primitive, well beyond the verbal and beyond immediate understanding. Performance artist Margaret Cameron (2012, 61) writes of such moments: 'It is *as if* [author's own emphasis] the material and immaterial devolve from one to other [...]. I listen. It seems more useful to *listen* [author's own emphasis] than to understand.' On such occasions for me, it was enough to listen and rest in the feeling of it and in the self-acknowledgement that what I was perhaps experiencing was my body's spontaneous expression of trauma memory, or perhaps the first gestational signs of the neural re-patterning I understood was necessary for the re-integration of my trauma memory, my body and mind. I made no attempts to capture and record these moments. It would have been as difficult as trying to capture and describe for example, the sensation of my pupils dilating or contracting in response to strong light passing across my eyes. Often during the hands-on work, I simply had a distant awareness of something cellular but it was so deeply embodied and so grounded in spontaneity that the anatomical and physiological dimensions could not be easily identified let alone articulated.

In *Body/Landscape Journals*, Margaret Somerville (1999, 14) writes of her attempts to retrospectively record how her body had felt during massage sessions. She talks of this in terms of writing image: 'It meant bringing myself out of a deep trance-like consciousness to cross over the bridge between semiotic and symbolic, to give the images words, and then to remember them.' While image did not always attend what I was feeling in my body during hands-on or movement sessions, my way of negotiating this difficulty of articulating the semiotic through the symbolic has been to approach it obliquely in poetic form, often, though not always through the use of evocative language and metaphor. The following writing, which emerged after a movement session, was prompted by a sense of acute and precarious instability registering in my body. The metaphor of the tightrope retrospectively presented itself as I wrote.

Falling … apart?

I'm deeply emotional
barely able to speak
breath held in my chest
my body pulsing

suspended on a tight rope
hovering in space
thin rope
    beneath the pads of my feet

I'm desirous of stillness
hungry for despotic control
Be still body!
Don't betray this emotion

Freedom betrays
undoes the corset of control
unravels the ropes of restraint
frays the ends of fibres

Breathe!
    Breathe!
Be steady
Find balance
Don't
    fall!
Don't
    fall!

To
    fall
        is to
            what?

Is to
    fall
to fall apart?

(BD 2010)

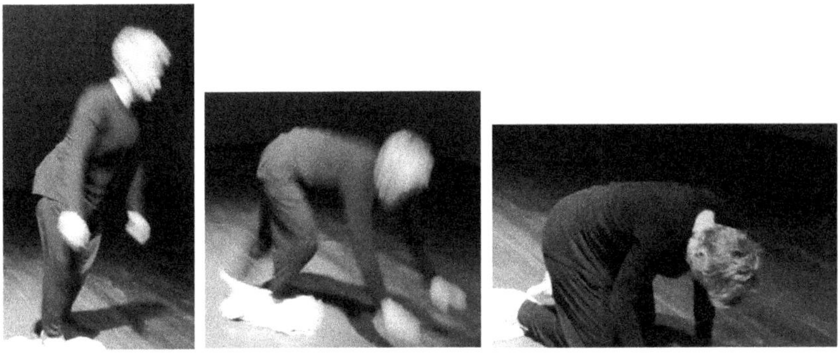

Having examined the embodied methodology supporting my autoethnographic somatic inquiry process, the final section of this chapter offers a reflective 'before' and 'during' perspective to the research. In this section, I reflexively analyse my relationship with my body within two time frames: before commencing the autoethnographic somatic inquiry phase prior to June, 2010; and, during my three and a half year immersion in this phase of the research through participation in Body-Mind Centering workshops, residential programs, and private session work. This section of the chapter is again supported by the addition of a substantial number of journal extracts. The journal extracts are not limited to the somatic inquiry time frame but extend to include relevant extracts written prior to my research. In combination, these extracts cover the period 2007–2013. Working within and around these extracts, this section combines my research process, findings, and analysis serving to highlight the entanglement of all three.

Feeling the fleshed body

> Your hand opens and closes. If it were always a fist or always stretched open, you would be paralysed. Your deepest presence is in every small contracting and expanding, the two as beautifully balanced and coordinated as birds' wings.
>
> — RUMI

This section takes the reader back to late 2009, before I began the Body-Mind Centering somatic inquiry work and well before my realisation that the hypervigilant attention I gave to my body was more akin to attachment than to detachment. I was aware that, in addition to broadening my knowledge base through the literature, I also needed to broaden my knowledge base with regard to my body. With this in mind, I began a personal process of somatic attunement. This involved taking note of any bodily responses I thought were interesting or relevant and documenting them in my research journal. My habitual pattern of what I perceived to be detachment from my body, meant it was necessary to begin by first teaching myself to pay attention to my body, or rather, to pay different attention to my body. I make this distinction because, as already mentioned, my hypervigilance meant that I was likely already paying attention to my body, had always paid attention to my body albeit to control it, and perhaps without a researcher's forensic eye for detail and nuance.

I felt now, though, that if I needed to pay different attention, I needed also to read my body in other, less pejorative ways. If my research were to continue to be driven by my intuitive sense that connections could be made between my silenced childhood rape experience and the symptoms and dissonance I felt in my adult body, I needed to listen to my body's language with greater consciousness and sharper focus. As a result, I felt it was essential that I learn to be more open and attuned to my habitual bodily behaviours as well as my embodied responses to stimuli in order to begin to recognise and fully acknowledge each.

To help facilitate this attunement, it was imperative that I begin to scrutinise my body in new ways. This filled me with uneasy anticipation. I worried that my habitual patterns of disconnection and denial would make the tracking of my bodily responses difficult, or indeed impossible. At times I felt overwhelmed by the task ahead of me. I was asking myself to perform a bodily contortion of sorts, orienting myself to face both inner and outer. If there was to be any chance of entering into a different relationship with my body and for somatic inquiry to take place, this was a necessary part of the process.

The next segment of this section of the chapter includes journal extracts written across a period of months prior to my entry into the work of Body-Mind Centering. To my surprise, as the extracts will attest, there was an abundant supply of material to draw on, some sitting in states of hibernation, others immediate and easily accessed. The journal entries are written in a combination of past and present tense. Those written in the present tense, although reflecting on past experience, illustrate my practice of holding myself in experience in order to write of it.

> *18 October, 2009*
>
> *I'm going to Pilates in the hope that my persistent back pain may be a result of inactive core muscles. I've been asked to move my body in a particular way. To tilt my pelvis so my spine becomes angled, then to raise my spine to the ceiling.*
>
> *I manage the tilting of the pelvis, I can picture in my mind how this should look and I move accordingly. The second part of the instruction however is lost. I can't see it in my mind and my body certainly can't feel where it should be going. I look helplessly at the instructor.*
>
> *The disconnection from my body is obvious; my mind is struggling to grasp this simple instruction. The instructor lies on the floor next to me. She moves her body into position as she speaks, gently inviting me to copy her.*
>
> *I feel stupid. It's such a simple movement.*
>
> *Once I've raised my hips in the air leaving my upper back, shoulders and bent legs to take the weight, I'm amazed at my inability to see and initiate this movement. I'm also amazed that, at 50, my mind and body continue to elude each other. I feel torn in two.*

'I feel stupid'

'I feel torn in two'

4 November, 2009

I've been asked to look at the position of my body in the mirror by the Pilates instructor. I don't want to. The mirror's too big and I'll be forced to see myself as a whole person if I raise my eyes to meet myself. I'll be forced to acknowledge my body.

I don't want to.

I'm tensing up.

I really don't want to.

The instructor stands by. I envy her casual relationship with her physicality. Her limbs are loose as she walks, her shoulders without tension. She is a relaxed walker. I don't need to look in the mirror to see the difference between us both. I know how my body is. I know my body will never have the freedom of hers.

And, more to please her than to please myself, I turn towards the threatening mirror. I notice my hair first of all, rumpled still from sleep, refusing to toe the line. It's easier to look at my hair ... it's the furthest point from my body, apart from my toes. But the instructor's gently urging me to note the position of my legs, the right-angle of my hips and shoulders ... I look.

I become fleetingly absorbed in the clothes I have on ... but I'm simply procrastinating and not looking at my body. She places her hand on the small of my back, forcing my sight line to shift, the weight of her hand forcing me to take in the muscle and tissue and bone beneath the fabric of my t-shirt.

I'm there.

I'm back with my body.

It's alien and familiar all at once.

I don't look for long though. I convince myself that to learn this position I must be able to find it without the aid of mirrors if I'm to do these exercises at home. I have no floor to ceiling mirrors at home. My bedroom has only a small mirror ... The bathroom has a larger mirror but it reflects back only half of me. I am nothing below the waist in my bathroom.

My lower body does not exist.

I know this because I can't see it.

'I'll be forced to see myself as a whole person ... I'll be forced to acknowledge my body'

'I'm there. I'm back with my body'

'It's alien and familiar all at once'

'My lower body does not exist. I know this because I can't see it'

9 November, 2009

When I think about the many impacts of my rape experience, it's the detachment from my body that troubles me the most. And yet I feel that without my body I would be better off. I'd be dis-embodied, a series of thoughts, a cerebral playground. Remove my face as well for it gives away too much. The skin infuses with blood when I feel anxious or uncomfortable. My cheeks burn with awkwardness. My lips refuse to form the words that await birth in the uterus of my mind. They press together, denying themselves the chance to fully dilate. But still I want to trust my body, to link arms with it [...] I want to love my body. I feel I have never loved my body.

'It's the detachment from my body that troubles me the most'

'without my body I would be better off'

'Remove my face as well'

'I want to love my body. I feel I have never loved my body'

Over six years has passed since I wrote the words of these journal entries, and still they are difficult for me to read. They tear at me with their raw candidness and dispassionate observation. They sit heavily as the sad despair they evoke and the yearning they speak rises from a desire for self-love that collapses unrequited. These words condense time, plunge me back into a body that was still the enemy despite the olive branch of my research. My words reflect the depth of the long-term bodily hatred I harboured, the dis-integrated relationship between my body and my mind, and my longing for change.

The following journal extracts give an insight into the fragility of my sense of identity at this time and the enduring detachment I felt from my body. They offer an entrée into my emotional state in the month prior to my first Body-Mind Centering workshop. They are a glimpse into the consciousness of my apprehension concerning the possibility of change once my autoethnographic somatic investigation began.

12 May, 2010

I've been reflecting on the coming workshop and how it might feel to find some peace with my body. After all, it's not guaranteed. I'm assuming this as a possibility only. With the workshop still three weeks away, I'm already feeling the familiar fear and anxiety states I harboured when I first began to talk of my rape experience to therapists, and, in more recent years, to others. The rapes had been such central, if hidden, defining features of my self-identity. So, will this BMC workshop shift my relationship with my body? Will I be able to experience some sort of integration and acceptance? Will I be less punitive and demanding in this relationship?

When I first began to talk of my trauma, I was terrified that should this 'thing' that I'd held so closely for so many years be taken away through disclosure or psychotherapy, I might actually disintegrate. There was, and still is to a degree, an internal solidity to its presence, almost as if it forms an important part of my anatomical structure, in the same way that my spine or shoulders or pelvis do. Before I started psychotherapy, my story and its secretive nature was enormous, occupying most of my torso, dark and heavy and impenetrable. It kept me upright. Now though, after years of therapy, its presence is smaller, about the size of two fists and located somewhere behind my navel. It doesn't keep me upright any longer; my re-kindled self-esteem does that for me most of the time. But it's still a dark and dense presence and remains a defining feature.

'Will I be able to experience some sort of integration and acceptance?'

'Will I be less punitive and demanding in this relationship?'

'It's still a dark and dense presence and remains a defining feature'

13 May, 2010

The history of my relationship with my body is a history of confrontation and control. Trust is absent. My body has rarely led an autonomous existence except on the occasions when my psyche was in turmoil and on the verge of collapse. Then my body seized the opportunity and rebelled, harnessed the collective energy of my cells and led a revolt that included erratic and unpredictable muscle spasms, uncontrollable trembling, throbbing head pain, weight loss and gain, chronic insomnia, and of course, cancer. When the guard was down, a state of anatomical anarchy was born.

25 May, 2010

When I was at the chiropractor this morning I tried to stay present to my body as much as possible and reflect on how my body felt during the treatment.

When the interferential machine was on I found myself drifting away from my body and found I had to consciously draw myself back into my body. It took me by surprise a little. The disconnection must be such an automatic process. It took conscious effort to bring myself back to my body and keep myself there.

26 May, 2010

Reflecting on yesterday's experience, I can see now that I have always been aware of my ability to consciously disconnect from things that make me anxious or cause me emotional pain. I use my will to push the anxiety down, away from the front of my mind, to almost bury it until I can eventually flat-line emotionally ... But it wasn't until yesterday that I realised that I quite probably do this on a physical level as well, in anticipation of pain. But which comes first? Emotional flat-lining or somatic severing?

Perhaps it's my conscious self responding in a somatically controlling way but it must happen in a nanosecond and so feels seamless and automatic. It's a learned behaviour I suppose and, like all learned behaviours, if practiced enough times they become part of one's modus operandi. After today's illumination though, I'm confused about which responds first to experience and difficulty. My mind? Or my body?

It's clear from these journal extracts that I was experiencing a heightened state of awareness at this time, attending as deeply as I could to the ways my body and my mind interacted. Conflict is demonstrably present. In the entry for 12 May, 2010, I asked myself: Will I be able to experience some sort of integration and acceptance? Almost in the same breath I also show misgivings about the risk of the rape experience being erased in some way through the Body-Mind Centering work. I self-identified so strongly, if secretly, as a rape victim that I worried that if it were taken from me altogether, there would be little left behind to define me or hold me up. There is a clear tussle playing out, a collision of fear and anticipation, a tug-of-war between the desire for change and the preservation of the damaging but known status quo.

The 12 May, 2010 extract also reveals some of the ways that the trauma of childhood rape, maintained not only a substantial part of my self-identity but also a strong presence in my body. I wrote of the trauma memory having an *internal solidity ... occupying most of my torso, and forming an important part of my anatomical structure which kept me upright*. While I wrote that earlier psychotherapy had somewhat diminished the size of the bodily occupation of the trauma, I noted that it still remained a dark and dense presence and remains a defining feature. This of course presents an interesting paradox. While I was clearly apprehensive, I was also keen to see how the Body-Mind Centering work would impact on me. My difficult relationship with my body and the tension associated with the potential (as I saw it) for the loss of self-identity sat alongside my desire for change, but the stress of holding these seemingly disparate emotional states was tiring and confusing me. Without doubt my years of psychotherapy had helped externalise my trauma and diminish its size so that it no longer propped me up. My body though still felt a dark and muddled place, mysterious and dangerous and not at all safe.

In another extract (13 May, 2010), I wrote of the bodily illness, discord, and unrest I experienced when I was mentally unwell. I describe this as a time when *a state of anatomical anarchy was born, when my body seized the opportunity and rebelled ... led a revolt ... when the guard was down*. From this extract, it's clear the relationship between my mind and my body at that time was very much a relationship of detachment, and one based on mistrust, opposition, and repression. The very words I chose to describe the relationship highlight this state; the words themselves are bound in masculinist metaphors of war. I could have been writing about a separatist uprising in a conflict-stricken region rather than my own body.

In the extract for 25 May, 2010, I wrote of my ability to mentally disconnect. Detachment was a way of life for me then, offering a space of conscious escape from feeling and a way of managing anxiety. I used the term emotional flat-lining to describe the way in which I managed difficulty by suppressing and numbing feeling. Because my experiencing of physically or emotionally challenging situations was so difficult for me, my determination to circumvent feelings of anxiety in advance of, or when confronted by them, led me to engage avoidance and detachment strategies. One of these was emotional numbing. I'm aware now, from the autoethnographic and psychological literature, that numbing is an avoidance strategy and is a common response in the aftermath of trauma (Culbertson 1995, Herman 1992, Levine 1997, Nijenhuis and van der Hart 1999, Rothschild 2000, Scaer 2001, van der Kolk 1994, Brison 2002). While it is affirming to read my response in these terms, this understanding does not alter the fact that for years I was unable to experience the full range of my emotions for fear of what might become of me if I did. As Body-Mind Centering educator Linda Hartley (1995, 107) notes however, 'there can be no movement toward the healing of old wounds as long as we remain unconscious and numb to our pain and fear and dissociated from imprisoned areas of the body'.

The journal extract I include below gives a further and final insight into the struggles I was grappling with prior to my engagement with the Body-Mind Centering work. The movement through layers of feeling that I underwent, and the sanctuary and guidance I found in the work of other researchers and theorists, is representative of the shape of my inquiry process and the depth of emotion I interrogated in my search for understanding.

26 April 2010

I find my thoughts and my eyes returning almost compulsively to the image of the child, the fleshed and small body in the white summer dress, the photograph of myself as a confident three-year-old. I have this photograph leaning against a pile of text books, the titles on their spines spelling out the sexual trauma research they relate to. This juxtaposition is deliberate.

I find myself oscillating between the archival child image and the present place of sexual trauma research I find myself in, back and forth between the photograph suspended in time and the photograph in a new temporal and spatial location resting against these particular books. I consider the accumulation of experience that has taken the body of this child from the pavement surrounding the Commonwealth Bank in 1962 to stand, fifty years later, against a wall of sexual trauma literature.

I search the smooth, soft face before me for a sign of the fate that lurked in the shadows of a yet-to-be-lived future. My child smile stretches the corners of my mouth, caught in an eternal state of ease-full wellbeing. No tension undulates beneath the smooth skin of my child forehead. My brow does not lower in mistrust to shield my child eyes from the gaze of the adult male stranger photographing me. The child I see appears completely at home in her skin, in herself and in the social world around her. She seems easeful and integrated. I ought to feel reassured, able to find solace in these early signs of openness with others and easefulness with self. I ought to take pleasure in witnessing what could be a place of return. But I can't. Instead I'm disturbed, and in the murk and muck of this, I'm unable to find clarity.

My thoughts return to Marianne Hirsch (1997, 264). She writes that photography has a 'capacity to evoke absence as well as presence'. My eyes flick and alight on the small right foot in the photograph. It rests frozen and static in time, the action of the camera's shutter preventing further mobility. The photographic medium, by its very nature, can only freeze image. This child is literally unable to move. Similarly, the mouth stretched into a smile is unable to speak.

Unable to move.

Unable to speak.

What has been evoked for me, I now realise as I look at this photograph, what I experience as acutely painful, is the prescient quality of my embodied response. It grips my viscera and causes me to hold my breath. Intellectually, I know I hold the knowledge of the future violation of this child, the associated future shattered sense of self, the absence of autonomy, and the stifling censoring of speech this violation will produce. What disturbs me though is the rush and intensity of the sense of foreboding that rises in my body. I sense my cellular memory has been activated and has conflated with my conscious memory to remind me of the myriad absences I have experienced in the aftermath of my childhood trauma, not least, those predictable states of immobility and the choking self-silencing that this provokes when I am feeling vulnerable. My body feels exhausted by these states, tested to its limits. Looking at the photograph, the child's frozen presence has given rise to somatic sensations that remind me of absence.

I want to take some sort of action in order to lift this child from the pavement and hold her body close to me. I want to absorb through her skin and mine, her trust in the world, but more especially, her trust in her self. I want to feel her open gaze through my own eyes. I want to draw on her child body in order to recapture my own. I want to return, in some way, to this place of social and somatic harmony, this perceived place of ease-full corporeal comfort. I ache with this desire but I feel lost and impotent. I am as frozen as the image before me.

And here again, Marianne Hirsch guides me. 'Writing the image,' she suggests, '... undoes the objectification of the still photograph and thereby takes it out of the realm of stasis, immobility, mortification ... into fluidity, movement, and thus, finally, life' (4).

Fluidity.

Movement.

Life.

In the holding of these words, the two dimensionality of the photograph, the accompanying stasis I feel in my body, the objectification of the image before me, and the silencing sensation I'm experiencing merges and strikes me with greater clarity. I understand now that the path to fulfilling, even partially, the imperative I feel for the return to that integrated state, is through the writing of the image in my research.

This writing will fill the lungs of the child before me, oxygenate her blood with story, and stimulate the venous return to her heart through the steady pumping action of narrative. I will give her fluidity and movement. I will bring her to life and accompany her into her future. And together, we'll see what happens there. I know though, that in the process of writing this narrative, in the cellular exploration I must undertake, in the reflection and self-reflexivity I must engage with in order to gain insight, I must enter my body and the trauma that lingers there.

I turn to Carol Gilligan (2003, 63) for encouragement: 'Perhaps it is necessary to go into the heart of tragedy in order to find a path that leads back to pleasure.' My conviction that this is the case is unwavering but in re-entering the heart of this story I must take my self to that place in time and the events that drove me from my body in the first instance. I must take on a new role and become a patient, attentive, and observant witness and participant, victim and survivor, both the researcher and the researched. This is not without its challenges.

And finally, Cathy Caruth (1995, 10) tells me that 'trauma is not experienced as a mere repression or defence, but as a temporal delay that carries the individual beyond the shock of the first moment. The trauma is a repeated suffering of the event, but it is also a leaving of its site.' She further notes that in order to 'listen to the crisis of the trauma ... not only to listen for the event, but to hear in the testimony the survivors departure from it; the challenge of the ... listener ... is how to listen to departure.'

Perhaps, the listening to departure holds the tantalising possibility of return.

Autoethnographic somatic inquiry through Body-Mind Centering

In this segment, I include journal extracts selected to illustrate the range of responses I experienced across the three and a half years of my autoethnographic somatic inquiry phase during my immersion in the practice of Body-Mind Centering. The extracts were written as workshop reflections as well as more general personal musings. They offer an insight into the unfolding of my somatic awareness through experiential exploration, and provide a glimpse into the embodied articulations of my unresolved trauma, revealed to me during the workshop explorations. They help amplify the significant contribution the somatic inquiry component of the research made to the evolution of my conceptual understandings. I have included some of the poetic writing that emerged during the inquiry process as a way of illustrating the shift I made into more lyrical modes of expression when poetic form spontaneously entered my imagination or when conventional forms proved inadequate. I begin with reflections from my first Body-Mind Centering workshop facilitated by Alice in June, 2010 and move through time to end with reflections written during two Body-Mind Centering residential programs in early 2013. I periodically interrupt the flow of the extracts to foreground the purpose for specific inclusions.

5 June, 2010

'Navel Radiation' workshop

Exploration: Alice asked us to imagine being in the uterine space, focusing on how this felt, how it felt to move in this space, to feel unbound by gravity, weightless, to reach out and imagine touching the fluid surroundings and uterine wall.

Reflection: I barely moved, felt the need to hold tight to my hands and keep each of my legs and feet pressed together. I needed to hold myself together, to keep warm but also to remain connected to myself in case I became separated.

When we finished the exploration, I drew before I wrote, my grasp light on the pen, my movements slow, distant. I drew a foetal shape in a womb with a large head and small curving body, limbless. Few words emerged: bound tight curled cold small vulnerable

I was aware of my desire to remain in my bodily experience and beyond symbolic language.

Exploration: Hands-on

Reflection: I was the first to receive with a hand on my navel centre and another on a limb. Although I was convinced I wouldn't like it, I felt beautifully held; the lightest and steadiest of touches, with enough connection to feel the warmth and presence without it becoming a distraction.

This was the most extraordinary experience. I have never stayed 'in my body' for such a long period of time. Whenever my mind began to stray, the touch, warmth and presence of the toucher brought me back to my self. This was incredible! The touch felt like it attached me to my body, preventing my body from wandering off.

6 June, 2010

Exploration: Cellular breathing. Alice guided us to imagine ourselves as a single cell, feeling breath entering and leaving our body. She asked us to move as and when we felt we wanted to. I curled my body into a foetal position.

Reflection:
upper body lightness freedom deep within expansion arms filling space more alive body
moving from the shoulders up body below lagging behind heavy

I found, like yesterday, I didn't want to rush into engaging my intellect and so I drew.

Exploration: From our radial centre (our navel), moving each of our limbs, initially without elevating them from the floor, then eventually moving them through space.

Reflection: I found it impossible to move my legs independently – navel to leg, leg to navel, left leg, and right leg. This was quite distressing. I felt pinned down, weighed down, helpless, vulnerable. Once I attempted to move all my limbs through space and gravity though, my legs responded and I felt relief.

7 June, 2010

Exploration: Lying on our blankets, moving our bodies and limbs randomly working with gravity and weightlessness and with whatever feeling arrived in us.

Reflection:

Exhausting deep sadness emerged grief movements of masking hands protecting face tears quivering profound feeling wanting to escape forcing myself to remain returning to foetal shapes safe haven where was my safety? always and forever the child emerges how to make her feel safe? when she's safe, will I too be safe to be me?

Exploration: Asymmetric movement lying on our backs, moving from our radial centre.

Reflection:

left leg is weighed down heavy pressed by gravity into the floor upper limbs icy cold lower limbs burning with heat peripheral toes moving in small circles

gentle and contained movement soothing

Exploration: Authentic Movement

Reflection:
Following my body, my body leading the movement, stretching, swaying, carving smooth arcs in the surrounding body space, sensual and liberating. My body taking me to places I've never been. Beautiful shapes, fluid movements using space in ways I never would have imagined possible. Sorrowful shapes, vulnerable shapes, embracing, inviting, shyly joyful, soothing, comforting, deeply, deeply satisfying.

A later reflection:

A dream
A dream to feel this free
A dream to feel this embodied

This Authentic Movement exploration was the most surprising and extraordinary experience. After the distress I felt during the morning at the intensity of the disconnection I was experiencing (and the associated isolation, vulnerability and grief I was processing), the joy I felt during the Authentic Movement in the afternoon was truly profound.

It is quite surreal how the disparate states (of connection and disconnection) can appear to reside in such close juxtaposition, and yet be experienced as intensely separate and so greatly divided.

It's a negotiation through movement, a dance, a pas de deux of disconnection-connection-disconnection-connection. The hands-on helped to bring me back to my centre, helped me to re-connect with my body but it was the body-driven movement that brought me so completely back to my self.

I want to keep moving in order to not lose my self again. I want to move to keep my body with me. Most of all, I want to move in order to be my body.

It's interesting to note in my journal extracts the lack of integration present. I consistently refer to my body and my mind as if they are entirely discrete entities, which of course is how I perceived them to be early on in the research. The following poem was written across three or four days in the period immediately following the first 'Navel Radiation' workshop. It is a clear example of the pervasiveness of this artificial separation. During the workshop, I perceived that the elation I had felt as a result of being prepared to remain present to my body, was my body experiencing relief and joy at finally discovering a voice that could be heard.

My body speaks

You were searching for you
thought I was lost.
But I was here all along,
waiting with impatient longing
for your hand to fill mine.

With the first tentative touch
there emerged
no reproachful undertone;
merely a joyful,
euphoric release.
Yes! At last!
You've found me!
I knew you would!

Time was all you required,
time and a guiding wisdom.

I never lost hope
although I was certain
at times you had and then
I tried to shake you
out of your lethargy,
tried to re-ignite that spark of desire
to re-energise your quest
for embodied peace,
for homeostasis,

for mutually sustaining cellular respiration.

Is love the act of breathing together?

(BD 2010)

The following extracts amplify how, in spite of my gratitude, the sense of connectedness I felt during, and immediately following the workshop was tenuous and short-lived. Hands-on work and Authentic Movement undoubtedly played vital roles in the development of this gratitude, however, the presence of a witnessing other is intrinsic to both of these practices. Away from the workshop environment, it wasn't possible for witnessing to take place and this contributed, I'm certain, to the sense of loss I experienced.

> *11 June, 2010*
>
> *The desire to experience my body in movement is almost painful. I can feel the agony of longing and necessity. I'm clinging perilously to the cellular memory of moving with my body as if its escape will send me spiralling backwards into that all too familiar disembodied world again.*

Clearly my first workshop encounter with the practice of Body-Mind Centering provoked a variation of responses. The range of emotions and sensations I experienced was quite extraordinary. At times I felt I was diving down into despairing states of further disembodiment and chaos, with little or no control over how far I would go or where I would land. At other times the embodiment I felt through movement and touch was exquisite, the sensation of working *with* my body rather than against it, sublime. The work carried me into a new and wondrous world of sensing and feeling and most surprisingly, a softened state of compassion towards my body.

> *17 June, 2010*
>
> *I can feel my body is getting away from me again.*

Without doubt, the workshop experience was an unpredictable ride, yet out of this unpredictability, from within this confusing mess of conflicting, though inter-related states of emotional chaos and joyful somatic freedom, I was beginning to read my body in other ways. The specific experiential quality and focus of the work, rather than a psychological and text-based focus, proved profound in its capacity to help facilitate a range of experiences. The supportive environment in which the work took place allowed me the time and the space to explore the difficulties of my relationship with my body as well as rest in, rather than reject, my sometimes distressing responses to these difficulties. The experiential nature of the work allowed me to imaginatively travel into my cellular tissue to begin to sense and feel my body in new ways. This immersion facilitated the eruption of periods of intense struggle and revealed layers of surprising pleasure. The co-existence of these two states seemed paradoxical and sometimes confusing.

Before continuing, it is important to locate the selection of writing that follows by foregrounding it with a concise account of the ways trauma can disrupt temporality. Herman (1992) writes:

> Long after the danger is past, traumatized people relive the event as though it were continually recurring in the present. They cannot resume the normal course of their lives, for the trauma continually interrupts. It is as if time stops at the moment of trauma. The traumatic moment becomes encoded in an abnormal form of memory, which breaks spontaneously into consciousness, both as flashbacks during waking states and as traumatic nightmares during sleep. Small, seemingly insignificant reminders can also evoke these memories, which often return with all the vividness and emotional force of the original event. Thus, even safe environments may come to feel dangerous, for the survivor can never be assured that she will not encounter some reminder of the trauma. (37)

The following extracts and poetic writing help illustrate what is known about the temporal disruption that can occur during episodes of intrusive memory (flashbacks), and the intensity of feeling that can accompany the return of traumatic and unresolved memory during these episodes (Herman 1992, Levine 1997, Ogden, Minton, and Pain 2006, Rothschild 2000, Scaer 2001). The writing amplifies the ways that powerful and visceral trauma memory can linger and shape daily responses to seemingly innocuous experiences.

Although I have experienced many episodes of triggered memory over the years, the poem, *Living in the Aftermath* is a lyrical record of one specific event. My physical responses during this event give another example of the intensity of feeling that can be evoked when trauma memory is inadvertently re-stimulated. The second extract, although from my 2011 journal writing, describes an involuntary bodily response that has plagued me since the rapes in 1971; my inability to speak only occurs when I'm in the company of others and only when I'm highly anxious. The remaining extracts are reflections chosen to provide further graphic examples of how my unresolved trauma memory remained in the tissues of my body and erupted viscerally without warning when re-stimulated. They amplify how the accumulation of experience and feeling this created sometimes overwhelmed me.

Living in the Aftermath

I pull the linen shirt up
and over my head
but I've forgotten to
undo the top buttons
The cloth lodges over my face,
gripping my chin and mouth.
I am instantly nauseous
I panic

Heat flashes on the surface of my body
Sweat beads bubble from my pores
In my panic I tug harder on the shirt,
try to wrest my face from its grip
The grip remains firm
I'm dizzy with fear,
my thoughts incoherent
I can barely breathe

My fingers give a final mighty wrench
Pearly buttons fly off and land
disconsolately on the carpet
The fabric tears,
shrieks with fibrous pain
and flies from my hand
My mouth sucks in air
Hot tears burn my eyes

The shirt lies on the floor,
a crumpled, dejected, torn,
and useless aggressor.

(BD 2008)

4 March, 2011

I try to speak and the heavy and debilitating hymen slams into position, a reverse loss-of-virginity action. It must be flesh, a muscular fleshy barrier that blocks the passage of my words. What else can it be? I can't be imagining it, it feels too real.

In relation to the 4 March entry, I was not aware of an explanation for this phenomenon until I began reading the literature surrounding hysteria and feminist literature specifically focusing on the enteric nervous system. It is interesting to note that women diagnosed with hysteria in the late nineteenth century often experienced a loss of voice, or a sensation of choking, 'as if a ball were in the throat'. This condition, given the name 'globus hystericus' (Showalter 1998, 15), was experienced by the majority of women diagnosed with hysteria at the Salpetriere Hospital (Hustvedt 2011). Wilson's (2004b, 43–45) investigation of the enteric nervous system and its role in depression argues that the gut 'is one of the most important means by which the outside world connects with the body.' She argues that traumatic events are not primarily felt at a psychological level and subsequently at a bodily level. Rather, given the high concentration of neurons in the entire central nervous system, and more especially in the enteric nervous system, any response to stimuli 'travels through the body', and as it does, 'it takes the psyche with it' (47). In relation to hysteria and *globus hystericus*, the peristaltic action of the oesophageal lining is intrinsically linked to and co-ordinated by the enteric nervous system (Tortora and Derrickson 2009, Furness 2007, Malagelada et al. 2007). When anxiety or a traumatic event occurs, and the gut becomes over-stimulated, the muscular lining of the oesophagus can go into spasm causing the individual to perceive a sensation of blockage, or choking (King 2014). Irregularities in gut function are pivotal to clinical diagnoses of somatoform disorder, including somatisation disorder, the contemporary name for hysteria (Wilson 2004b).

Had I been a woman living in nineteenth-century France, would I have been diagnosed with hysteria?

4 December, 2010

The experience of childhood rape has damaged me on so many levels. I find that, every now and then, today, I still feel completely overwhelmed by this knowledge, totally defeated by the long term ramifications. On occasion, the damage seems so thoroughly pervasive that it's hard not to feel a sense of despair creeping back in at the thought of the work that's still needed in order to come to terms with this. Because, after all, that's the best case scenario really, coming to terms with it.

The experience will never go away because the acts of rape certainly didn't end when the perpetrator walked from the room. Indeed, the perpetrator has never really ever walked away; he travels with me wherever I go: he's the fear that prevents me from going to certain places; he's the shadow in the dark; the creak of the floorboard at night; the movement in the bushes by day; the force behind my hand on the turned key in the lock at night. As soon as he entered that child's bedroom four decades ago, my cells absorbed the memory of his presence, and then his pressing weight. How could they not? So drunk were they on the chemicals of fear that they couldn't resist. And there the memories have remained, whether I've had conscious awareness of them or not. He's there, his body is there, central to those memories. My body has known this all along.

This knowledge fills me with rage and nausea.

I feel I want to scour my internal landscape with something so caustic that blisters will form and blood will seep from the membranes forming thick impenetrable protective scabs. I want the new tissue that develops beneath the scabs to be pink and pristine, untainted by these nauseating memories. I don't want them anymore. They're too painful, too heavy a burden to carry. Today I don't have the strength to carry them. Today my belly is heavy and my back and spirit are bending under their weight.

6 March, 2011

'Membranes and the layered body: Navigating the interface' workshop

Exploration: Moving from the mind of the fascia tissue

The concept of an all-enveloping and spiralling, semi-viscose fascia was really appealing. I love that it's present throughout my body, extending from the top of my head to the tip of my toes. I love the image of it providing support for the blood vessels and muscles, wrapping around and cradling my viscera. I was really looking forward to this and wanted to explore, but almost as soon as we began the somatisation, I felt my skin enliven and a sense of panic flood through me. I felt my heart begin to race and my breathing become rapid and shallow. I felt deeply anxious and wasn't sure what to do. I was also shocked that this could happen without warning, again. And precipitated by what?

12 March, 2011

I've been unable to put aside my memory of what erupted when Alice's hands rested on my collarbones during the private session last Friday. I've been digging away, trying to comprehend what actually happened, how my body felt when I suddenly pulled Alice's hand away.** My action seemed to happen without thought. It felt involuntary [...]. I'm certain that at no point, despite the tide of shapeless fear rocketing through my body [...] did I <u>consciously</u> consider raising my hand to remove hers. I believe now, that in that brief moment that morning, I felt and witnessed a spontaneous reflexive response to something my body perceived as a real, serious, and immediate threat to my personal safety. I believe, in the few seconds Alice's hands rested on my collarbones, that my body-I had genuinely felt, in every cell, the potential, again, for suffocation. I understand now from my research reading, that at the precise moment my hand grabbed at Alice's, my body-I was in a hyper-aroused state of confusion. I understand that this spontaneous response sprang from a messy melange of instinctual behaviour, my sexual trauma history, and the sexual trauma stories of other girls and women, a combination of personal memories, 'pre-memories', and 'post-memories' (Brison, 2002).*

When my body-I reacted that morning, my body-I was occupying a distorted and fractured temporal space where I simultaneously existed as a fifty-one-year-old woman, an eleven/twelve-year-old girl child, and an early human being programmed to survive. The experiencing of Alice's hands on my collarbones had shifted me in time, confused and disorientated me, shunted me into a time-space in which normal chronology was suspended, a time-space that flicked back and forth between childhood, primitive past, and adult present, between self narrative and the narratives of others. This all happened with dizzying velocity and devastating reality. At the precise moment I pulled her hand away, my response was instinctual and self-preserving, infused with a blend of self-knowledge and somatically-held experience as well as with the 'known', but not somatically-held experiences of other girls and women across time.

I ask myself now though, how is it possible that I could have felt such pressing danger when I was voluntarily lying on the floor of a quiet room and trusted so completely the hands touching me? How is it possible that my life could have felt in such danger?

I live now with conscious awareness of the somatic memory of the perpetrator's body heavy against my left leg and belly. Since that Friday, I live also with the re-awakened sensations of suffocation and choking. These are real. They are not imagined. These somatic memories have occupied cellular space in my body for forty years. I can now feel their irrepressible presence and their agitated desire for further release. I fear this release. I have always feared this release. It's this fear that has forced me to patrol my body like a vicious and merciless guard, pacing up and down the length of myself, sneering at irregularities, and pouring scorn on ineptitude. Only with the exertion of absolute, rigid and unforgiving constraint have I felt 'safe' from the dark and disruptive potential of these visceral and distressing memories. I have always been able to easily recall the presence of the perpetrators tongue filling my mouth, his hand over my lips and nose. These memories have always occupied conscious space and somehow, I've been able to hold them at arm's length in order to accommodate them. But I have not had conscious awareness of his hand/s on my neck. However, when Alice's hands rested there, there was no denying my body's immediate response. Her hands became the hands of the perpetrator. In those moments, rationality abandoned me and I was flung back through decades of life to arrive on a bed in a dark room on a hot summer's night in 1971. What I felt on that night (and perhaps on that other night later the same year) was a terror so razor sharp and intense and so far beyond my experience it left no room for thoughts other than the possibility of death. But these thoughts I gagged also ... until they vomited themselves up that Friday.

[*For the related journal extract (9 March, 2011), refer to Chapter One, *Philomela and me.*
[** Talking to Alice some weeks after this event, her perception was that I didn't pull her hand away quickly, but rather my movements were slow and purposeful.]

17 January, 2013

'Perceptions, Planes & the Vestibular System' residential program, Victoria

It had been a difficult morning after another restless night. I was sleep-deprived and worn out. My senses were exhausted; my ears had been on high alert, again, throughout the night. We were outside amongst the grapevines for an exploration involving hearing. We were to have a partner crumble dried vine leaves near our ears to bring our awareness to not only how they sounded but more particularly, to how the sound felt in our ears. N. slowly crumbled the leaves near my right ear. I couldn't bear it; the noise was excruciating. It sliced through the ambient sound, reverberated sharply through my middle ear, and stabbed my tympanic membrane in short painful jabs. I began to weep – from the specific physical pain I was experiencing, but more specifically, from the amorphous grief and emotional pain that gripped me. I asked N. to stop. I knew I was* *grieving for my ears that didn't want to listen any longer to the smallest of sounds; for my ears that didn't want to be the lookout anymore; for my ears that were exhausted by their vigilant state and position of responsibility. The innocuous sound of dried leaves crumbling had taken me deep into my body and the pain of this had plunged me into the oceanic grief of my story.*

[*I generally don't sleep for extended periods of time in my own home. When I travel and sleep in unfamiliar places, my insomnia is heightened by my hyper-vigilance. This was the case when I travelled to Riddells Creek.]

It was my intention to include the extracts and poetic writing in this section to serve as evocative and embodied entry points to the material process and outcomes of my autoethnographic somatic inquiry. My hope, though, is that these writings move beyond the parameters of this intention. My hope is that they also transport the reader, through embodied empathy, across the full personal and political landscape of the catastrophe of childhood rape. If I achieve this, I will have achieved what artist and art theorist Barbara Bolt (2012) refers to as 'a blurring of distinction between the observer and the observed through a shift to an immersion in the experience rather than reflection on the experience.'

Bolt (2012) argues that 'discomfort, the shock to the senses' created by performative work, 'forces people into consideration of catastrophe'. She further argues, 'If we don't create discomfort, we don't create movement.' Movement into other ways of considering, she suggests, is the point of performative work that addresses difficulty [From personal conference notes, November 9, 2012]. Through 'imaginative identification' [From personal conference notes, November 9, 2012], Bolt says, performative work can facilitate the temporal shift from past personal experience and narrative to wider considerations of catastrophe happening in the present. It does this by asking 'not did it happen, but is it happening' (Bolt 2012).

This book, this autoethnographic research, is the germination of the seed of gendered sexual violence buried in the soil of my childhood in 1971. The journal and poetic writings that appeared not only in this chapter, but appear throughout the book, are the tendrils of knowing that have emerged, and continue to emerge, through the germination of that seed. They document the pernicious growth of my rape aftermath story to confirm not only that the experience of childhood rape did happen, but also, that the somatic aftermath of this experience is still indeed happening.

CHAPTER TEN

Coming to knowing through writing-as-inquiry

> Questions without answers must be asked very slowly.
>
> — ANNE MICHAELS[1]

> Writing is a full-bodied, sensory, immersive activity that asks me to give myself over to phenomena, that calls forth deep joy and deep sorrow sometimes so profound that I am gutted by my inadequacy. I am pierced, dumbstruck. Lyric language is the crayon I use, and poetry is my secular compunction.
>
> — LORRI NEILSEN GLENN[2]

> We gather textures and threads and fabrics of being and shape them in our own time and place into something we hope is deep and sustaining: ties of human interaction with self, other, the material world, the planet, and spirit.
>
> — LORRI NEILSEN GLENN[3]

This chapter continues the unfolding of the methodological framework behind my research. The method revealed here, writing-as-inquiry, offered rich ground for the facilitation of embodied and creative autoethnographic inquiry. Through an immersion in journal and lyrical forms of writing, as well as through the performance-making-as-inquiry process which follows

1 From: Michaels, Anne (1997). *Fugitive Pieces*. London: Bloomsbury Publishing (159).
2 From: Neilsen Glenn, Lorri (2011). *Threading Light: Explorations in Loss and Poetry*. Regina, SK: Hagios Press (99).
3 From: Neilsen Glenn, Lorri (2011). *Threading Light: Explorations in Loss and Poetry*. Regina, SK: Hagios Press (108).

in the next chapter, it was possible to dwell deeply in the feeling space of the personal whilst also engaging reflexively with the broader social, cultural, and historical representations of sexual trauma. The chapter begins with a lyrical exploration of my use of writing to engage deeply with embodied process and follows with a discussion of the use of metaphor to access linguistically-challenging somatic understandings. Drawing on the work of women writers such as Virginia Woolf, Susan Sontag and others, the chapter then moves into discussion of journal writing as an embodied method of inquiry. The chapter closes with a series of journal extracts to illustrate the ways in which writing offers a liberating space of exploration for reflexive engagement in embodied knowledge-making practices.

***

In my hunger for understanding, I take my time.

I lower my gaze and turn my plate to view the shapes of the questions from every angle. Some I feel I've tasted before. They glint with seduction. I'm drawn to them. They look delicious. But I'm wary. Not all is what it seems. They have a suspicious translucence. I don't trust them. Others are dark, formless, amoeboid. They wobble and mutate before my eyes, change colour, texture, shape. The mystery of their uncertainty is enticing. A few mobilise, slide across my plate. I stab at them to hold them in place. They elude me, drop to the floor. I let them be. I lower my nose. Close my eyes. Pungent smells fill my nostrils, metallic, sharp, sour, sickly sweet, raw. I breathe them in. They seem ancient, yet new to me. I want to taste. Saliva floods my mouth. I scoop one up. The sharp bitterness of conundrum stings my tongue. My lips swell in allergic reaction but still I'm compelled to swallow. I'm filled with the heat of uncertainty. My skin crawls. A rash of ambiguity surfaces, spreads across my face, down my body. Welts and blisters erupt, weep with opacity. I scratch, endlessly. Dark blood accumulates beneath my nails. I pick at the crust that forms across failed attempts at clarity. I am consumed by the tantalising quest for answers. The rare smell of lucidity makes me hungry. I am obese from the need for more. Greed fills my belly by day, my dreams by night. I am insatiable. I cannot stop! I pursue doggedly and relentlessly. More! More! Until I heave up an answer. A projectile of insight lands on the plate of my journal. I'm astonished at its appearance. I take the knife of my pen, cut the fat from it. I slice it into delicate pieces. Saliva again floods my mouth, oozes from between my swollen lips. I open my jaw wide, spoon in the slivers of perception. I chew with care. I swallow with satisfaction. I slowly digest.

I write my way into knowing.

***

I argue that by writing my way into knowing through language that engages deeply with metaphor to reach new meaning subjectively and tangentially, I am honouring the embodied process that supports this kind of arrival at understanding. Neilsen Glenn (2008, 98) argues that writing forms which engage poetic language 'can be a transgressive and powerful tool, especially for women and others who prefer to write outside rationalist forms of language.' She observes however, that within the academic domain, 'expressive and poetic writing is often dismissed as "merely subjective".' I argue that by its very nature, subjective forms of writing and inquiry are grounded in the material and consequently, are rich sources of experiential understanding. For this reason, these forms are also, as Neilsen Glenn argues, 'political'. In this way, the use of poetic writing that engages with metaphor offers readers the opportunity for an embodied, aesthetic, and empathic encounter with the often confronting field of rape trauma research.

My journal was my close companion for the duration of my research. Writing was my 'aesthetic/epistemic praxis' (2009) and my way of coming to knowing through 'embodied theorizing' (Spry 2009, 604). I turned to my journal to write responses to the writing of others, to explore kernels of ideas, develop slender thoughts, delve into intuitive hunches, experiment with creativity, and wrestle with difficulty. I used it to jot down single words that sang to me, quotes from favourite books, lines from poetry, images that had stayed with me from performances I had attended, artwork that had resonated. It holds my delight in the research process, my biggest irritations, the many paradoxes revealed, my fears, my vulnerabilities, my most memorable dreams. My journal provided a reliable, safe and intimate place of return, a haven from the eyes of others, a place of seclusion and privacy where I could berate myself, wrestle with and shout at the world, give in to grief, rejoice in pleasure, rest, gather myself, stretch, yawn, re-energise. It was a place where I re-shaped my self-perception, re-visioned my place in the world, developed 'a feel for my own work' (Mairs 1994, 33), and found my voice as a researcher and a writer. All of the writing in my journal, every word, helped me negotiate my way through the personal, sociocultural, political, and historical landscapes and complexities of my sexual trauma research. My journal holds one hundred and thirty-eight thousand words.

***

My doctoral thesis, my journal, my poetic writing, and the chapters of this book are grounded in, and emerged from an aesthetic sensibility. Metaphor, in particular, helped facilitate the unfolding of my somatic knowing. Metaphor was a means of grasping hold of wisps of elusive experience, a way to hold myself in feeling that sometimes refused to linger. It reminded me, that as we rub shoulders with experience and try to link arms with language, the beauty of metaphor is its constantly evolving shape, the certainty that the relationship we have to the words one day can be, will be, different to the next. Lorri Neilsen Glenn (2011, 119) observes the Western tendency towards immutability in meaning-making 'and our continual dismissal and disregard of mystery and unknowing.' She argues 'Metaphorical thinking, as Jan Zwicky points out, is the leap than can be an antidote to such fixity: "when meaning holds still long enough to get its picture taken, [...], it is dead."' In this research, metaphor has been a means to 'expand and deepen meaning' (Spry 2011, 148), to illuminate and amplify understanding through viscerally evocative and descriptive language without consigning meaning to states of immobility. And finally, metaphor was useful as an embodied pedagogical aid for the transmission of my somatic knowing to others.

In her novel Sorry, Gail Jones (2007, 199) writes of the new 'dimension of communication' her protagonist, Perdita, discovers when she is introduced to the embodied vocabulary of sign language: 'There were meanings that could exist only in sign, connotations for which only the inventive body and a gestural repertoire sufficed.' During my research process, somatically-held trauma memory and bodily responses to it were extraordinarily difficult for me to articulate. Autoethnographically, metaphor acted as 'a device of memory' (Cook 2000, 18) to animate my trauma memory through the use of creative language more connected to my body than more conventional forms. It served as a form of gestural repertoire and provided me with a means of transmitting my knowing through a sideways manoeuvre, expressing what I could not articulate directly by approaching from an angle.[4] Sophie Tamas (2009, 23) says she continues to write about trauma 'because words are my least dangerous ways of speaking. But what I need is a language that both shows and tells [...] I need to speak from within that which I purport to describe'.

Not all my writing has been richly metaphoric. At times it's bare and spare when the remembering and expression of feelings of pain, grief, and fear has overridden attempts at more ornate forms of expression. Stripping language down and isolating the sparseness of experience in these ways was nonetheless equally as transformative as my use of metaphor. I offer now, three poems as examples of how the poetic form was a liberating writing technique throughout my life/research and a powerful and evocative mode of inquiry, expression, and communication. The first poem, 'Unnamed', I originally wrote from the perspective of my 'frozen' shoulder.[5] When I read this back to myself some days after its completion, I realised that what I had written related equally to my 'frozen' rape aftermath experience. The second poem, 'Fragmented Woman', I wrote following a private Body-Mind Centering session with Alice in January, 2011. Alice had been guiding me to help locate my centre of gravity, as well as find greater strength and

4 I borrow this concept from Lekkie Hopkins and her unpublished poem which begins: 'The best way for me to approach a poem is sideways' (2010).

5 'Frozen shoulder' is the lay term given to the inflammation of the shoulder capsule. The inflammation causes stiffness and immobility. It is most common in women, and most often those over forty years of age. (<http://medical-dictionary.thefreedictionary.com/frozen+shoulder>). From mid-2010, for a period of almost eighteen months, my left shoulder was indeed 'frozen'. I was unable to move it without intense pain.

autonomy through my pelvis, legs and feet, all areas of my body impacted on by my unresolved trauma. Alice used a large, hand-held mirror in front of me so I could see, as well as feel, the bodily changes I was making. The mirror moved about in Alice's hands as she talked. In my reflection, I saw myself as a series of fractured, flighty images. These images perfectly captured and symbolised the persistent, fragmented and detached states I had experienced since my childhood trauma. These shards of self were reprised through projected image during the performance of *aperture*. The final poem, 'rape', is a contemporary, graphic, lyrical, and sensorial remembering of my first rape experience in 1971.

Unnamed

I am frozen
I cannot move

Stillness buries pain deep within me
I cannot shake it off
Pain seeps from my centre
Through slender pathways

It cannot be seen

I long to move
I ache to move
I am inflamed with desire
For movement
And yet
The effort and skill required
Is beyond me

I am frozen
I cannot move

(BD 2010)

Fragmented Woman

She slides into view
Fleeting presence
Picasso image
Exposed foot
Angled knee
Timid fingers

She swings out of view
Escapes to nowhere
Land of absence
Island of denial
Empty sky space
Cloud of dreams

She pieces herself together
Shards of self
Fragile fragments
Sharp edged armour
Blocking out
And locking in

(BD 2011)

rape

she's jolted awake
can't breathe
a rough, strong hand
clamps down on her
covering her face
forcing her mouth shut
half blocking her nose
the weight of the hand
presses her head
into the pillow
she shakes it from side to side
tries to pull the hand away
it presses harder
mashes her lips against her teeth
he's pulling at her pyjama pants
she's terrified
struggles with her hands
her body sparks with terror
she wants to cry out
the hand prevents her
his hot breath fills her ear
her throat feels full
thick with fear
his tongue forces its way
past her teeth.
she feels utter disgust
wants to vomit
her body buried under his body
his weight presses on her
movement is impossible
his choking tongue persists
he forces her thighs apart
terrified eyes are wide open
Something pushes at her
between her legs
painful
insistent

pushing, pushing
the tongue fills her mouth
his weight crushes
the pain is too much
she still can't breathe properly

night air floods her mouth
her body feels weightless
he is gone
stickiness oozes and congeals
between her legs

(BD 2011)

How did I write my way into knowing? Although I've spent a lifetime writing my way into knowing, I have only recently, through this research project, come to name it an experiential, embodied, and poetic process. In the past, during times when I've been in states of difficulty or states of elation, I've turned to writing poetry or in a journal to try and capture and explore the ephemerality or powerfully solid presence of what I've been feeling in my body. May Sarton (1973, 41), novelist, poet, and lifetime journal writer, says she wrote 'novels to find out what I thought about something and poems to find out what I felt about something'. For me, writing is an embodied practice, not simply the placement of words on a page. It is in the 'doing' and 'feeling' of writing, the mulling, the literal and metaphorical moving around of feeling responses, ideas, thoughts, and images through my bodymind, that I 'make the world make sense' (Mairs 1994, 36). When my writing is not anchored in embodiment, it drifts around me, the pain of hauling the words onto the page is excruciating. When I write in collaboration with my bodymind, when the words emerge from my feeling states and intuition, they often feel effortless. If I let them roll out without intervention, the understandings that arrive in me seem as though they've been there all along. Virginia Woolf, who kept a diary/journal from 1915 until four days before her death in 1941, wrote the following in January, 1919:

> I have just re-read my year's diary and am much struck by the rapid haphazard gallop at which it swings along, sometimes indeed jerking, almost intolerably over cobbles. Still, if it were not written rather faster than the fastest type-writing, if I stopped and took thought, it would never be written at all; and the advantage of the method is that it sweeps up accidentally several stray matters which I should exclude if I hesitated, but which are the diamonds of the dustheap. (7)

When Woolf talks of writing *faster that the fastest type-writing*, and, *if I stopped and took thought, it would never get written at all*, it suggests to me that what she is experiencing here are the occasions when her writing emerges from a deeply embodied place of intelligence. Cixous (1991a) is a prolific journal and notebook keeper. Susan Sontag (Rieff 2012), kept journals throughout her life, and, like Cixous (1991a), articulates the outpouring of her writing as a gift from the subconscious. In 1964, she wrote: 'I experience the writing as given to me – sometimes, almost, as dictated. I let it come, try not to interfere with it. I respect it, because it's me and yet more than me. It's personal and transpersonal, both' (Rieff 2012, 38). I argue that what lies within these writer's words is an affirmation of the corporeally constituted origins of writing and coming to knowing. Trinh T. Minh-ha (1999, 258) captures this, observing, 'It wrote itself through me. [...] We write – think and feel – (with) our entire bodies rather than (with) our minds or hearts'. Neilsen Glenn (2008, 99) suggests the use of the term 'lyric' to describe forms of writing that 'make connections among intellect, emotion, spirit, and the body', those that create an aesthetic engagement with the inquiry process itself as well as produce work that resounds with rich, sensorial language. This type of engagement, she argues, aligns itself with the sort of transgressive writing typical of l'ecriture feminine, 'writing that springs from the body' and which Cixous and Clement (1986) urge women to adopt in order to subvert masculinist and rationalist forms of dominant writing practices.

Like Woolf, when I allowed my words to gallop along, I too was conscious of sweeping up diamonds. When this happened, and new states of perception emerged, I was conscious of an alignment of the somatic and the intellectual, an embodied symbiotic state. I then imaginatively took those diamonds, moved into, around, and through them to begin to make connections between these new states of knowing and my already established cultural, historical and political understandings. These were moments, Annie

Dillard (1989, 3) notes, when 'The writing has changed, in your hands, and in a twinkling, from an expression of your notions to an epistemological tool'.

The most intensely pleasurable feature of using writing as a form of inquiry was, and remains, this transformational quality. Its most frustrating quality is its unpredictability; I could never take its presence for granted, only revel in the mystery of the moments of jouissance when my hand could barely keep up with the outpourings from my body. Often I sat down to write with nothing but a wisp of a feeling, with no idea where the writing would take me. And then I would be swept along. The writing became the wind in the sails of my travelling inquiring self. Questions would always emerge; some telescopic-like, sprouting linearly from other questions; sometimes the questions were obscurely, tangentially and slimly interconnected. Leaps of intuition fired me off in different inquiry directions, exposed me to new sights, and insights, new tastes, smells, new ways of moving through my research that were ontological and epistemological, both. The pace was often thrilling and the spontaneity immensely satisfying.

I rarely planned these travels. When I did, more often than not I failed to reach any destination and instead became immobilised in a state of inquiry paralysis, the pain of the failure and the concomitant loss of voice a reminder to return to my intuitive, organic, unrestrained, and deeply embodied writing practice. Setting writing goals risked eroding and undermining this practice. It threatened to usurp the corporeal trust I had in my body's capacity to invite understanding to the surface of my consciousness. In 1932, Gertrude Stein (1990, 112–113) wrote, 'when you write a thing it is perfectly clear and then you begin to be doubtful about it but then you read it again and lose yourself in it as when you wrote it'. This captures for me the looping path knowing takes when words snake from body-to-intellect-to-body in a process of embodied meaning-making. My interpretation of Stein's line situates her perfectly clear in her authentic and intuitive writing body and assumes that doubt enters in the shift to the intellectual analysis of the writing, almost as if a fracture occurs between the two and uncertainty sprouts from the liminal space between them. When Stein loses herself in the re-reading of the work, I perceive this as her return to the intuition-based and corporeally constituted origin of her writing where understanding is confirmed and affirmation gained. Of course, my interpretation springs from experience in my own writing practice when I've paused in my writing and viscerally felt the interruption of the embodied process as my intellect 'took over'. The momentary but temporal delay this created, was sufficient enough to interrupt the intuitive flow and I sometimes felt a strange uncertainty about what it was I was trying to say. When I allowed myself to re-enter my embodied state, the meaning returned and I continued.

Virginia Woolf (1953), May Sarton (1973), and Susan Sontag (Rieff 2012), to name but a few women writers, immersed themselves in journal writing to help bring clarity to complex and sometimes elusive thoughts, to explore feelings, as a means of critically reflecting on their own writing practices as well as those of others, to critique art and literature, and to capture the seeds of words and phrases of interest for use in future poetry, novels or essays. While I began the research with a deep mistrust of my body in other ways, I had always been able to turn to writing to keep me company through difficulty and to help bring clarity. My life-long practice of journal writing, its intimacy offering the spaciousness necessary for candid and creative expression, has always taken me into places of poetic self-reflection and self-discovery. Stephanie Dowrick (2007, 3) argues 'It is virtually impossible to write a journal and not discover more about yourself'. Writing, says Richardson (2000, 923), is 'a way of "knowing" – a method of discovery and analysis. By writing in different ways, we discover new aspects of our topic and our relationship to it. Form and content are not separable'.

My experience tells me moving and writing are not separable either. Intrinsic to my writing praxis has been my moving body. I have long felt that moving helps bring clarity but had not understood why this was, and had never had a vocabulary with which to articulate this, until my somatic inquiry phase began through the work of Body-Mind Centering with Alice. What I now understand is that my custom of taking long solitary walks along beaches or in bushland, or, more recently, moving my body in other ways in a floor practice at my home, as well as during Authentic Movement and somatisation work in studios during Body-Mind Centering workshops, helps 'integrate and embody material' (A. Cummins, personal communication, December 13, 2010) as it emerges. During workshops, Alice often says 'Let the moving make meaning' (A. Cummins, personal communication, March 7, 2011). Moving, then helps move things around at a cellular level and this, for me, always contributes to the development of clearer cognition. During my doctoral work, moving, when preceding or punctuating periods of journal or thesis writing, undoubtedly helped facilitate an embodied self-reflexivity. If I needed to work my way through ideas before writing, or if I was stuck at a writing crossroad, or worse still, a writing dead-end, moving my body through space always helped shuffle things around, breathing life and energy into immobilised and stagnant corners, and functioning as a sort of moving prelude, an active pre-writing writing in the materiality of my body.

I return now to writing as a form of inquiry and include a series of research journal extracts below as examples of coming to knowing through journal writing. They plot the evolution of my thinking over time in relation to one theme and convey the experiential meaning-making possibilities of an embodied writing methodology.

5 June, 2010

'Navel Radiation' Workshop [my first Body-Mind Centering workshop]

Alice talked about a baby's rooting reflex and how the baby will always turn away from the nipple before attaching to it. There was much discussion about this. I was troubled and didn't contribute. Instead, I sat quietly, imagining and feeling in my body what Alice was talking about, rotating my head slightly back and forth, thinking and feeling that in order to turn away from the nipple, the baby must first surely acknowledge the presence of it. In this way, the nipple (or any other object for that matter) becomes located in consciousness, it's acknowledged and considered rather than remaining unacknowledged and turned away from, or rejected.

14 January, 2013

'The Planes of Perception' residential program
Evening reflection

This morning, in the context of developmental movement patterns, we talked of the rooting reflex in a baby (the turning away of the head before the attachment to the nipple). I've been perplexed by this at previous workshops. I'm puzzled as to what evolutionary purpose is served by a behaviour that requires us to turn from the source of nurturance and sustenance before returning to it. I expressed my concerns about this to the group ... I spoke of how, in the turning away, in the suspended interval between turn and return, a space of vulnerability opens up. My anxiety about this rests in the possibility of something occurring in the space or interval during the return phase that could interrupt and hamper the attachment to the food source. What if something were to occur in that space? What if the process was interrupted? What then? In human terms, this would surely mean the potential decline of the species.

Alice asked me to personalise the question and try to understand what this question would mean in relation to my own life. I couldn't do this. I couldn't relate this to myself and my own experiences. Not in that moment. I was completely inside the possibility of species destruction. I went blank in relation to my own life; I threw up a barrier, a wall that made it impossible for me to be self-reflexive. I lost my train of thought. My brain stopped and refused to go on. I knew I needed to move my body and looked forward to the discussion ending so I could go back into the studio and move my way through her challenge.

15 January, 2013

'The Planes of Perception' residential program
Early morning reflection

I'm sitting in the kitchen at 8am; people are off preparing for the day's work. This morning I went for another long walk up the hill, quite early, 6:30 or so. I wanted to reflect on the concerns I had yesterday about the possibility of interruption in the rooting reflex. I tried to relate this concern to my own life. I wanted to find some answers by walking through Alice's suggestion so as not to carry my nagging irritation into the studio. I didn't want my confusion to get in the way of the absorption of the day's material. I was looking for some clarity where none had opened out to me yesterday.

This is what came to me as I walked in the silence of the forest and I explore more fully here:

When I chose to sleep at my childhood friend's house on those two occasions, a fracture in my life occurred. The sleepovers represent for me the points of suspension when I turned away, the rapes the moments of interruption. Afterwards, I was unable to return. I was prevented from returning to the source of nurturance (family, friends) in quite the same way. I had to become self-sufficient from that moment on. To support this I became secretive and cautious.

So, my options/choices were severely limited by my experience of interruption. I had to remain self-sufficient or suffer further. The self-sufficiency however, while allowing me to survive, came at a high cost and that cost was a body that bore the burden of my rape experience with a hyper-vigilant sensory system, a body that had no boundaries and yet had imposed and rigid boundaries, and a severely restricted geographical space of occupation. Yes, I survived the interruption but the cost was crippling and complex and the ramifications long term. This is why the possibility of interruption distresses me so much and grips me with such persistence.

23 January, 2013

'The Fluids' residential program

My exploration of the baby's rooting reflex has led me to understand that, although I had actively pursued detachment from my body for decades in order to avoid the trauma I had experienced, I must indeed have been paying very close attention during those years. After all, in order for me to disregard something, for example an object, an irritation, a thought, or even in this instance, my own body, it fits that it first surely required a certain amount of my attention to be directed towards that object, or thought, or body. If my attention or regard was not directed towards my body then how was it possible for me to constantly dis-regard it and turn away?

This insight has been critical to the evolution of my thinking and the shifting relationship I now have with my body. This realisation might not have taken place if I had not been able to cultivate a sense of awareness to my embodied experience through this BMC work and the private hands-on work with Alice. By developing the capacity to hold myself in experience and then explore this reflexively through moving and writing, I've been able to gain insight, find greater clarity, and give birth to new meaning.

***

The next chapter presents the performance-making-as-inquiry methodology. The chapter offers insight into my reasoning behind the choice of a solo autoethnographic movement performance as an additional, companion piece to my research. This writing unfolds to reveal the myriad embodied understandings that emerged during both my somatic inquiry process and the creative development phases of *aperture*, to form the substance of the performance itself. *aperture* was the creative expression of the cumulative processes engaged in during the previous three and a half years of autoethnographic somatic inquiry work. It also became the heartbeat of my research. Discussion surrounding performance-making opens the chapter. *aperture* itself is revealed through word and image in a post-performance reflection originally written as a spoken word piece. This reflection closes the chapter.

CHAPTER ELEVEN

Coming to knowing through performance-making-as-inquiry

> Performing self in front of an audience is, I would argue, the most 'foreign, scary, (seemingly) uninhabitable, but necessary' kind of performance because self is, perhaps, the most difficult text to embody.
>
> — TAMI SPRY[1]

> She lies helpless and fragmented, limbs leaden with story, forced ever further into herself by the viscous shame that suffocates and disables her. Fleshed lips cling to each other, tongue recoils from the sharp taste of the narrative of her body. Within the impotent portal of her mouth, her story sits, an impenetrable oral hymen.
>
> — BRENDA DOWNING, 2012

I brought into my doctoral research, a keen desire not only to write of the somatic aftermath of childhood rape but also an intense desire for a more multidimensional somatic and aesthetic engagement with the work of this research. I felt a written thesis, woven with the threads of embodied and poetic language, along with the addition of a performance component, as a companion piece to the thesis, could, in combination, satisfy this desire.

With the addition of a performance modality, I was convinced I could lift the words off the thesis page in order to, literally, bring the information to life. Through performance I knew I could give the bones of the written language of sexual trauma a heartbeat, a pulse, give them breath. I believed

1 From: Spry, Tami (2011). *Body, Paper, Stage: Writing and Performing Autoethnography* (171).

a performance held the potential to drape flesh on the words and pump blood through their sentences. I wanted the narrative of sexual trauma to move and sweat, collapse and stand rather than remain in stasis. I wanted the unresolved nature of silenced sexual trauma to permeate the flesh and speak with more than written language. I wanted the raped female body to be *fully* present. A performance seemed the only way to convey the multidimensionality of my muted experience.

'Performance is a promissory act,' Della Pollock (2005, 2) tells us, 'Not because it can promise possible change but because it catches its participants – often by surprise – in a contract with possibility: with imagining what might be, could be, should be'. Tami Spry (2011, 126) calls this dialogical engagement with an audience, 'collaborative meaning-making'. I felt certain that I could create for an audience Pollock's *contract with possibility*. I believed that through a performance modality a portal would open to the reality of how it is to live with silenced and unresolved sexual trauma. Beyond that portal an invitation would await for others to engage collaboratively with the difficulties and compromises of this reality through embodied imagination and somatic empathy. A performance, I felt, could act as a physical, emotional, and intellectual bridge of communication between those who have experienced sexual violence and those who have not. As Spry (2011, 170) notes, 'Words can construct, but cannot hold the weight of the body'. The words of my thesis then would construct and speak my story as well as shape my research but a performance would hold the weight of my flesh in the embodied articulation of my story.

In addition to her Body-Mind Centering practice, Alice Cummins is also a dance artist and performer. Alongside our continuing therapeutic relationship, in June, 2010, Alice agreed to collaborate with me as artistic director on the development of the solo performance piece, *aperture*. We began the first of three, two-week phases of creative development in September, 2011 at The Blue Room Theatre in Perth, Western Australia. In May, 2012, I travelled to Victoria for the second phase at three studios: Melbourne's Dancehouse; Alice's George St Studio in Fitzroy, Melbourne; and her Riddells Creek studio in country Victoria. The final phase, culminating in the performance of *aperture* to an invited audience, took place at The Chapel Space, in Perth in September, 2012.

Although the performance of *aperture* was not for examination, the understandings that I arrived at through the making and performing were crucial and form the crux of my research. Spry (2011, 28–29) articulates clearly the contribution performative work can make to the autoethnographic academic endeavour. When embarking on this method of research, Spry argues that 'performance is not an added scholarly bonus. It does not operate as an interesting feature or entertaining option [...] performance does not "illuminate" the text, rather it assists in the creation of the text; it is in itself performative.'

***

In order to realise my embodied story and perform that story well, I first needed to build my capacity to be 'present'. Alice (2013) notes that, 'Without Brenda developing the capacity and endurance to be "present", we could not have found a vocabulary that might unearth and express her story through embodied performance making.' In order for my body 'voice' to be heard through a somatic narrative, Alice maintained that presence was necessary for me to 'be able to access the intelligence and imaginary life of her [my] body ... to make, to grasp, to reveal her [my] experience' (2013). During private sessions with Alice prior to the first creative development phase in the studio, and as a result of extensive periods of both hands-on work using cellular touch and Authentic Movement, I was able to build the capacity and resilience to sustain an embodied presence and to remain present to my embodied story. This was crucial body-focused work, crucial not only for the therapeutic re-integration of my rape aftermath experience but also, in performance terms, for the enablement of deep excavation of my experience and for the refined physically creative expression of this in the performance space.

During the three creative development phases, we spent many hours in the studio continuing to use Authentic Movement as a means of accessing the many layers of my story. As I moved from 'the experiential ground of my trauma' (A. Cummins, personal communication, September 19, 2011), Alice (2013) witnessed me, following 'the nuance of somatic response' in her own body as she engaged with the depth and intimacy of my closely held story. As my somatic narratives emerged, Alice followed these often fragmented articulations through and with her bodymind playing them back to me through language and occasionally movement. We gave time after Authentic Movement explorations and throughout the rehearsal day for spontaneous moving, writing, and conversation to further explore and discuss the abundant material that emerged, weaving personal experience with the wider cultural story of rape with the feminist ethics and theory that informs, shapes, and supports each of our lives.

Given my ongoing struggle to find a written vocabulary subtle enough to articulate the bodily manifestation of my trauma experience, the shift to the studio, and into a movement-based form of expression, was a liberating experience. It enabled me to step into a non-verbal mode of expression to access the many 'feeling' elements of my story which were beyond language but still able to be accessed in my body and articulated through movement. Spry (2010, 509) suggests it is through performance that 'words make flesh'. During my immersion in a predominately non-verbal performance mode, using forms of embodied creative inquiry such as Authentic Movement, it was not only words that made flesh, but crucially, also my cellular responses to rape and its aftermath, mined and articulated through my moving body. This was a clear realisation during the creative development phases in the studio, as my experiential and cellular knowing percolated through me and became externally and spontaneously expressed through my moving body, when embodied and non-verbal articulation replaced linguistic articulation, and when the semiotic was given precedence over the semantic.

> *19 September, 2011*
>
> *There was little need for words because my body had a movement vocabulary all its own that spoke more than any recognisable verbal language could possibly say.*

While the shift to a movement-based form of articulation provided relief from the struggle to express my somatic narrative through words, I took with me into the early creative development phase another struggle. For those who witnessed *aperture*, my predominately non-verbal moving body was the focus of the piece and the 'raw data' (Spry 2010, 501) for the audience to engage with reflexively, through critique, and with analysis. While the collaborative motivation in the studio was to make a powerful work that was socioculturally transgressive to graphically expose the stark and confronting reality of lived experience precisely in order to render it impossible to ignore, I was also aware of the personal risks involved in this exposure. Although driven to have the work generate discussion, and aiming to implicitly locate the work within a wider cultural and discursive context, it was still my body and my story under the full glare of lighting in the performance space. I was deeply conscious of what was at stake by choosing to expose myself in this way, not least, the potential for being viewed as 'abject, abnormal, unsociable, unruly' (Spry 2011, 170). This stirred feelings of vulnerability that lurked in the shadows of my commitment.

The autoethnographic performance research of Spry (2011) once again gave me guidance. Spry developed the terms 'performative-I', 'performative-I disposition', and 'performative-I persona' (28). She uses these terms to identify and name the series of stages of becoming the autoethnographic researcher-performer moves between and through when interpreting and negotiating experiential knowledge, cultural context, and linguistic representation, while seeking to embody the persona that emerges in performance. In relation to the 'performative-I' and the 'performative-I disposition', Spry writes:

> The performative-I is the positionality of the researcher in performative autoethnography and is based in a negotiation between self/other/culture/language, a system of relation between body/I/we/word. Through a performative-I disposition, the researcher constructs a story of her critical engagement with others in culture [...] by identifying and critically reflecting upon a particular personal experience intersecting the politics of culture. This performative-I disposition is founded in the ethical check and balance of agency (the empowerment of telling one's story) and representation (the sociocultural responsibility of telling one's story). (30)

Spry (2011) argues the 'performative-I persona' is the position the autoethnographer seeks through self/text, critical reflection, and embodied rehearsal, which lead eventually to autoethnographic performance. Spry stresses that the process of embodying a performative-I persona refuses linearity and stasis by creating a Mobius-like looping negotiation that moves between 'the writing, rehearsal, and performance process', in a movement dynamic that 'is always turning in on itself, looking forward and back, being transformed by the constant conversation of being and becoming' (176). This fluidity and reflective exchange was particularly apparent during the final rehearsal phase in the days leading up to the performance of *aperture*. While the material I was intending to embody in performance was choreographically and chronologically clear by this stage, I was nonetheless aware my moving self was influenced on the day, in the hour, in the moment, by whatever I bought with me into the rehearsal space. Through Spry's words, affirmation of this as integral to the process, was timely and gave me the confidence to soften into the necessarily temporally and contextually-dependent improvisational aspect of autoethnographic rehearsal and live performance.

In relation to my concerns about my story and my body being viewed as abnormally 'other', Spry (2011, 167) allayed my concerns by introducing me to the concept of 'practiced vulnerability'. She describes this as 'a methodology of moving out of one's comfort zone of familiarity, a strategic surrendering into a space of risk, of uncomfortability, of uncertainty that one experiences when critically reflecting upon and then embodying one's own experience.' Practiced vulnerability, Spry argues, does not leave the performer exposed but rather can offer a space of empowerment through reflexivity and 'letting go' (168). She states:

> Letting go and metaphorically presented bare constitutes an expansion of self into the autoethnographic text; it is the threshold into the textualizing body where body, paper, and stage animate one another expanding the epistemological possibilities of performative autoethnography. (168)

Further allaying my concerns, drawing on the work of Wallace Bacon (1979), Spry (2011, 175), emphasises that the autoethnographic body in performance is not a 'container' for the expression of the autoethnographic story but rather the body participates in meaning-making through an experiential and material presence that is culturally challenging and epistemologically relevant. This ethics of embodiment reinforced the onto-epistemic value I placed on my body as well as reminding me of my body's performative capacity to act in ways resistant to sociocultural norms.

In addition to the skilled guidance of Alice, Spry's concept of moving through these multiple positionings of self was extremely useful as I negotiated the transition from desk to rehearsal space, from autoethnographic writer to autoethnographic performer, all the while juggling the desire to offer my body/story for public reflection with the acknowledgement of the risks involved. The concept gave me room to breathe as I moved between the 'I' at the desk, the 'I' in the rehearsal studio, and the 'I' in the performance space. It allowed me to develop some cushioning fat to soften and minimalise the risk as I made room between these 'I's' and transitioned to a state of being 'twice removed [from experience] – once through writing and again through performance' (Spry 2011, 173).

***

During an afternoon of improvisation in the studio prior to the first creative development phase, at Alice's suggestion, I worked with a blanket. Alice gave me no direction, merely asked me to 'play with it', to see what emerged.

13 April, 2011

George St studio, Fitzroy, Melbourne

I stood, picked up the soft grey blanket and wrapped it about me. As I moved I pulled the blanket, stretching it with my arms and legs. I eventually came down to lie on the floor with the blanket completely covering me and with just an edge of it tucked under my head to secure it in place and give some resistance to my movement. I pushed my arms up from beneath the blanket, pressed the palms of my hands flat in a gesture of defence. I gripped the fabric with my fingers and twisted and clawed at it. I brought my legs into the movement, bent and flexed them and extended my feet to form embodied peaks beneath the fabric. I took my arms out from underneath the blanket and pulled the fabric down over my face like a mask. I smoothed the fabric over my face, opened my mouth, tilted my head back and arched my body slightly; I ran my hands slowly over my covered face and hair. I became completely absorbed in the improvisation of what I was doing. I wrapped the blanket around and around my right fist until it was the size of a large ball, then I raised it above me and held it suspended over my face. I held it there for some time then tugged my hand out and allowed the blanket to fall into folds over me. My movements were slow and measured. I'm not sure where they came from. I certainly had no awareness of consciously choreographing the movement. The movements and the shapes I was making simply arrived in me, in the creative space of me, and in the intersubjective space between Alice and me, and I was compelled to follow them.

In just one afternoon in the studio, through my moving body and across the intersubjective space between us, Alice had witnessed and felt a fragmented and embodied realisation of several elements of my story. These embodied fragments captured the sense of invisibility I cultivated in order to keep my story secret; the struggle to free myself from the weight of my trauma memory; the silent scream that choked me; and the image of the perpetrator's body suspended over me which haunts my nightmares and terrifies me. This early creative and improvisational work was significant and helped form the ground for the later phases. I continued to work with the blanket. It became a feature of the performance, absorbing my embodied story in its weave. Somerville (1999, 151) talks of how a blanket is 'often the first object of desire that makes the transition between child, mother, and outside world'. As well as a reference to childhood, the blanket in performance became many things. It transformed from a crumpled and innocuous heap into a heavy shroud of shame; from a childhood bed and place of safety and dreaming to the nightmare of a hovering perpetrator; from a rejected lover to the birth of new life. It helped effect transitions from states of deep maternal and passionate love to ones of profound self-disgust, despair and hopelessness. The blanket became a weapon, a place of mystery, a cleaning cloth. It became a place in which to hide, a place in which to find myself, a place to cultivate agency. It symbolised the permeable membrane that is the liminal space between self and other, between the feeling self and others, between self and culture, the porous tissue through which the blood and tears of experience seeped, and through which meaning flowed. It represented the smothering potential of phallocentric discourse and the cultural silencing that refuses to hear the stories of rape, diminishing the bodies of girls and women as a result. The boundless transformative possibilities the blanket presented helped facilitate the imaginative embodiment of many of the disturbing fragments of my story. It helped re-contextualise each moment/movement of my body's narrative.

My moving, feeling, experienced, and knowing body articulated many facets of my personal story in performance, but *aperture* also helped create an opening for the wider story of rape in our culture to slide alongside my own. And it made room for the feminist theory that sat so deeply in Alice's life and in my own, enabling theory and reality to co-mingle. *aperture* reflected my desire to take the personal and make it political and for this reason, the work was multidimensional and multi-layered. It was creatively conceptualised with subtlety and nuance in mind. Through a series of fragments or shards of experience, we were conscious of attempting to mirror the incoherence, the fragmentation, and the ephemerality of my experience to 'reveal elusive states that you were left in, abandoned in, we are alluding to something' (A Cummins, personal communication, April 15, 2012). Their emergence in the improvisational work was echoed in the final performance as not only a series of clashing vignettes but also a series of projections of shattered images taken from photographs of me across my lifetime.

***

The final section of this chapter is the distillation of a reflection written several days after the performance of *aperture*. The writing emerged at a time when my body still resonated with the visceral stimulation of live performance and still held the choreographic score for the work. The images, added to sit alongside and enhance the words, are stills taken from the video recording of the performance.

The writing and images combine to present the findings of my autoethnographic somatic inquiry and performance-making work as well as the new knowledges that arose as a result. They are the creative coming together of the ontological and the epistemological. They are the culmination of a three and a half year period of intensive exploration of my body at a micro cellular level and at a macro sociocultural, philosophical, and discursive level. Implicit in the words and images is the feminist theory that informs this research and the feminist embodied ethics that supports the life lived beyond the page and beyond the performance space.

The making and performance of *aperture* was the flesh to the forensic examination of the bones of my life narrative. Through my predominately non-verbal moving body, *aperture* creatively revealed the raped body to be a site of intelligence, an archival holding place for memory, a communicator of unresolved trauma, a site of resistance, and a disseminator of trauma narrative through performance.

***

aperture: a post-performance reflection

Waiting in the green room

The sound of the audience gathering beyond the doors: women's voices, conversation, occasional laughter, a palpable air of expectancy

Humming to myself, moving my body, a dance of constant motion, steadying my nerves, keeping warm, calming myself, gathering my resources

Looking into the huge mirror opposite, grinning at the improbability of what I was about to do, the realisation of a long-held vision, a sense of surrealism in the anticipation

Alice coming to check on me at regular intervals … fifteen minutes … ten minutes … five minutes …

Rising up and down on my toes, holding my position on 'stiletto heels', feeling the weight of my story on the balls of my feet

Allowing the score to sit in my body quietly, letting my mind drift but remaining connected to the present, allowing trust to filter throughout my body, firmly grounded in the rehearsal preparation, the storying and embodiment of the deeply known

Two minutes … my belly fizzing … this is it, almost time, after a year of time, after a life time

A last look in the mirror, seeing clearly the face of the 1971 school girl. Whispering: 'This is for you'

Alice coming to get me. *It's all yours*. A look. A smile

Ready

I'm ready

Standing outside the performance space, waiting, the audience settling, Anouar Brahem music and stage lighting slowly fading, my heart pounding

The plunge into an abyss of silence and darkness

A shift from inner to outer, from the sensory experience of the rape of me, to the aftermath, to the storying of the rape of me, to the performance of the story of me, to the stories of raped women everywhere, from the personal to the political

Pumping bass noise.[2] One minute of throbbing, relentless sound, increasing in volume and intensity, filling ears, vibrations of sound shuddering up through the floor, working their way up the body, cacophonous noise disturbing, energising, wanting it to stop, wanting it to continue

Sudden deafening silence

The tiny pen light guiding into the darkness ... one ... two ... three steps ... pause. Wanting to suspend time, hold this moment forever, a thrilling and terrifying moment, the beginning of something after the end of something else, past, present and future conflating in those first steps

Silhouettes of seated women waiting. Feeling the collective. Feeling the individual. Watching, open, expectant

The pen light a curious creature illuminating, moving slowly through the space, examining, familiar structural elements now strange, unknown; cloth, metal, brick, wood, seeing them for the first time

Finding the crumpled blanket at the foot of the pole, resting inanimate in the corner. Approaching, draping the blanket over upper body, covering head and face, turning slowly, sliding body down the pole to squatting, yellow beam of stage light stroking the floor, body caught in its surveillance

2 In the creative development phase at The Blue Room in 2011, Alice and I were discussing how some people in Western cultures observe a one minute silence in respect of fallen soldiers. Alice wondered what it might be like to open the performance with one minute of loud, discordant sound in respect of raped women. I immediately thought of the Karyn L. Freedman quote found on 43. A minute of unsettling sound was perfect.

Fragment: *Power struggle*

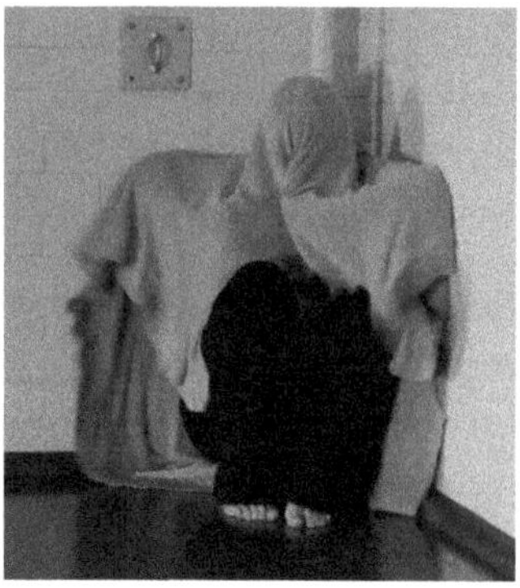

Sharp intake of breath, arms flailing for support, pressing into the floor with legs, trying to rise, the hand of patriarchy, cultural silencing pushing down, down, struggling against it, rising, down, rising, down, down, down, body horizontal on the floor, legs splayed, head propped awkwardly against the pole, yellow beam of light spilling over legs, pubis, torso, vulnerability on display, exposed, an unavoidable image

Fragment: *Peering out from rape*

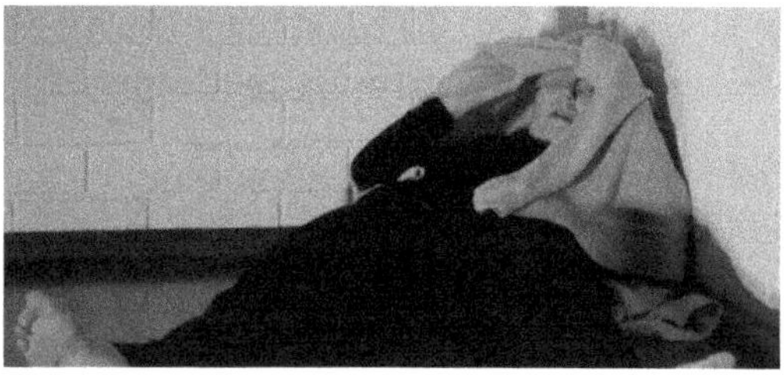

Uncovering my face, looking out, inert pelvis, lifeless legs, lower body immobilised, defended, defeated, powerless, dragging fragmented presence, hauling body to sitting with arms, staccato breath, whimpering voice, choking throat full of experience

Fragment: *The descent into shame*

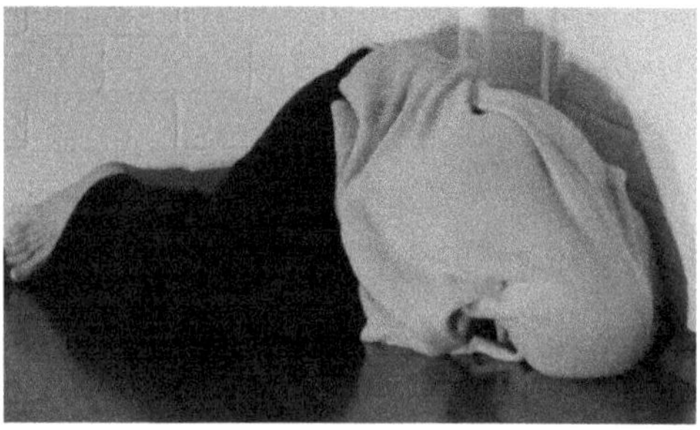

Foetal curl of body on floor, flesh rising to sitting in its shroud, turned face to the corner, loss of face, hidden shame, blanketed voice. Full weight of body/memory in hands, gripping the pole, pulling to upright, restoring

respectability, leaving memory behind, survival, deep breath, deeper breath, turning body downstage, here I am, almost, but not quite, not quite whole, me, not quite me, something familiar, something strange, changed, not the same, same path, different rules

Fragment: *The bed*

Make your bed, lie in it. Under the cloth, another kind of shroud, escape, safety, veiling history. Humming, train whistle blowing up from early childhood, stroking the cloth, hands, elbows, knees, feet, playing, creating shapes, lost in reverie, temporal and spatial starlit sky, place of dreams

Fragment: *The altar of female sacrifice*

Body contorts, Kath Kollwitz 'Rape'[3] position, right arm detaches itself,

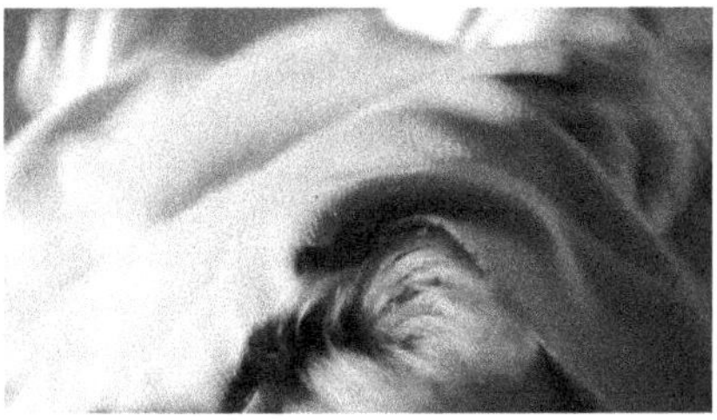

emerges from blanket, hand clamps down hard on mouth, wild struggle, thrashing head, legs flailing, body arching, left arm tugging, suffocating darkness, choking fear, long silent scream, recurrent nightmare, nocturnal companion

Fragment: *The hovering perpetrator*

Suspended above face, large, terrifying, powerful, threatening, body small, vulnerability huge, gripping the memory/threat, rolling, rolling, rolling downstage, surge of energy/

3 This refers to Kath Kollwitz's 1907 lithograph, *Rape*.

fear/anger propelling body, coming to rest, belly flat to the floor, legs splayed behind, lungs exploding

Fragment: *The lover*

Softening body, muscles of jaw, quietened breath, lowering face, parting lips, moment of passion ... scrape of memory, body retracts, detaches, recoils, disgust swamping mouth, violently pushing lover away

Fragment: *New life*

Scrubbing legs, frantic, trying to erase disgust, trying to rid flesh of memory, tumbling the blanket between thighs, knees, spiralling the baby up from between legs, into arms, maternal love flooding body, expanding heart, the miracle of birth, new life, innocence ... rasp of memory, temporal distortion, despair, hopelessness, helplessness, a child attempting to care for a child, dragging presence of trauma pulling, weakening, confusing, pressing further into the past

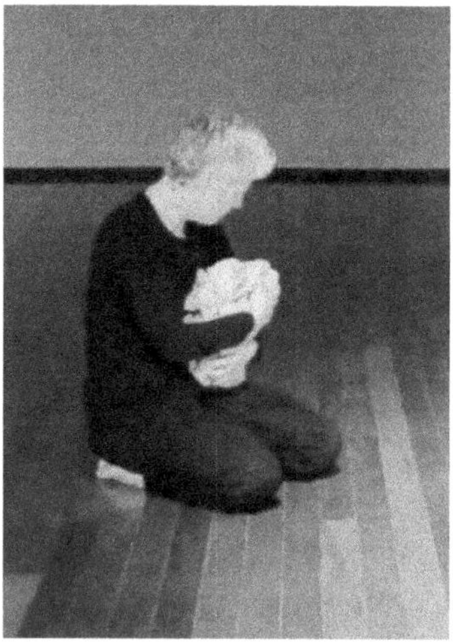

Fragment: *Where have I gone?*

Lost to myself, here but not here. What will I find if I go looking? Visceral attraction, magnetising, I can't resist, gingerly lifting the edges of myself, trepidation at what lurks in folds of memory, the inevitability of the known, the terror of the ignored. Too much to endure, not ready

for it yet. The desire to regain control swells, gathers strength, scrubbing where memories erupted, erasing, wiping away so no trace remains, keeping it un-seen. The control, the strength, the empowerment of domination brings me to standing, trapping memory under determined feet

Fragment: *Tucking myself away*

Madness bleeding into life, bruised words, incoherent, coherent, reminding body/life/memory of who's in command, strong feet keeping waywardness at bay, the mind assaulting, fearful, the body passive victim, another violation, another kind of assault, food withdrawal, deprivation of love, starvation

Fragment: *Fuck you!*

No voice, silent mouth, lips sealed, cells fighting to speak, anger oozing from pores, the unspoken choking, twisting nerve fibres, cramping viscera.

My eyes shouting: Fuck you betraying body! You got me into this! Fuck you rapists! Don't destroy, turn away, stride off without a backward glance holding innocence in your sweaty hand! Fuck you all who turn their backs! Don't silence raped women with your closed eyes, your deaf ears!

Fragment: *A mirror, lipstick and stilettoes*

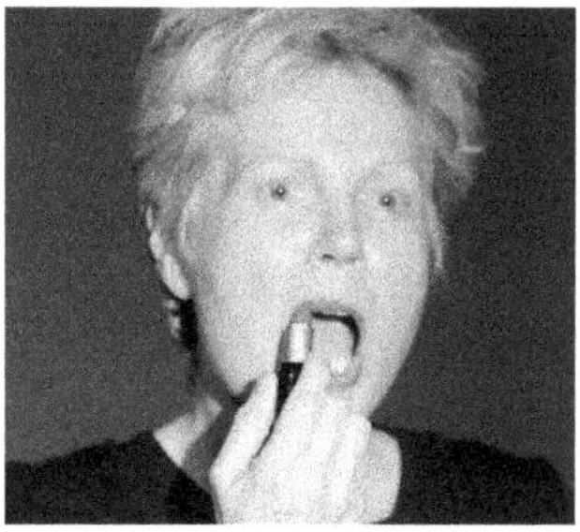

Turning to gaze, curiosity ignited, body softened. Who do I see? What do I feel as I cast my eyes over the image before me? Who is this woman in the mirror who still feels a child? How do I reconcile what I feel with what I see? How do I make room for myself in this woman's body? Why does this child refuse to leave? How do I reclaim missing years? How do I reconcile loss? How can I renegotiate a path to maturity? Fetid madness rots and decays, attempts to find answers exhausts, creates vertigo states. And, then, miraculously, another construction of respectability. Finding strength in the trappings of normality, strength in the mask of coping, a red slick of colour for courage, a pair of heels to elevate self-esteem, borderline parody, the tragedy of the superficial, the resilience found there, paradoxical, the performance of what's expected suppressing inner turmoil, the performance of this expectation impossible to resist, even harder to negotiate, suffocating memory under an oily veneer of red.

Fragment: *The fall*

Difficult to balance, exhausted body, the fulcrum shifted, struggle unsupported, the performance of coping teetering, brittle, a precarious fragile existence, finding strength, regrouping, endlessly, all the while edging towards the precipice, the fall – inevitable, the landing – brutal

Fragment: *Catharsis*

Gathering strength with dispassionate eyes at what lies before me. A surge of bitterness meets exhaustion, knowing and understanding arrive simultaneously, grappling with the life/history/trauma memory, throwing, retrieving,

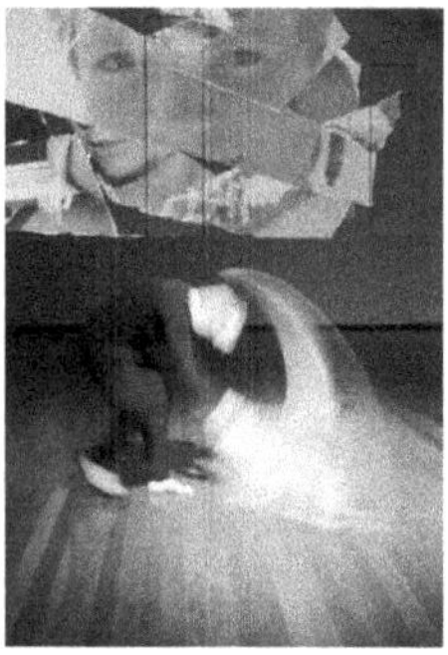

conflict stabbing my heart, the desire to be rid of it, the desire to hold it close. Resenting how it's shaped identity, fearful of what will remain if it goes. Could the letting go facilitate the moment of implosion? Create further fragmentation? Greater dis-integration? Twin desires competing, to hold/to purge, to keep/to liberate, duelling and bloody binaries fraught with fear, uncertainty, the unknown, the unknowable. Throw, gather back, throw, gather back then ... *No!* Voice escaping my distraught body, forcing its way into my mouth. *NO MORE!* The air punctuated by resistance, sound escaping in the physicality of the moment, the power of the life/history/memory diminished by every collision with the floor until, finally, it lies a discarded defeated heap, its hold released.

Fragment: *Realisation*

Spent, emptied out by the effort, the struggle, exhausted from the turbulent confrontations between the mind and the body, from carrying the weight of the life/history/memory, sinking to the floor to join it, to put it alongside, the noise of breath and pumping heart in the space between, a new understanding developing: acknowledgement of abandonment, of harsh unjustified treatment, of the need to

find stillness, to make peace, to sit in love, knowing these memories exist, will always exist, but will no longer destroy and undermine, co-existent consciousness is possible.

Fragment: *Sitting with trauma*

I reclaim my whole self in the coming together at this moment. I reclaim my agency. I re-shape my identity. I no longer need to define myself by the terms of my rape history. I am so much more than a child who was raped. I move into myself as a woman with agency, with self-respect, with compassion, with love softening memory

Fragment: *The walk back to the present*

My life passes before me, behind me, writ large for all to see. My woman's body casts a silhouette beside the nine year old image, the child yet to suffer

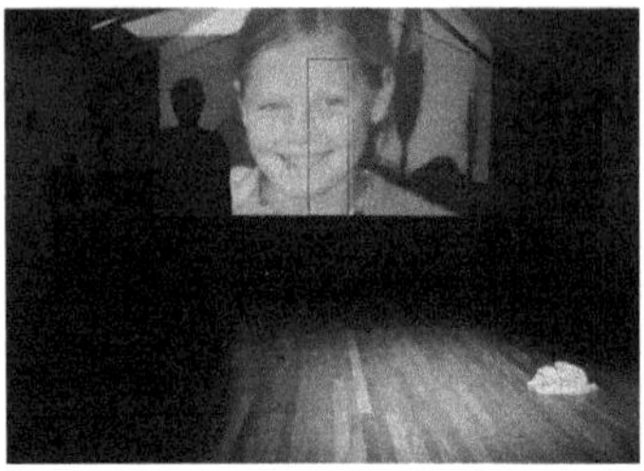

the pain and burden of rape trauma. The 1971 image appears, the school girl with her cracked and blistered lips, tired eyes, strained smile. My silhouette passes across her, I halt when she appears again, want to send her a signal to say: I'm here now. I hear you. It's alright.

Fragment: *Masking-un-masking*

A diagonal walk downstage into the pool of light, masked, confident, sure-footed, my body filled to its edges at last with story, with newly-found trust, trust in the self, trust in others to hold my story with respect, trust in the process of re-integration, and the power of love to achieve it

This is me
All of me

Observe
Feel
Imagine

I want you to see
all of me

Observe
Feel

Imagine
Ask me

Fragment: *Leaving the story behind*

A turn away. A diagonal walk back to leave the space. Silence around me, deep profound silence, not a sound.

***

This is what the silence held for me:

I sensed my story had been seen, heard, felt, and imagined.

I felt my body had told its story. My body felt acknowledged and replete. It vibrated with affirmation.

I experienced myself as complete.

And as I registered this in the silence I asked myself: *Is this an end or merely a beginning?*

CHAPTER TWELVE

Weaving the warp and weft of the aftermath of childhood rape

> Here, on the page, memory can ligate, light can be threaded and woven through darkness. What we remember can serve as both binding and bridge long after our bodies, these fragile tumbling bonehouses, have gone.
>
> — LORRI NEILSEN GLENN[1]

I opened this book with the briefest of glimpses into my experience of rape in 1971, my rejected disclosure that same year, and the combative relationship I developed with my body as a response to the trauma of that experience. As I begin this chapter and cast a retrospective eye over the five years of this project, I can see that, like Philomela, I have found ways to create a many-hued, multiply textured, and narrative-bearing cloth. The cloth I have crafted with the making of these chapters bears not only my voice and my story in its weave, but also the voices and stories of nine other raped women, and the wider story of rape violence in our culture. These pages resound with voices and stories. In this way, the text defies the familial, social, and cultural silencing that persistently acts to sever rape victim's tongues leaving their bodies colonised by limiting discourses and haunted by irrepressible and unspeakable trauma memory.

Philomela, to protect her story from the eyes of others, and simultaneously to protect herself, was forced to craft a cloth whose symbols could

1 From: Neilsen Glenn, Lorri (2011). *Threading Light: Explorations in Loss and Poetry.* Regina, SK: Hagios Press (8).

only be deciphered by her sister, Procne. I have no need now to protect my story from the eyes of others. To help facilitate the decipherability of the stories that emerged from this research, I have used readily recognisable symbols. Through the conventional forms of word and image, I have created a book that holds not only the multiple and embodied stories of the aftermath of childhood rape but one that also conveys the multidimensionality of my methodology. While my methods of coming to knowing have been deeply embodied modes of inquiry, I remain aware that the primary form I have chosen for the dissemination of my research findings – the written word – may, at times, be inadequate to the task of conveying the intensity, nuance, subtlety, and depth of feeling of my autoethnographic somatic explorations. I am conscious that, in the absence of my moving articulating body in live performance, which could at least have added another visceral, visual, and dynamic dimension, I am reliant on the performativity of my words on the page to transmit meaning. This was the risk when I undertook this research and remains a frustrating but transparent limitation. I believe this frustration stands as an example of the incompatibility of phallocentric language, which so often problematises the expression of the feminine, with feminist embodied research. As I have discussed previously, to overcome this difficulty I lapsed into poetic forms of writing and, to re-anchor myself in the corporeal ground of my research, I turned to my body and reminded myself to 'imagine every cell in my body has the potential to dialogue with all there is' (Hay 2000, 104). With the accrued experience of hands-on work with Alice, I now know this *potential to dialogue* to be a reality. At the end of this project, acknowledging my frustrations with language but refusing to feel silenced by them, I am comfortable with the knowledge that *all I can do is tell* (Cixous 1991a, 105) and, like Cixous, the rest is up to the reader. Through the interwoven threads of these chapters, which represent the 'telling', I have offered the reader the opportunity to step into the poetics and embodiment of my language, the chance for immersion in the rigor of the embodied process of inquiry that supported this project, and the invitation to enter into an imaginative, and empathic engagement with the catastrophic aftermath of childhood rape through the reader's own materiality and through the subjectivity and rigor of their own lives.

If I can return to the topic of hysteria for the moment, Kirby (1997), in relation to the 'hysteric's inscripted body' (58) and its propensity for subversive action through disturbing transformation, eloquently argues that what is so shocking about the transformation for the reader-witness is that:

> [...] within the strangeness of her embodied scripture we read something of ourselves. Reluctantly perhaps, we find ourselves inhabiting the flesh of this text and sharing the same corporeal stuff of its writing. For what is posed is the awful evidence that perhaps we are not what or where we think ourselves to be. (59)

I do not assume that the reader will have experienced sexual violence, but I do assume that the reader holds the capacity for imaginative and empathic engagement with meaning-making, and the potential, then, to inhabit *the flesh of this text*, reluctantly or otherwise. Imagination is critical to the development of empathy (hooks 1991) and each must surely be present if the desire to inhabit is also to be present. Clare Hemmings (2012, 151) notes that empathy 'foregrounds the importance of knowledge; it opens a window on the experience of others and stresses their importance for an ethical feminist epistemology.' She further notes that 'empathy prioritises embodied knowledge, affective connection and a desire to transform the social terrain' (151). This was one of my aims for this book: to offer the reader an embodied, evocative, and compelling entry point into the somatic narratives of others in order for an intellectual, somatic, and collaborative exchange to take place and for possibilities for transformation to reveal themselves. I believe I have fulfilled this task; I have crafted chapters with the potential to 'transport others to new worlds' (Thomas 2001, 274), and I have produced embodied work that moves beyond the parameters of language and discourse alone to give a 'vibrant, biologically attuned' (Wilson 2004b, 14) account of rape trauma. In doing so, I believe I have also satisfied Richardson's (2000, 924) call for qualitative research that is *vital* and *attended to*, and for texts that *make a difference*.

My investigations, this book, the creativity and rigor I have brought to both and the empathy I hope it engenders, has been my attempt at personal, social, cultural, and political transformation through the pursuit of embodied knowledges inextricably bound to the sexual violence that penetrates and insidiously permeates not only the bodies of girls and women but also the fabric of Western culture.

***

A key finding to emerge from this research, and one which challenges dominant medical and psychological discourses, is my understanding that the violence of rape registers first in the body with psychological symptoms emerging secondarily. In earlier chapters, I have identified that dominant psychological discursive constructions of rape trauma locate the aetiology of trauma within the psyche (Campbell 2002, Koss and Figueredo 2004, Ullman and Brecklin 2002). While the rape trauma literature acknowledges that aftermath disturbance can be largely a result of the experience itself (Campbell 2008), there is still a tendency to frame the trauma as primarily psychological. Even when acknowledgement is made of the physical impacts of rape, these are often restricted to the immediate physical injuries sustained during the assault (Boyd 2011) rather than to the long term micro and macro bodily manifestations that are the focus of this research. Furthermore, while Post Traumatic Stress Disorder is consistently, and appropriately, cited as a profound impact of sexual violence (Ahrens, Stansell, and Jennings 2010, Chivers-Wilson 2006, Foa and Rothbaum 1998, Najdowski and Ullman 2009, Ullman and Brecklin 2002), the bodily symptoms that lie at the heart of this condition (Rothschild 2000) are diminished by the dominant attention given to the emotional presentation.

As a direct result of the intensive body-based explorations I undertook for this project, I have developed an embodied consciousness; an increased sensitivity to, and awareness of somatic change; crucially, a more integrated body-mind relationship; and the capacity to re-pattern habitual bodily modes of behaviour. These new ways of being, in combination with my extensive reading in the fields of trauma, somatics, and neuroscience, have allowed me to now perceive that the experiencing and responding, sensing and feeling biological body cannot escape the inscription of the violence of rape. Even if, as the trauma literature confirms, the storage of conscious memory is autonomously and instantaneously selective (to protect victims from further harm) (Herman 1992, Levine 1997, Rothschild 2000, Scaer 2001, van der Kolk 1994), the combination of intense physiological responses that erupt to ensure survival and the surge of energy this generates (Levine 1997, Pert 1999, Rensberger 1996), as well as the myriad sensory elements of the violence itself (Brison 2002, Culbertson 1995, van der Kolk, van der Hart, and Marmar 2007, Ogden, Minton, and Pain 2006) can remain unprocessed, undischarged, and unresolved, and therefore, frozen, in the body at a cellular level. These understandings, which emerged from the literature, are now amplified by my experiential knowing, and are supported by the findings from the participant somatic inquiry. They combine to form the empirical framework of this research. Embodied knowledges are grounded in sensory perception (Bainbridge Cohen 2008, Merleau-Ponty 1962, Shusterman 2008). This project has been all about sensory perception. It is my contention, therefore, that all rape begins with the initial violation of the material sensory body and psychological symptoms attend secondarily in the aftermath.

Further to this, and as I have stated previously, this research challenges some areas of feminist theoretical understanding that suggests language and discourse alone form experience. I contend that bodily responses to rape cannot solely be read as products of discourse. Rather, bodies in the aftermath of rape are co-constituted by anatomical and biological experience overlaid by discourse. As Hekman (2008, 98) argues from within a materialist paradigm, 'for the new ontology, our language structures how we apprehend the ontological but it does not constitute it.' It is my view that within feminist rape trauma research there is no room for an ideological stance that fails to embrace the fleshed, agentic biological body. If we are to 'understand the human body as something other than a blank slate awaiting the inscription of culture' (Alaimo 2008, 244), we must open ourselves to the biological conditions of the raped body. In Barad's (1996, 2008) 'agential realism' terms, the biological body accounts for 'the real, material consequences of knowledge' (Hekman 2008, 104). This conceptualisation of the porous and active body highlights the interrelatedness of embodiment and discourse and makes room for accounts of corporeality which promote the agentic capacity of the bodymind to absorb, discern, and respond. To help facilitate greater dimensionality in rape trauma research, the biologically traumatised body must, therefore, be awarded the same level of ontological and epistemological gravitas as other forms of investigation.

These understandings, both theoretical and experiential, and revealed to me during this project, now confirm that the violence of rape was so traumatic for me, that despite *burying* the conscious memories of these experiences *deep within my body, and attempting to conduct my life as if they never existed*, my concomitant unconscious sensory memories remained incarcerated in my flesh, unwilling prisoners to the externally imposed and self-imposed silence that restrained and held them there. I am speculating, based on the extent and duration of aftermath symptoms revealed in the participant survey and interview material, that this was also the case for many of the women. The additional enforced and unnecessary violence of this self-protective response appals me.

A second key finding to emerge from the research is the understanding that the body in the aftermath of childhood rape is not static or inert. Speaking in terms not specific to rape trauma but entirely relevant nonetheless, Barad (2008, 139) argues that 'Matter is not immutable or passive.' I have discussed in earlier chapters that my memory-soaked body refused to be silenced or stilled. I have already used the metaphor of an echo to position aftermath symptoms as resonances of rape experience. Additionally, I want to draw in Kirby's (1997, 64–65) conceptualisation of a hologram here to expand on this and provide another graphic layer of interpretation.

Kirby describes a hologram as having 'the 'peculiar property' of distributing information through the entirety of an image, such that any fragment contains the whole image, albeit differently.' She goes on to suggest that, 'Theoretically [...], if we smash a hologram to pieces, each tiny fragment retains the imprint of the "original" image, [...] still alive in its smallest particle.' By appropriating Kirby's metaphor, placing it within the context of rape trauma research, and transposing aftermath symptoms with the shattered fragments of the hologram she describes, it is possible to speculate that the individual somatic symptoms identified by myself, the participants, and the literature, can each be interpreted as an active fragment which *retains the imprint* of the original violation, the trauma *still alive* in the spectrum of presentation.

In terms of my own experiential understanding, I am firm in my conviction that the bodily symptoms that surfaced and came to my attention yet remained medically 'unexplained', the sense of bodily dissonance I harboured across the decades, and quite possibly many of the 'explained' symptoms that satisfied known medical criteria, were actively carrying traces of the trauma of my experience in their presentation. These often intangible signs were everywhere in my body, I simply wasn't always somatically literate enough to be able to read them nor did I have appropriate frameworks or assistance to guide and help me make connections. The survey and interview material suggests this was also the case for many of the women who took part in my research.

An additional point of significance is the relationship between inappropriate discourses and somatic symptoms. I have stressed in earlier chapters that inaccurate but culturally entrenched discursive constructions of sexual violence help perpetuate feelings of shame and self-blame, and, when combined with dominant medical and psychotherapeutic discourses, serve to narrow the range and interpretation of possible trauma responses, limit disclosure, shape disclosure responses by others, and silence raped women. I reiterate these points here for two reasons. Firstly, to draw attention to the impact of inappropriate discourses on already traumatised bodies, illustrated I believe, through the sustained presence of the multiple bodily symptoms identified by the women and also by me. And, secondly, to support my argument that raped bodies are not passive recipients of discursive practices but rather, are active agents of resistance, both resistant to the trauma of rape and resistant to such silencing discourses. This interpretation of raped bodies as active agents of resistance, I believe, endorses Barad's assertion that *matter is not immutable or passive*. Like Philomela's tongueless state that defied enforced muteness and necessitated articulation in other ways, the manifestation of somatic symptoms in the aftermath of rape can be viewed (simultaneously and alternately) as: primary and secondary manifestations of the rape itself (as a re-living of the sensory elements of the event and the repeated echo of the event); an alternative means of communicating the unspeakable; and as acts of bodily resistance to silencing, misinterpretation, and inappropriate discourse. This supports my argument that rape inflicts damage at a primary anatomical and physiological level and that inappropriate discourses exacerbate this damage. This argument positions the body in the aftermath of rape as: the biological holding ground of trauma experience; a site of struggle, disorder, and distress; and the materially subversive locus of a refusal to comply. Any failure by trauma researchers and healthcare professionals to acknowledge the multiple origins and multidimensionality of somatic responses to rape is to contribute to the perpetuation of the aftermath ramifications identified through the literature and through this research, that continue to impact so profoundly on the bodies of traumatised girls and women.

Another crucial outcome of the research is the finding that bodily responses to the experience of rape in childhood manifest in the aftermath irrespective of whether or not discourse exists to appropriately frame or 'explain' those responses. The autoethnographic and participant somatic inquiry amply revealed that bodily responses to childhood sexual trauma occur whether the symptoms are medically explained or otherwise, and are a lived, daily, and distressing reality for raped women. My research additionally revealed that bodily responses occur irrespective of whether or not victims, or healthcare professionals, make associations between an experience of rape and the bodily symptoms that present in the aftermath. These symptoms are not 'all in the mind'. Wilson (2004b, 11) writing in relation to one of Freud's female hysteria patients, observes that if the patient's pain symptoms were 'indeed all in her head', then, if taken 'literally (reductively), […] this entails a number of reciprocal ontological contortions: that her thigh is her head, that her mind is muscular […].' Although not in relation to hysteria, Kirby (2003, 435) makes an interesting and relevant observation. 'What is happening,' she asks, 'when I speak on the telephone without my glasses and find I cannot hear as clearly? Do I merely imagine my incapacity, or is "one" modality always/already recalling the "other"? And if I do "merely" imagine, then again, why is this not a biological phenomenon of/with material manifestation?' If I hold the thread of Kirby's observation and extend Wilson's argument to my own symptoms and those of the other women, it conjures a bizarre image. But Wilson is not being flippant here. She is making the point that naming symptoms 'psychosomatic' reduces the symptoms to products of psychological fantasy and imagination and labels the women who experience these symptoms as mentally disturbed. My unwavering argument is that, just as the hysterics were not 'crazy', girls and women who have been raped are not 'crazy' either. We are, as Brison states, *traumatised* (2002, 111).

As the literature has revealed, within healthcare practice there is a tendency to hierarchically privilege psychological expressions of disturbance (Wilson 2004b). I am suggesting that the biological conditions of the body in the aftermath of rape cannot be ignored. Even if, for some women, the trauma of rape cannot yet be communicated in other ways, even if some women are not always able to make links between their symptoms and their rape experience, and even if women are unable to disclose a rape experience, it does not mean the symptoms do not exist. They must, therefore, be taken seriously. These findings have significant healthcare implications and support my argument for greater empathic vigilance in healthcare practice, warranting specific attention by professionals working in the area of women's health, as well as those regularly treating female patients as part of their healthcare practice.

A final outcome of my research, and more specifically, my autoethnographic somatic inquiry, is the finding that it has been possible to shift the relationship between my body and mind from one of detachment, disconnection, and punitive control to one of respect, reciprocity, and integration. This remains something of a miracle. My autoethnographic research took me deeply into the materiality of my raped body. This work was full of risk but also richly rewarding. I have already discussed the various anxieties I experienced before commencing this phase of the research. And I have revealed the spectrum of my responses that unfolded during my therapeutic engagement with Alice and the practice of Body-Mind Centering, the more disturbing of which included my revulsion at feeling the re-animation of the memory of the weight of the perpetrator's body on my own; the unprovoked eruptions of deep anxiety which immobilised me; and the experience of re-stimulation during hands-on work and somatic explorations when my confused body reacted as though the past was happening in the present and my life was under threat. But I have also already revealed the immense surprise, joy, and relief I felt when I sensed my first fleeting moments of bodily connection; my enormous pleasure in the freedom I found when expressing myself through my moving body; and the words that came to me when I felt a deep sense of integration following a hands-on session ('I have a body now, Alice'). The therapeutic effect of this work cannot be underestimated. Through the hours of hands-on work with Alice, the many witnessed Authentic Movement sessions, and the inestimable number of somatic explorations I engaged in during the Body-Mind Centering workshops and residential programs, I now feel and read my body in new ways.

In undertaking a method of exploration grounded in embodiment, I necessarily launched myself into the unknown through my epidermis, the porous outer layer of my body, my immediate and tangible interface with the world. I immersed myself in the mystery of the anatomical and physiological micro landscape that forms the geography and topography of my inner corporeality. My immersion allowed me to experience this wondrous terrain in new ways. I now perceive that my body is full of complexity. It is in constant micro motion, vibrating with trillions of my unique cells, all engaged in a reciprocal dance of information exchange aimed at maintaining homeostatic balance. I can now imagine and feel this landscape filigreed with thousands of millions of neurons exquisitely sensitive to the full range of external environmental information and responsive to the minutest internal fluctuation. I can now feel the presence of my bones as they support and give me structure, each as important as the next, all working towards articulation; my spiralling muscles, my tendons and ligaments that knit my bones together, offer tensile strength, suppleness, grace, and dynamism; my soft and beautiful organs that fill me with oxygen, pump my blood, filter my fluids, digest my food, expel my waste, help me with cognition, and have been home to the creation of new life; my endocrine glands that quietly secrete hormones to help orchestrate physiological harmony. I feel too, the presence of my sense organs that take in all around me: touch; sound; smell; taste; vision. I know that everything is registered; everything is stored as somatic memory. And I understand that some memories lie in readiness for retrieval, others lurk in shadow, some bristle and shudder, while yet others grind against each other, the friction of their torment igniting other memories that smoulder below consciousness.

At the close of my research process, *because* of my research process, I know that everything that is my body is me. All the tissues and systems that shape and structure and secrete and perceive, help me be in, make sense of, and move through the world. Since the moment of conception, when 'new life pauses on the threshold of becoming' (A. Cummins, personal communication, 18 March, 2014), my cells have harboured the capacity to intelligently juggle complexity, absorb experience, measure, adjust and transform. Because of the intensive somatic work I have engaged in, I now feel the deep intelligence of my body. I recognise and know that my body has always been full of intelligence. I am enraged that when the perpetrator seized and penetrated my young body, the trauma this unforgiveable violence generated in the long post-rape aftermath obscured, and then severed this knowing.

My findings from the participant information indicated that many of the women had not attended any sort of bodywork practice and for those who did, the benefits were mixed. I argue that my engagement with, and experience of a body-based therapeutic practice was crucial to the re-establishment of my more integrated bodymind relationship; my diminished sense of fragmentation; the cultivation of voice and agency; and my capacity to move through the world with greater confidence. I am sensitive to the indisputable knowledge, however, that bodies and minds post childhood rape are deeply traumatised. I am keenly aware that trust is a major concern. And I am alert to the fear that lingers from childhood and shapes decision-making, especially in relation to any voluntary participation in therapeutic practices that require touch or focus on the body. I stress that, although I am promoting the benefits of therapeutically attending to the raped body, I am doing so with awareness that many women will be so thoroughly traumatised by their rape experience that their bodies will remain inaccessible. Body-based therapies may never be appropriate for some women.

***

This book challenges dominant medical and psychological discourses that position the psychological consequences of rape in hierarchical relationship to those that manifest in the body. It destabilises feminist theorising which promotes language and discourse and diminishes corporeality in meaning-making practices. And it subverts traditional forms of knowledge-making and dissemination through performative, lyrical, and embodied modes of interrogation and information sharing. It does these through a commitment to an embodied methodology which embraces and acknowledges rather than denies the ontological and epistemological possibilities of the fleshed body in rape trauma research. As these chapters have amply demonstrated, through my autoethnographic somatic inquiry, the participant somatic inquiry, and through the literature, the multiple dimensions of childhood sexual violence inflict extensive and unspeakable damage on girls and women long after the event itself, which, especially if left unattended to, or if poorly attended to, has lasting and profound health implications.

I'm told by people who have known me for a long time that I've changed much since beginning my work with Alice. I try to take their comments as a compliment but my sensitivity surrounding this lingers. I can't help wondering if people think I'm 'cured'. The word itself has an air of smugness and finality about it that speaks more about the remedy than the symptoms or the treatment. It glistens with power and achievement. It puts people at ease. It comforts the witness.

It does not apply to me.

Although I've undoubtedly made enormous progress, there remains much to be done. There are still areas of my body that are distressing to enter through somatic work. There are areas of my body that I may never be able to enter. For the years of my research, I have persisted with the difficulties inherent in entering my traumatised body. I have been dogged in my determination to understand my body, the somatic impact of my rape experience, and its significant aftermath. I have an ongoing commitment to the re-integration of this experience and to my self-care. But I am not 'cured'. I may never be 'cured'. I don't believe it is possible for such finality to exist in relation to sexual trauma. 'Cures' are convenient. They comfort others but diminish personal experience. I will not buy into the notion of my own 'cure'. It is not useful for me to do so, nor do I feel it is helpful for other girls and women who experience sexual trauma.

What I can say with certainty is that the depth of understanding and the clarity generated through the many methodological components of my research process has developed a robustness in me that fills my body and grounds my sense of place in the world. By rendering my story visible and visceral through these chapters and through performance, I have honoured my right as a woman to speak and be heard and I have given my raped body voice, presence, and integrity. This honouring strengthens and guides me towards greater exposure of my story and propels me to continue future research into the somatic ramifications of gendered sexual violence.

At the end of this period of research, I realise this is just the beginning.

Bibliography

ABS. 2002. 4522.0.55.001 – 'Information Paper: Measuring Crime Victimisation, Australia: The Impact of Different Collection Methodologies.' Australian Bureau of Statistics.

ABS. 2006. 4906.0 – 'Personal Safety, Australia, 2005'. (Reissue.)

ACSSA. 2005. 'Adult victim/survivors of childhood sexual assault.' Wrap No. 1; Nov. 2005. Edited by Australian Centre for the Study of Sexual Assault.

ACSSA. 2006. 'Services for victim/survivors of sexual assault: identifying needs, interventions & provision of services in Australia. Summary Sheet 6. Jill Astbury.' 1–26. Retrieved September 10, 2009, from <http://www.aifs.gov.au/acssa/pubs/issue/summarysheet6.html>.

Adler, Janet. 1999. 'Who is the Witness? A Description of Authentic Movement.' In *Authentic Movement: Essays by Mary Starks Whitehouse, Janet Adler and Joan Chodorow*, edited by Patrizia Pallaro. London: Jessica Kingsley Publishers Ltd.

Adler, Janet. 2002. *Offering from the Conscious Body: The Discipline of Authentic Movement*. Rochester, Vermont: Inner Traditions.

Adler, Janet. 2007. 'From Autism to the Discipline of Authentic Movement.' In *Authentic Movement: Moving the Body, Moving the Self, Being Moved*, edited by Patrizia Pallaro. London: Jessica Kingsley Publishers.

Ahrens, Courtney E. 2006. 'Being Silenced: The Impact of Negative Social Reactions on the Disclosure.' *American Journal of Community Psychology* no. 38:263–274.

Ahrens, Courtney E. and Rebecca Campbell. 2000. 'Assisting Rape Victims as They Recover From Rape: The Impact on Friends.' *Journal of Interpersonal Violence* no. 15:959.

Ahrens, Courtney E., Rebecca Campbell, N.K. Ternier-Thames, S.M. Wasco, and T. Sefl. 2007. 'Deciding Whom To Tell: Expectations And Outcomes of Rape Survivors' First Disclosures.' *Psychology of Women Quarterly* no. 31:38–49.

Ahrens, Courtney E., Janna Stansell, and Amy Jennings. 2010. 'To Tell or Not to Tell: The Impact of Disclosure on Sexual Assault Survivors' Recovery.' *Violence and Victims* no. 25 (5). doi: 10.1891/0886-6708.25.5.631.

Ahsen, Akhter. 1968. *Basic Concepts in Eidetic Psychotherapy*. California: Brandon House.

AIC. 2007. 'Australian crime: facts and figures 2006.'

Alaimo, Stacy. 2008. 'Trans-Corporeal Feminisms and the Ethical Space of Nature.' In *Material Feminisms*, edited by Stacy Alaimo and Susan Hekman, 237–264. Bloomington: Indiana University Press.

Alaimo, Stacy, and Susan Hekman. 2008a. 'Introduction: Emerging Models of Materiality in Feminist Theory.' In *Material Feminisms*, edited by Stacy Alaimo and Susan Hekman. Bloomington: Indiana University press.

Alaimo, Stacy, and Susan Hekman, eds. 2008b. *Material feminisms*. Bloomington: Indiana University Press.

ALRC. 2010. 'Family Violence – A National Legal Response' (ALRC Report 114). Edited by Australian Law Reform Commission: Australian Law Reform Commission.

Anderson, Irina, and Kathy Doherty. 2008. *Accounting For Rape: Psychology, Feminism and Discourse*. East Sussex: Routledge.

Anxieu, Didier. 1989. *The Skin Ego*. London: Karnac.

Armsworth, M.T, K. Stronck, and C.D. Carlson. 1999. 'Body Image and Self Perception in Women with Histories of Incest.' In *Splintered Reflections: Images of the Body in Trauma*, edited by Jean M. Goodwin and Reina Attias. New York: Basic Books.

Asher-Greve, Julia M. 1998. 'The Essential Body: Mesopotamian Conceptions of the Gendered Body.' In *Gender and the Body in the Ancient Mediterranean*, edited by Maria Wyke. Oxford: Blackwell Publishers Ltd.

Assiter, Alison. 1996. *Enlightened women: Modernist feminism in a Postmodern Age*. London: Routledge.

Astbury, Jill. 2006a. ACSSA Wrap No. 6. 'Services for victim/survivors of sexual assault: Identifying needs, interventions and provision of services in Australia.' <http://www.aifs.gov.au/acssa/pubs/issue/acssa_issues6.pdf>.

Astbury, Jill. 2006b. 'Services for victim/survivors of sexual assault: Identifying needs, interventions and provision of services in Australia.' Edited by Australian Centre for the Study of Sexual Assault.

Australian Bureau of Statistics. 2011. 4510.0 – 'Recorded Crime – Victims, Australia, 2011.'

Australian Bureau of Statistics. 2012. 4530.0 – 'Crime Victimisation, Australia, 2011–12.'

Australian Somatic Psychotherapy Association. 2012. *What is somatic psychotherapy?* 2012 [cited 22 November 2012]. Available from <http://www.somaticassociation.org.au/what-is-somatic-psychotherapy>.

Bainbridge Cohen, Bonnie. 1993. *Sensing, Feeling, and Action: The Experiential Anatomy of Body-Mind Centering*. First ed. Northampton, MA: Contact Editions.

Bainbridge Cohen, Bonnie. 1995. 'Sensing, Feeling, and Action: The Experiential anatomy of Body-Mind Centering (Excerpts).' In *Bone, Breath & Gesture: Practices of Embodiment*, edited by Don Hanlon Johnson, 185–203. Berkeley: North Atllantic Books.

Bainbridge Cohen, Bonnie. 2008. *Sensing, Feeling, and Action: The Experiential Anatomy of Body-Mind Centering(R)*. Northampton, MA: Contact Editions.

Bainbridge Cohen, Bonnie. 2013. *Nerve Reversal & Healing [YouTube]*: Body-Mind Centering.

Barad, Karen. 1996. 'Meeting the uiniverse halfway: realism and social constructivism without contradiction.' In *Feminism, Science, and the Philosophy of Science*, edited by Lynn Hankinson Nelson and Jack Nelson, 161–194. Dordrecht: Kluwer.

Barad, Karen. 2003. 'Posthumanist Performativity: Toward an Understanding of How Matter Comes to Matter.' *Signs* no. 28 (3):801–831.

Barad, Karen. 2008. 'Posthumanist Performativity: Toward an Understanding of How Matter Comes to Matter.' In *Material Feminisms*, edited by Stacy Alaimo and Susan Hekman, 120–154. Bloomington: Indiana University Press.

Bartky, Sandra L. 1990. *Femininity and Domination: Studies in the Phenomenology of Oppression*. New York: Routledge.

Bauer, Susan. 1999. 'Somatic Movement Education: A Body-Mind Approach to Movement Education for Adolescents.' *Somatics* no. 12 (2).

Bauer, Susan. 2012. *What is Somatic Movement Education?* 2012 [cited 27 November 2012]. Available from <http://susanbauer.com/somatics/somatic-movement-education>.

Bauer, Susan. 2013. *What is Experiential Anatomy?* 2013 [cited 5 February 2013]. Available from <http://susanbauer.com/somatics/experiential-anatomy>.

Beckford, Martin. 2012. '80% of women don't report rape or sexual assault, survey claims.' *The Telegraph*, 12 March, 2012.

Benjamin, Ben E. 2012. *The Primacy of Human Touch* (2) 2012 [cited 7 December 2012]. Available from <http://www.benbenjamin.net/pdfs/Issue2pdf>.

Birke, Lynda. 1999. 'Bodies and Biology.' In *Feminist Theory and the Body: Reader*, edited by Janet Price and Margrit Shildrick, 42–49. New York: Routledge.

BMC. 2012. *Home page* 2012 [cited 15 June 2012]. Available from <http://www.bodymindcentering.com>.

Bolt, Barbara. 2012. 'Back and beyond the sublime: Catastrophe in contemporary art'. In *'catastrophe & creativity', CREATEC symposium*. Edith Cowan University, Mount Lawley, Western Australia.

Bonitz, Verena. 2008. 'Use of physical touch in the "Talking Cure": A journey to the outskirts of psychotherapy.' *Psychotherapy, Theory, Research, Training* no. 45 (3):391–404.

Bourke, Joanna. 2012. 'Sexual Violence, Bodily Pain, and Trauma: A History.' *Theory, Culture & Society* no. 29 (3):25–51.

Bowden, Peta, and Jane Mummery. 2009. *Understanding Movements in Modern Thought: Understanding Feminism*. Durham: Acumen.

Boyd, Cameron. 2011. 'The imapcts of sexual assault on women.' Edited by Australian Centre for the Study of Sexual Assault. Melbourne: Australian Centre for the Study of Sexaul Assault.

Breitenbecher, Kimberly Hanson. 2006. 'The Relationships Among Self-Blame, Psychological Distress, and Sexual Victimization.' *Journal of Interpersonal Violence* no. 21 (5):597–611.

Brennan, Shannon, and Andrea Taylor-Butts. 2008. 'Sexual Assault in Canada 2004 and 2007.' Cat. No. 85F0033M- No. 19 Canadian Centre for Justice Statistics Profile Series. <http://www.statcan.gc.ca/pub/85f0033m/85f0033m2008019-eng.pdf>.

Brison, Susan J. 2002. *Aftermath: Violence and the Remaking of a Self.* Princeton, New Jersey: Princeton University Press.

Britannica Online Encyclopedia. 2012. *Orphic religion* 2012 [cited 26 November 2012]. Available from <http://www.britannica.com/EBchecked/topic/433191/Orphic-religion>.

Brown, Brene. 2010. *The power of vulnerability [Videofile]*: TEDTalks. Retrieved from <http://www.ted.com/talks/brene_brown_on_vulnerability.html>.

Brown, Brene. 2012. *Listening to shame [Videofile]*: TEDTalks. Retrieved from <http://www.ted.com/talks/brene_brown_listening_to_shame.html>.

Brownmiller, Susan. 1976. *Against Our Will: Men, Women and Rape* Middlesex: Penguin Books Ltd.

Burns, Catherine. 2011. 'The Active Role of the Baby in Birthing.' In *Exploring Body-Mind Centering*, edited by Gill Wright-Miller, Pat Etheridge and Kate Tarlow Morgan, 21–40. Berkeley: North Atlantic Books.

Buxton, Richard. 2004. *The Complete World of Greek Mythology*. London: Thames and Hudson Ltd.

Calhoun, Cheshire. 2004. 'An Apology for Moral Shame.' *The Journal of Political Philosophy* no. 12 (2):127–146.

Calhoun, Karen S., and Beverley M. Atkeson. 1991. *Treatment of Rape Victims: Facilitating Psychosocial Adjustment*. New York: Pergamon Press, Inc.

Cameron, Margaret. 2012. 'A *quest*(ion) of *it*: methodology is whatever generates possibilities & delays closure.' In *Live Research: Methods of Practice-Led Inquiry in Performance*, edited by Leah Mercer, Julie Robson and David Fenton. Nerang: Ladyfinger.

Campbell, Rebecca. 2002. *Emotionally Involved: The Impact of Researching Rape*. New York: Routledge.

Campbell, Rebecca. 2008. 'The psychological impact of rape victims.' *The American Psychologist* no. 63 (8):702–717.

Campbell, Rebecca, Adrienne E. Adams, Sharon M. Wasco, Courtney E. Ahrens, and Tracy Sefl. 2010. '"What has it been like for you to talk with me today?": The Impact of Participating in Interview Research on Rape Survivors.' *Violence Against Women* no. 16 (1):60–83.

Campbell, Rebecca, and S. Raja. 1999. 'Secondary victimization of rape victims: Insights from mental health professionals who treat survivors of violence.' *Violence and Victims* no. 14 (3):261–275.

Campbell, Rebecca, and S.M. Wasco. 2005. 'Understanding Rape & Sexual Assault: 20 Years of Progress & Future Directions.' *Journal of Interpersonal Violence* no. 20.

Cancienne, Mary Beth, and Celeste N. Snowber. 2003. 'Writing Rhythm: Movement as Method.' *Qualitative Inquiry* no. 9 (2):237–253.

Caruth, Cathy. 1996. *Unclaimed experience: Trauma, Narrative, and History*. Baltimore: The John Hopkins University Press.

CDC. 2013. *Sexual Violence: Definitions*. Centre for Disease Control 2009 [cited 7 May 2013]. Available from <http://www.cdc.gov/violenceprevention/sexualviolence/definitions.html>.

Cheever, Olivia. 2000. 'Connected Knowing and "Somatic Empathy" among Somatic Educators and Students of Somatic Education.' *ReVision* no. Spring:15–23.

Chivers-Wilson, Kaitlin A. 2006. 'Sexual assault and posttraumatic stress disorder: A review of the biological, psychological and sociological factors and treatments.' *McGill Journal of Medicine* no. 9 (2):111–118.

Chodrow, Joan. 1999. 'Active Imagination.' In *Authentic Movement: Essays by Mary Starks Whitehouse, Janet Adler and Joan Chodrow*, edited by Patrizia Pallaro. London: Jessica Kingsley Publishers Ltd.

Cixous, Helene. 1976. 'The Laugh of the Medusa.' *Signs: Journal of Women in Culture and Society* no. 1 (4).

Cixous, Helene. 1990. 'Difficult Joys.' In *The Body and the Text: Helene Cixous, Reading and Teaching*, edited by Helen Wilcox, Keith McWatters, Ann Thompson and Angela Williams. Hemel Hempstead: Harvester Wheatsheaf.

Cixous, Helene. 1991a. 'Coming to Writing.' In *Coming to Writing and Other Essays*, edited by Deborah Jensen. Cambridge, Mass: Harvard University Press.

Cixous, Helene. 1991b. *Coming to Writing and Other Essays*. Edited by Deborah Jenson. Cambridge, Mass: Harvard University Press.

Cixous, Helene. 1991c. 'The Last Painting or the Portrait of God.' In *'Coming to Writing' and Other Essays*, edited by Deborah Jenson. Cambridge, Mass: Harvard University Press.

Cixous, Helene. 1993. *Three steps on the ladder of writing*. New York: Routledge.

Cixous, Helene. 1997. *Rootprints: Memory and Life Writing*. London: Routledge.

Cixous, Helene. 1998. *Stigmata*. Abingdon, Oxfordshire: Routledge

Cixous, Helene, and Catherine Clement. 1986. *The Newly Born Woman*. Minneapolis: University of Minnesota Press.

Clark, Haley, and Antonia Quadara. 2010. 'Insights into sexual assault perpetration: Giving voice to victim/survivors' knowledge.' Edited by Australian Institute of Family Studies: Australian Government.

Clarke, Laura Hurd, and Meridith Griffin. 2008. 'Body image and aging: Older women and the embodiment of trauma.' *Women's Studies International Forum* no. 31:200–208.

Colebrook, Claire. 2008. 'On Not Becoming Man: The Materialist Politics of Unactualized Potential.' In *Material Feminisms*, edited by Stacy Alaimo and Susan Hekman, 52–84. Bloomington: Indiana University Press.

Conway Ker, J. 1999. *When Memory Speaks: Exploring the Art of Autobiography*. New York: Vintage Books.

Cook, Bree, Fiona David, and Anna Grant. 2001. 'Sexual Violence in Australia.' Australian Institute of Criminology Research and Public Policy Series, 36 (2001). <http://www.aic.gov.au/documents/4/3/6/%7b43630977-E669-46BD-ADCC-6B0766447C31%7dRPP36.pdf>.

Cook, Meira. 2000. 'At the Membrane of Language and Silence: Metaphor and Memory in Fugitive Pieces.' *Canadian Literature* no. 164 (Spring):12–33.

Corry, Darlene, Tania Pouwhare, and Macarena Vergara. 2008. 'The Crisis in Rape Crisis.' <http://www.thurrock-community.org.uk/sericc/pdf/wrc_crisis_summary.pdf>.

Crome, Sarah, and Marita McCabe. 1995. 'The impact of rape on individual, interpersonal, & family functioning.' *Journal of Family Studies* no. 1 (1):58–70.

Culbertson, Roberta. 1995. 'Embodied Memory, Transcendence, and Telling: Recounting Trauma, Re-establishing the Self.' *New Literary History* no. 26 (1):169–195.

Cummins, Alice. 2012. *Home page* 2012 [cited 15 June 2012]. Available from <http://www.alicecummins.com>.

Damasio, Antonio. 1994. *Descarte's error*. New York: Putnam.

Daniels, Victor. 2012. *Wilhelm Reich Lecture* 2008 [cited 23 November 2012]. Available from <http://www.sonoma.edu/users/d/daniels/reichlecture.html>.

Dansky, Bonnie S., Timothy D. Brewerton, Dean G. Kilpatrick, and Patrick M. O'Neil. 1997. 'The National Women's Study: Relationship of Victimization and Post-traumatic Stress Disorder to Bulimia Nervosa.' *International Journal of Eating Disorders* no. 21:213–228.

Davies, Bronwyn. 1992. 'Women's Subjectivity and Feminist Stories.' In *Investigating Subjectivity: Research on Lived Experience*, edited by Caroline Ellis and Michael G. Flaherty. London: Sage.

Denzin, Norman K. 1997. 'Performance texts.' In *Representation and the text: Reframing the narrative voice*, edited by William G. Tierney and Yvonna S. Lincoln. Albany: State University of New York Press.

Dickson-Swift, Virginia, Erica L. James, Sandra Kippen, and Pranee Liamputtong. 2007. 'Doing sensitive research: what challenges do qualitative researchers face?' *Qualitative Research* no. 7 (3):327–353.

Dillard, Annie. 1989. *The Writing Life*. New York: Harper Perennial.

Doidge, Norman. 2007. *The Brain That Changes Itself.* Carlton North: Scribe Publications Pty Ltd.

Dolmage, Jay. 2009. 'Metis, *Metis*, *Mestiza*, Medusa: Rhetorical Bodies across Rhetorical Traditions.' *Rhetoric Review* no. 28 (1):1–28.

Dolphijn, Rick, and Iris van der Tuin. 2012. *New Materialism: Interviews & Cartographies*. Ann Arbor: Open Humanities Press.

Downing, Brenda, and Alice Cummins. 2012. 'The Catastrophe of Childhood Rape: Traversing the Landscape between Private Memory and Public Performance.'

Downing, Brenda, and Alice Cummins. 2013. 'The Catastrophe of Childhood Rape: Traversing the Landscape between Private Memory and Public Performance'. 16 (1), <http://journal.media-culture.org.au/index.php/mcjournal/article/viewArticle/590>.

Dowrick, Stephanie. 2007. *Creative Journal Writing*. Crow's Nest: Allen & Unwin.

Duffy, Bobby, Kate Smith, George Terhanian, and John Bremer. 2005. 'Comparing data from online and face-to-face surveys.' *International Journal of Market Research* no. 47 (6):617–639.

Easteal, Patricia. 1992a. 'Survivors of Sexual Assault: A National Survey.' Edited by Australian Institute of Criminology.

Easteal, Patricia. 1992b. 'Violence Prevention Today. No. 1. Rape.'

Easteal, Patricia. 1992c. 'Violence Prevention Today. No. 1. Rape.'

Eddy, Martha. 2002a. 'Dance and Somatic Inquiry in Studios and Community Dance Programs.' *Journal of Dance Education* no. 2 (4).

Eddy, Martha. 2002b. 'Somatic Practices and Dance: Global Influences.' *Dance Research Journal* no. 34 (2):46–62.

Eddy, Martha. 2009. 'A brief history of somatic practices and dance: historical development of the field of somatic education and its relationship to dance.' *Journal of Dance and Somatic Practices* no. 1 (1).

Edelman, Gerald M. 1989. *The Remembered Present*. New York: Basic Books.

Ellis, Carolyn, and Art P. Bochner. 2000. 'Autoethnography, Personal Narrative, Reflexivity: Researcher as Subject.' In *Handbook of Qualitative Research (2nd Edition)*, edited by N.K. Denzin and Y.S. Lincoln. California: Sage Publications Inc.

Esposito, Noreen. 2005. 'Manifestations of Enduring During Interviews With Sexual Assault Victims.' *Qualitative Health Research* no. 15 (7):912–927.

Fanflik, Patricia L. 2007. 'Victim Responses to Sexual Assault: Counterintuitive or Simply Adaptive?' American Prosecutors Research Institute.

Feiring, Candice, and Lynn S. Taska. 2005. 'The Persistence of Shame Following Sexual Abuse: A Longitudinal Look at Risk and Recovery.' *Child Maltreatment* no. 10:337–349.

Feldenkrais, International Federation. 2012. *The Feldenkrais Method* 2012 [cited 7 December 2012]. Available from <http://feldenkrais-method.org/en/feldenkrais-method>.

Feldenkrais, Moshe. 1995. 'The Elusive Obvious (Introduction).' In *Bone, Breath, & Gesture: Practices of Embodiment*, edited by Don Hanlon Johnson, 137–147. Berkeley: North Atlantic Books.

Field, Tiffany. 2000. *Touch Therapy*. London: Churchill Livingstone.

Fileborn, Bianca. 2011. 'Sexual Assault Laws in Australia.' Australian Centre for the Study of Sexual Assault.

Firestone, Shulamit. 1970. *The dialectic of sex: The case for feminist revolution*. New York: Morrow.

Fleckenstein, Kristie S. 1999. 'Writing Bodies: Somatic Mind in Composition Studies.' *College English* no. 61 (3):281–306.

Foa, E.B., and B.O. Rothbaum. 1998. *Treating the trauma of rape: Cognitive behaviour therapy for PTSD*. New York: Guilford.

Fonow, Mary Margaret, and Judith A. Cook. 2005. 'Feminist Methodology: New Applications in the Academy and Public Policy.' *Signs: Journal of Women in Culture and Society* no. 30 (41).

Forbes, David, Mark C. Creamer, Andrea J. Phelps, Anne-Laure Couineau, John A. Cooper, Richard A. Bryant, Alexander C. McFarlane, Grant J. Devilly, Lynda R. Matthews, and Beverley Raphael. 2007. 'Treating adults with acute stress disorder and post-traumatic stress disorder in general practice: a clinical update.' *Medical Journal of Australia* no. 187 (2):120–123.

Foster, Jonathon K. 2008. *Memory: A Very Short Introduction*. Oxford: Oxford University Press.

Frank, Ruella. 2012. *Defintions* 2012 [cited 4 December 2012]. Available from <http://www.somaticstudies.com/index.html>.

Freedman, Karen L. 2006. 'The Epistemological Significance of Psychic Trauma.' *Hypatia* no. Spring 2006 21 (2).

Friedan, Betty. 1963. *The Feminine Mystique*. New York: W.W. Norton & Company Inc.

Frieder, Susan. 2007. 'Reflections on Mary Starks Whitehouse.' In *Authentic Movement: Moving the Body, Moving the Self, Being Moved*, edited by Patrizia Pallaro, 35–44. London: Jessica Kingsley Publishers.

Fuchs, Thomas. 2004. 'The memory of the body.' <http://www.klinikum.uni-heidelberg.de/fileadmin/zpm/psychatrie/ppp2004/manuskript/fuchs.pdf>.

Furness, John B. 2007. 'Enteric nervous system.' (2 (10)) <http://www.scholarpedia.org/article/Enteric_nervous_system>.

Furness, John B. 2014. *Enteric Nervous System*. Scholarpedia 2011 [cited 27 March 2014]. Available from <http://www.scholarpedia.org/article/Enteric_nervous_system>.

Gannon, Susanne. 2004. '"Dream(e)scapes": a Poetic Experiment in Writing a Self.' *Auto/Biography* no. 12:107–125.

Golding, Jacqueline M. 1994. 'Sexual Assault History and Physical Health in Randomly Selected Los Angeles Women.' *Health Psychology* no. 13 (2):130–138.

Goodrich-Dunn, Barbara. 2004. 'Somatic Psychotherapies: A Road Map.' *Psychotherapy Networker* no. 28 (4).

Goodwin, Jean M., and Reina Attias. 1999. 'The Body Speaks: Bodily Disturbances After Childhood Trauma.' In *Splintered Reflections: Images of the Body in Trauma*, edited by Jean M. Goodwin and Reina Attias. New York: Basic Books.

Gordon, Lyndall. 2010. *Lives Like Loaded Guns: Emily Dickinson and Her Family's Feuds*. London: Virago Press.

Gorelick, Sherry. 1991. 'Contradictions of Feminist Methodology.' *Gender and Society* no. 5 (4):459–477.

Grammatikakis, Ioannis Emm. 2011. 'The Woman in Minoic Crete.' *Journal of Maternal-Fetal and Neo-Natal Medicine* no. 24 (7):968–972.

Green, Jill. 2002. 'Somatic Knowledge: The Body as Content and Methodology in Dance Education.' *Journal of Dance Education* no. 2 (4):114–118.

Greenberg, Judith. 1998. 'The Echo of Trrauma and the Trauma of Echo.' *American Imago* no. 55 (3):319–347.

Griffin, Michael G., Patricia A. Resick, Angela E. Waldrop, and Mindy B.Mechanic. 2003. 'Participation in Trauma Research: Is There Evidence of Harm?' *Journal of Traumatic Stress* no. 16 (3):221–227.

Grosz, Elizabeth. 1994. *Volatile Bodies: Toward a Corporeal Feminism*. St Leonards: Allen & Unwin Pty Ltd.

Grosz, Elizabeth. 2008. 'Darwin and Feminism: Preliminary Investigations for a Possible Alliance.' In *Material Feminisms*, edited by Stacy Alaimo and Susan Hekman, 23–51. Bloomington: Indiana University Press.

Grosz, Elizabeth. 2010. 'The Untimeliness of Feminist Theory.' *NORA – Nordic Journal of Feminist and Gender Research* no. 18 (1):48–51.

Gueter, Ulfried, Michael C. Heller, and Judyth O. Weaver. 2010. 'Elsa Gindler and her Influence on Wilhem Reich and Body Psychotherapy.' *Body, Movement and Dance in Psychotherapy*.

Gunew, Sneja. 1992. 'Feminist Knowledge: Critique & Construct.' In *Feminist Knowledge: Critique & Construct*, edited by Sneja Gunew. London: Routledge.

Gwyther, Gabrielle, and Alphia Possamai-Inesedy. 2009. 'Methodologies a la carte: an examination of emerging qualitative methodologies in social research.' *International Journal of Social Research Methodology* no. 12 (2):99–115.

Hamilton, Edith. 1998. *Mythology*. New York: Little, Brown and Company.

Hanna, Thomas. 1986. 'What is somatics?' In *Bone, Breath, & Gesture: Practices of Embodiment*, edited by Don Hanlon Johnson, 341–352. Berkeley: North Atlantic Books.

Hanna, Thomas. 1988. *Somatics: Reawakening the Mind's Control of Movement, Flexibility, and Health*. Reading, MA: Addison-Wesley.

Hartley, Linda. 1995. *Wisdom of the Body Moving: An Introduction to Body-Mind Centering*. Berkeley, California: North Atlantic Books.

Havig, Kirsten. 2008. 'The Health Care Experiences of Adult Survivors of Child Sexual Abuse: A Systematic Review of Evidence on Sensitive Practice.' *Trauma, Violence, & Abuse* no. 9 (1):19–33.

Hay, Deborah. 2000. *My body the Buddhist*. Middleton: Wesleyan University Press.

Hayden, Wendy. 2010. '(R)Evolutionary Rhetorics: Science and Sexuality in Nineteenth Century Free-Love Discourse.' *Rhetoric Review* no. 29 (2):111–128.

Heilbrun, Carolyn G. 1988. *Writing a Woman's Life*. New York: Ballantine Books.

Hekman, Susan. 2008. 'Constructing the Ballast: An Ontology for Feminism.' In *Material Feminisms*, edited by Stacy Alaimo and Susan Hekman. Bloomington: Indiana University Press.

Hekman, Susan. 2010. *Material of Knowledge: Feminist Disclosures*. Bloomington, IN, USA: Indiana University Press.

Hemmings, Clare. 2012. 'Affective solidarity: Feminist reflexivity and political transformation.' *Feminist Theory* no. 13 (2):147–161.

Herman, Judith Lewis. 1992. *Trauma and Recovery*. New York: Basic Books.

Hess, Michael. 1994. 'Black and Red: The Pilbara Pastoral Workers' Strike, 1946.' *Aboriginal History* no. 18 (1):65–83.

Hester, Marianne. 1992. *Lewd Women & Wicked Witches: A Study of the Dynamics of Male Domination*. London: Routledge.

Hird, Myra J. 2004. 'Feminist matters: New materialist considerations of sexual difference.' *Feminist Theory* no. 5 (2):223–232.

Hirsch, Marianne. 1997. *Family Frames: photography, narrative and postmemory*. Cambridge, Mass: Harvard University Press.

Hirsch, Marianne. 2008. 'The Generation of Postmemory.' *Poetics Today* no. 29 (1).

Hirsch, Marianne. 2014. *Postmemory.net* 2014 [cited February 1 2014]. Available from <http://www.postmemory.net>.

Holcomb, Justin S., and Lindsay A. Holcomb. 2011. *Rid of my Disgrace: Hope and Healing for Victims of Sexual Assault*. Wheaton, Illinois: Crossway.

Holgate, Alina. 1989. 'Sexual harrassment as a determinant of women's fear of rape.' *Australian Journal of Sex, Marriage & Family* no. 10 (1):21–28.

hooks, bell. 1991. 'Narratives of Struggle.' In *Critical Fictions: the Politics of Imaginative Writing*, edited by P. Mariani. Seattle: Bay Press.

Hopkins, Lekkie. 2009. *On Voice and Silence. Giving Life to a Story and Story to a Life*. Saarbrucken: VDM Verlag Dr. Muller.

Hovdestad, Wendy E., and Connie M. Kristiansen. 1996. 'Mind Meets Body: On the Nature of Recovered Memories in Trauma.' In *A Feminist Clinician's Guide to the Memory Debate*, edited by Susan Contratto and M. Janice Gutfreund. Binghamton, NY: Harrington Park Press.

Hughes, Janice. 2012. *Bodywork Therapies: A Glossary* 2012 [cited 5 December 2012]. Available from <http://www.shareguide.com/Bodywork.html>.

Hughes, Patricia, and Ian Kerr. 2000. 'Transference and countertransference in communication between doctor and patient.' *Advances in Psychiatric Treatment* no. 6:57–64.

Hunter, Dianne. 1983. 'Hysteria, Psychoanalysis, and Feminism: The case of Anna O.' *Feminist Studies* no. 9 (3).

Hurst, Claire, Jane MacDonald, Janet Say, and John Read. 2003. 'Routine questioning about non-consenting sex: a survey of practice in Australasian sexual health clinics.' *International Journal of STD & AIDS* no. 14 (5):329–333.

Hustvedt, Asti. 2011. *Medical Muses: Hysteria in Nineteenth-Century Paris*. New York: W.W. Norton & Company, Inc.

Inckle, Kay. 2007. *Writing on the Body? Thinking Through Gendered Embodiment and Marked Flesh*. Newcastle: Cambridge Scholars Publishing.

Irigaray, Luce. 1985a. *Speculum of the Other Woman*. Ithaca, NY: Cornell University Press.

Irigaray, Luce. 1985b. *This Sex Which is Not One*. Ithaca: Cornell University Press.

Irigaray, Luce. 1993. *An Ethics of Sexual Difference*. London: Athlone.

ISMETA. 2012. *International Somatic Movement Education and Therapy Association* 2012 [cited 30 November 2012]. Available from <http://www.ismeta.org/home.html>.

Jackson, Alecia Y., and Lisa A. Mazzei. 2008. 'Experience and "I" in Autoethnography: A Deconstruction.' *International Review of Qualitative Research* no. 1 (3):299–318.

James, Nalita, and Hugh Busher. 2006. 'Credibility, authenticity and voice: dilemmas in online interviewing.' *Qualitative Research* no. 6 (3):403–420.

James, Nalita, and Hugh Busher. 2009. 'Engaging with Research Participants Online.' In *Online Interviewing*, edited by Nalita James and Hugh Busher. London: SAGE Publications Ltd.

Johnson, Don Hanlon, ed. 1995. *Bone, Breath, & Gesture: Practices of Embodiment*. Berkeley: North Atlantic Books.

Johnson, Don Hanlon. 2012. *Somatics* 2012 [cited 30 November 2012]. Available from <http://donhanlonjohnson.com/about.html>.

Johnson, Susan K. 2008. *Medically unexplained illness: Gender and biopsychosocial implications*. WAshington DC: American Psychological Assoication.

Joinson, Adam N. 2001. 'Self-Disclosure in computer-mediated communication: The role of self-awareness and visual anonymity.' *European Journal of Social Psychology* no. 31 (2):177–192.

Jones, Gail. 2007. *Sorry*. North Sydney: Random House Australia Pty Ltd.

Jones, Stacy Holman. 2008. 'Autoethnography: Making the Personal Political.' In *Collecting and Interpreting Qualitative Materials*, edited by Norman K. Denzin and Yvonne S. Lincoln. Thousand Oaks, California: Sage Publications.

Jordan, Jan. 2001. 'Worlds Apart? Women, Rape and the Police Reporting Process.' *British Journal of Criminology* no. 41 (679–706).

Jordan, Judith V. 2008. 'Valuing Vulnerability: New Definitions of Courage.' *Women & Therapy* no. 31 (2–4):209–233. doi: 10.1080/02703140802146399.

Juhan, Deane. 1987. 'Job's Body: A Handbook for Bodywork (Excerpts).' In *Bone, Breath & Gesture: Practices of Embodiment*, edited by Don Hanlon Johnson, 355–378. Berkeley: North Atlantic Books.

Kaukinen, Catherine, and Alfred DeMaris. 2009. 'Sexual Assault and Current Mental Health: The Role of Help-Seeking and Police Response.' *Violence Against Women* no. 15 (11):1131–1357.

Kimerling, Rachel, and Karen S. Calhoun. 1994. 'Somatic Symptoms, Social Support, and Treatment Seeking Among Sexual Assault Victims.' *Journal of Consulting and Clinical Psychology* no. 62 (2):333–340.

King, Helen. 2011. 'Galen and the widow: towards a history of therapeutic masturbation in ancient gynaecology.' *Journal on Gender Studies in Antiquity* no. 1:205–235.

King, Rosalyn M. 2014. *The Enteric Nervous System: The Brain in the Gut*. Rosalyn King 2014 [cited 6 February 2014]. Available from <http://www.psyking.net/id36.htm>.

Kirby, Vicki. 1991. 'Corporeal Habits: Addressing Essentialism Differently.' *Hypatia* no. 6 (3).

Kirby, Vicki. 1997. *Telling Flesh: The Substance of the Corporeal*. New York: Routledge.

Kirby, Vicki. 2003. 'Enumerating Language: "The Unreasonable Effectiveness of Mathematics".' *Configurations: A Journal of Literature, Science, and Technology* no. 11 (3):417–439.

Kirby, Vicki. 2008. 'Natural Convers(at)tions: or, what if Culture was Nature all along?' In *Material Feminisms*, edited by Stacy Alaimo and Susan Hekman, 214–236. Bloomington: Indianna University Press.

Kirby, Vicki. 2012. 'Initial conditions.' *differences: A Journal of Feminist Cultural Studies* no. 23 (3):198–205.

Klein, Renate. 2004. 'Sickening relationships: Gender-based violence, women's health, and the role of informal third parties.' *Journal of Social and Personal Relationships* no. 21 (1):149–165.

Kogan, Steven M. 2004. 'Disclosing unwanted sexual experiences: results from a national sample of adolescent women.' *Child Abuse & Neglect* no. 28:147–165.

Kong, Rebecca, Holly Johnson, Sara Beattie, and Andrea Cardillo. 2003. 'Sexual Offences in Canada.' Cat No. 85-002-XIE, Vol. 23, No. 6 Canadian Centre for Justice Studies. <http://www.statcan.gc.ca/pub/85-002-x/85-002-x2003006-eng.pdf>.

Koss, Mary P. 2005. 'Empirically Enhanced Reflections on 20 Years of Rape Research.' *Journal of Interpersonal Violence* no. 20 (100).

Koss, Mary P., and Laura Boeschen. 2000. 'Rape.' In *Encyclopedia of psychology*, edited by Alan Kazdin, 1–6. Washington, DC: American Psychology Association.

Koss, Mary P., and Aurelio Jose Figueredo. 2004. 'Cognitive Mediation of Rape's Mental Health Impact: Constructive Replication of a Cross-Sectional Model in Longitudinal Data.' *Psychology of Women Quarterly* no. 28:273–286.

Kristeva, Julia. 1982a. 'Approaching Abjection.' In *Powers of Horror. An Essay on Abjection*. New York: Columbia University Press.

Kristeva, Julia. 1982b. *The Powers of Horror: An Essay on Abjection*. New York: Colombia University Press.

Lam, Carla. 2012. 'Past the Impasse, The (New) Material Feminisms.' In *The Canadian Political Science Association conference* University of Alberta, Edmonton.

Larcombe, Wendy, and Mary Heath. 2012. 'Developing the common law and rewriting the history of rape in marriage in Australia: PGA v. The Queen.' *Sydney Law Review* no. 34 (4):785+.

Le Guin, Ursula. 1989. *Dancing at the Edge of the World*. London: Paladin.

Lee, Adeline, Jan Coles, Stuart Lee, and Jayashri Kulkarni. 2012. 'Women survivors of child abuse: Don't ask, don't tell.' *Australian Family Physician* no. 41 (11).

Lee, Deborah A., and Sophie James. 2013. 'The Compassionate-Mind Guide to Recovering from Trauma and PTSD: Using Compassion-Focused Therapy to Overcome Flashbacks, Shame, Guilt, and Fear.' In. Oakland, CA: New Harbinger Publications. <http://ECU.eblib.com.au/patron/FullRecord.aspx?p=1108651>.

Leijssen, Mia. 2006. 'Validation of the body in psychotherapy.' *Journal of Humanistic Psychology* no. 46 (2).

Letherby, G. 2003. *Feminist Research in Theory & Practice*. Buckingham: Open University Press.

Levine, Peter A. 1997. *Waking the Tiger: Healing Trauma*. Berkeley: North Atlantic Books.

Levine, Peter A. 2008. *Healing Trauma: A Pioneering Program for Restoring the Wisdom of Your Body*. Boulder, CO: Sounds True, Inc.

Levine, Peter A. 2009. 'A Summary of Trauma & Somatic Experience.'

Lievore, Denise. 2003. 'Non-Reporting & Hidden Recording of Sexual Assault: An International Literature Review.' Australian Institute of Criminology

Lievore, Denise. 2005. 'No longer silent: A study of women's help seeking decisions and service responses to sexual assault.' Canberra: Australian Institute of Criminology.

Littleton, Heather, Danny Axsom, Carmen Radecki Breitkopf, and Abbey Berenson. 2006. 'Rape Acknowledgement and Postassault Experiences: How Acknowledgement Status Relates to Disclosure, Coping, Worldview, and Reactions Received From Others.' *Violence and Victims* no. 21 (6).

Lorde, Audre. 2000. 'Age, Race, Class, and Sex: Women Redefining Women.' In *Feminist Theory: A Reader*, edited by Wendy Komar and Frances Bartkowsli, 288–293. Mountain View, Cal: Mayfield.

Mahoney, Maureen A. 1996. 'The problem of silence in feminist psychology.' *Feminist Studies* no. 22.

Mairs, Nancy. 1994. *voice lessons: On Becoming a (Woman) Writer*. Boston: Beacon Press.

Malagelada, J.R., F. Bazzoli, A. Elewaut, M. Fried, J.H. Krabshuis, G. Lindberg, P. Malfertheiner, P. Sharma, and N. Vakil. 2014. *Dysphagia*. World Gastroenterology Association 2007 [cited 6 February 2014]. Available from <http://www.world-gastroenterology.org/assets/downloads/en/pdf/guidelines/08_dysphagia.pdf>.

Martin, Sandra L., Siobhan K. Young, Deborah L. Billings, and C. Christopher Bross. 2007. 'Health Care-Based Interventions for Women Who Have Experienced Sexual Violence: A Review of the Literature.' *Trauma, Violence, & Abuse* no. 8 (1):3–18.

Maynard, Mary, and Jan Winn. 1997. 'Women, Violence & Male Power.' In *Introducing Women's Studies (2nd Edition)*, edited by V. Robinson and D. Richardson. Basingstoke: MacMillan Press Ltd.

Mazza, Danielle, Lorraine Dennerstein, and Vicky Ryan. 1996. 'Physical, sexual and emotional violence against women: a general practice-based prevalence study.' *Medical Journal of Australia* no. 164:14–17.

McAndrew, Sue, and Tony Warne. 2005. 'Cutting across boundaries: A case study using feminist praxis to understand the meanings of self-harm.' *International Journal of Mental Health Nursing* no. 14:172–180.

McKie, Linda, Barbara Fennell, and Jarmila Mildorf. 2002. 'Time to disclose, timing disclosure: GPs' discourses on disclosing domestic abuse in primary care.' *Sociology of Health & Illness* no. 24 (3):327–346.

McLaren, Rosie. 2001a. *Menopause, Art and the Body: Contemporary tales from the daughters of hysteria*. Flaxton: Post Pressed.

McLaren, Rosie. 2001b. 'Off the Page.' In *The Art of Writing Inquiry*, edited by Lorri Neilsen, Ardra L. Cole and J. Gary Knowles. Halifax, Nova Scotia: Backalong Books.

Mead, Veronique. 2012. *An introduction to the history, background, and theoretical perspectives of Somatic Psychology* 2012 [cited 21 November 2012]. Available from <http://www.veroniquemead.com/articles/somatic_bkgd.pdf>.

Mechanic, Mindy B., Patricia A. Resnick, and Michael G. Griffin. 1998. 'A Comparison of Normal Forgetting, Psychopathology, and Information-Processing Models of Reported Amnesia for Recent Sexual Trauma.' *Journal of Consulting and Clinical Psychology* no. 66 (6):948–957.

Meho, Lokman I. 2006. 'E-mail interviewing in qualitative research: A methodological discussion.' *Journal of the American Society for Information Science and Technology* no. Volume 57 (10):1284–1295. doi: 10.1002/asi.20416.

Mercer, Leah. 2012. 'The physics of practice-led methodology or; sometimes you fly and sometimes you perch.' In *Live Research: Methods of Practice-Led Inquiry in Performance*, edited by Leah Mercer, Julie Robson and David Fenton, 115–129. Nerang: Ladyfinger.

Merleau-Ponty, Maurice. 1962. *Phenomenology of Perception*. London: Routledge & Kegan Paul.

Merleau-Ponty, Maurice. 1968. *The Visible and the Invisible*. Translated by Alphonso Lingis. Edited by Claude Lefort. Evanston: Northwestern University Press.

Metcalf, Robert. 2006. 'Unrequited Narcissism: On the Origin of Shame.' <http://www.historyofethics.org/092006/092006Metcalf.shtml>.

Metta, Marilyn. 2010. *Writing Against, Alongside and Beyond Memory: Lifewriting as Reflexive, Poststructuralist Feminist Research Practice*. Bern: Peter Lang.

Micale, Mark S. 1995. *Approaching Hysteria: Disease & Its Interpretations*. New Jersey: Princeton University Press.

Michaels, Anne. 1997. *The Weight of Oranges. Miner's Pond*. Toronto: McClelland & Stewart Ltd.

Miller, Gill Wright 2011. 'Postmodernism, Body-Mind Centering, and the Academy.' In *Exploring Body-Mind Centering: An Anthology of Experience and Method*, edited by Gill Wright Miller, Pat Ethridge and Kate Tarlow Morgan. Berkeley: North Atlantic Books.

Mills, Letty, J., and Judith Daniluk, C. 2002. 'Her Body Speaks: The Experience of Dance Therapy for Women Survivors of Child Sexual Abuse.' *Journal of Counselling and Development* no. 80 (1).

Minge, Jeanine Marie. 2007. 'The Stained Body: A Fusion of Embodied Art on Rape and Love.' *Journal of Contemporary Ethnography* no. 36 (3):252–280.

Ministry of Justice, Home Office & The Office for National Statistics. 2013. 'An Overview of Sexual Offending in England and Wales.' Edited by Home Office & The Office for National Statistics Ministry of Justice: Ministry of Justice, Home Office & The Office for National Statistics.

Modjeska, Drusilla. 1995. *The Orchard*. Sydney: Picador.

Moore, Bruce, ed. 2002. *The Australian Pocket Oxford Dictionary (5th Edition)*. South Melbourne: Oxford University Press.

Moran, Patricia. 1996. *Word of Mouth: Body Language in Katherine Mansfield and Virginia Woolf*. Charlottesville: The University Press of Virginia.

Morrison, Zoe, Antonia Quadara, and Cameron Boyd. 2007. '"Ripple effects" of sexual assault.' ACSSA Issues No. 7. edited by Australian Centre for the Study of Sexual Assault.

Mouzos, Jenny, and Toni Makkai. 2004. 'Women's Experience of Male Violence: Findings from the Australian Component of the International Violence Against Women Survey (IVAWS).' Australian Institute of Criminology.

Myers, Thomas W. 1998. 'Kinesthetic dystonia: what bodywork can offer a new physical education.' *Journal of Bodywork and Movement Therapies* no. 2 (2):101–114.

Myers, Thomas W. 1999. 'Kinesthetic dystonia: the contribution of bodywork to somatic education.' *Journal of Bodywork and Movement Therapies* no. 3 (2):107–116.

Myhill, Andy, and Jonathan Allen. 2002. 'Rape & sexual assault of women: findings from the British Crime Survey (2000).' Home Office Research Study 237.

Najdowski, Cynthia J., and Sarah E. Ullman. 2009. 'PTSD symptoms and self-rated recovery among adult sexual assault survivors: The effects of traumatic life events and psychosocial variables.' *Psychology of Women* no. 33:43–53.

Neame, Alexandra, and Melanie Heenan. 2003. 'What lies behind the hidden figure of sexual assault? Issues of prevalence and disclosure.' Edited by Australian Centre for the Study of Sexual Assault.

Neilsen Glenn, Lorri. 2011. *Threading Light: Explorations in Loss and Poetry*. Regina, SK: Hagios Press.

Neilsen, Lorri. 2008. 'Lyric Inquiry.' In *Handbook of the Arts in Qualitative Research: Perspectives, Methodologies, Examples & Issues*, edited by J. Gary Knowles and Ardra L. Cole. Thousand Oaks, CA: SAGE Publications, Inc.

Newman, Elana, and Danny G. Kaloupek. 2004. 'The Risks and Benefits of Participating in Trauma-Focused Research Studies.' *Journal of Traumatic Stress* no. 17 (5):383–394.

Nijenhuis, Ellert R.S., and Onno van der Hart. 1999. 'Forgetting and Reexperiencing Trauma: From Anesthesia to Pain.' In *Splintered Reflections: Images of the Body in Trauma*, edited by Jean M. Goodwin and Reina Attias. New York: Basic Books.

O'Donovan, Analise, Grant J. Devilly, and Ronald Rapee. 2007. 'Antecedents to Women's Fear of Rape.' *Behaviour Change* no. 24 (3):135–145.

Ogden, Pat, and Kekuni Minton. 2001. 'Sensorimotor Processing for Trauma Recovery.' *Psychotherapy in Australia* no. 7 (3):42–46.

Ogden, Pat, Kekuni Minton, and Clare Pain. 2006. *Trauma and the Body: A Sensorimotor Approach to Psychotherapy*. New York: W.W. Norton & Company, Inc.

Olsen, Andrea. 1998. *Bodystories: A Guide to Experiential Anatomy*. Lebanon: University Press of New England.

Page, L.A., and S. Wessely. 2003. 'Medically unexplained symptoms: exacerbating factors in the doctor-patient encounter.' *Journal of the Royal Society of Medicine* no. 96:223–227.

Pennebaker, James W., and Lori D. Stone. 2004. 'Translating traumatic experiences into language: Implications for child abuse and long-term health.' In *From child sexual abuse to adult sexual risk: Trauma, revictimization, and intervention.*, edited by Linda J. Koenig, Lynda S. Doll, Ann O'Leary and Willo Pequegnat, 201–216. American Psychological Association.

Pert, Candace. 1999. *Molecules of Emotion*. London: Simon & Schuster UK Ltd.

Peseta, Tai. 2007. 'Troubling our Desires for Research and Writing within the Academic Development Project.' *International Journal for Academic Development* no. 12 (1):15–23. doi: 10.1080/13601440701217253.

Phelan, James E. 2009. 'Exploring the use of touch in the psychotherapeutic setting: A phenomenological review.' *Psychotherapy Theory, Research, Practice, Training* no. 46 (1):97–111.

Pollock, Della. 2005. 'Introduction: Remembering.' In *Remembering: Oral History Performance*, edited by Della Pollock, 1–17. Gordonsville: Palgrave Macmillan.

Psychotherapy, Australian College of Contemporary Somatic. 2012. *Contemporary Somatic Psychotherapy* 2012 [cited 21 November 2012]. Available from <http://www.somaticpsychotherapy.com.au/index.php?option=com_content&task=view&id=42&Itemid=38>.

Quadara, Antonia. 2008. ACSSA Wrap No. 6. 'Responding to young people disclosing sexual assault: A resource for schools.' <http://www.aifs.gov.au/acssa/pubs/wrap/w6.html>.

Reed-Danahay, Deborah. 1997. 'Introduction.' In *Rewriting the Self & the Social*, edited by D. Reed-Danahay. Oxford: Berg.

Reiki.org. 2012. *What is Reiki?* 2012 [cited 5 December 2012]. Available from <http://www.reiki.org/faq/whatisreiki.html>.

Reinharz, Shulamit. 1992. *Feminist Methods in Social Research*. Oxford: Oxford University Press, Inc.

Rensberger, Boyce. 1996. *Life Itself: Exploring the Realm of the Living Cell.* Oxford: Oxford University Press.

Resnick, Patricia A., and Monica K. Schnicke. 1996. *Cognitive Processing Therapy for Rape Victims: A Treatment Manual.* Newbury Park, CA: Sage Publications, Inc.

Richardson, Laurel. 2000. 'Writing: A method of inquiry.' In *Handbook of qualitative research (2nd ed.)*, edited by N.K. Denzin and Y.S. Lincoln, 923–948. Thousand Oaks, CA: Sage Publications Inc.

Rieff, David, ed. 2012. *Susan Sontag: As Consciousness Is Harnessed to Flesh. Journals & Notebooks 1964–1980*. New York: Farrar, Straus and Giroux.

Robinaugh, Donald J., and Richard J. McNally. 2010. 'Autobiographical memory for shame or guilt provoking events: Association with psychological symptoms.' *Behaviour Research and Therapy* no. 48 (7):646–652. doi: http://dx.doi.org/10.1016/j.brat.2010.03.017.

Robohm, Jennifer S., and Margaret Buttenheim. 1997. 'The Gynecological Care Experience of Adult Survivors of Childhood Sexual Abuse: A Preliminary Investigation.' *Women & Health* no. 24 (3):59–75.

Roe, Stephen, Kathryn Coleman, and Peter Kaiza. 2009. 'Crime in England & Wales 2008/09.'

Rogers, Mary F. 2005. 'Postmodernist Feminisms.' In *Encyclopedia of Social Theory*, edited by George Ritzer. Thousand Oaks, CA: SAGE Publications, Inc.

Rosenfield, Israel. 1988. *The Invention of Memory*. New York: Basic Books.

Roth, Susan, and Leslie Lebowitz. 1988. 'The experience of sexual trauma.' *Journal of Traumatic Stress* no. 1 (1):79–107.

Rothschild, Babette. 2000. *The Body Remembers: The Psychophysiology of Trauma and Trauma Treatment*. New York: W.W. Norton & Company, Inc.

Rozee, Patricia D., and Mary P. Koss. 2001. 'Rape: A Century of Resistance.' *Psychology of Women Quarterly* no. 25:295–311.

Salverston, Julie. 2001. 'Change on Whose Terms? Testimony and an Erotics of Inquiry.' *Theater* no. 31 (3):119–125.

Sarantakos, Sotirios. 1998. *Social Research (2nd Edition)*. South Yarra: Macmillan Education Australia Pty Ltd.

Sarantakos, Sotirios. 2005. *Social Research (3rd Edition)*. New York: Palgrave Macmillan.

SARC. 2013. 'What is sexual assault and sexual abuse?' Edited by Department of Health. Perth: Sexual Assault Resource Centre.

Sarton, May. 1973. *Journal of a Solitude*. New York: W.W. Norton & Company.

Scaer, Robert C. 2001. *The Body Bears the Burden: Trauma, Dissociation, and Disease*. Binghamton, NY: The Haworth Medical Press.

Scull, Andrew. 2009. *Hysteria: The Biography*. Oxford: Oxford University Press.

SECASA. 2012a. 'How the legal system responds to sexual assault victim/survivors.' <http://www.secasa.com.au/pages/how-the-legal-system-responds-to-sexual-assault-victim-survivors>.

SECASA. 'What are the effects of child sexual assault?' SECASA 2012b [cited February 28, 2014. <http://www.secasa.com.au/sections/for-students/what-are-the-effects-of-child-sexual-assault>.

Sellers, Susan. 2002. '"Magnetizing the world": an interview with Helene Cixous.' In *helene cixous: The Writing Notebooks*, edited by Susan Sellers, 116–122. London: Continuum.

Seu, Bruna Irene. 1996. *A Psychoanalytic Feminist Inquiry into Shame*, University of London, London.

Seu, Bruna Irene. 2006. 'Shameful selves: Women's feelings of inadequacy & constructed facades.' *European Journal of Psychotherapy and Counseling* no. 8 (3).

Seu, Bruna Irene. 2008. 'Shameful silences: self-protective secrets & methodological omissions.' In *Secrets and Silences in the Research Process: Feminist Reflections*, edited by R. Ryan-Flood and R. Gill. London: Routledge.

Showalter, Elaine. 1998. *Hystories: Hysterical Epidemics and Modern Culture*. London Picador.

Shusterman, Richard. 2008. *Body Consciousness: A Philosphy of Mindfulness and Somaesthetics*. New York: Cambridge University Press.

Singh, Bruce S. 2009. 'Managing somatoform disorders.' *Medical Journal of Australia*:90–95. Retrieved October 12, 2009, from <http://www.mja.com.au/public/mentalhealth/course/15singh.pdf>.

Smith, Daniel W., Elizabeth J. Letourneau, Benjamin E. Saunders, Dean G. Kilpatrick, Heidi S. Resnick, and Connie L. Best. 2000. 'Delay in Disclosure of Childhood Rape: Results from a National Survey.' *Child Abuse & Neglect* no. 24 (2):273–287.

Smyth, J.M., K.E. Heron, S.A. Wonderlich, R.D. Crosby, and J.M. Thompson. 2008. 'The influence of reported trauma and adverse events on eating disturbance in young adults.' *International Journal of Eating Disorders* no. 41 195–202.

Snyder, Howard N. 2000. 'Sexual Assault of Young Children as Reported to Law Enforcement: Victim, Incident, and Offender Characteristics.' Edited by United States Department of Justice.

Somatics. 2012. *Educational Resources* [cited 15 November 2012]. Available from <http://www.somaticsed.com>.

Somerville, Margaret. 1999. *Body/Landscape Journals*. North Melbourne: Spinifex Press Pty Ltd.

Somerville, Margaret. 2004. 'Tracing bodylines: the body in feminist poststructural research.' *International Journal of Qualitative Studies in Education* no. 17 (1).

Spelman, Elizabeth V. 1982. 'Woman as Body: Ancient and Contemporary Views.' *Feminist Studies* no. 8 (1):109–130.

Spelman, Elizabeth V. 1988. *Inesential Woman*. Boston: Beacon Press.

Spry, Tami. 1995. 'In the absence of word and body: hegemonic implications of "victim" and "survivor" in women's narratives of sexual violence.' *Women and Language* no. 18 (2).

Spry, Tami. 2009. 'Bodies of/as Evidence in Autoethnography.' *International Review of Qualitative Research* no. 1 (4):603–610.

Spry, Tami. 2010. 'Performative Autoethnography: Critical Embodiments and Possibilites.' In *The Sage Handbook of Qualitative Research*, edited by N.K. Denzin and Y.S. Lincoln. Thousand Oaks, CA: Sage.

Spry, Tami. 2011. *Body, Paper, Stage: Writing and Performing Autoethnography*. Walnut Creek, CA: Left Coast Press, Inc.

St. Pierre, Elizabeth Adams. 2000. 'Poststructural feminism in education: An overview.' *International Journal of Qualitative Studies in Education* no. 13 (5):477–515. doi: 10.1080/09518390050156422.

Stacey, Jackie. 1997. 'Feminist Theory: Capital F, Capital T.' In *Introducing Women's Studies*, edited by Victoria Robinson and Diane Richardson. Basingstoke: Macmillan Press Ltd.

Stanko, Elizabeth A. 1985. *Intimate Intrusions: Women's Experience of Male Violence*. London: Unwin.

Starks Whitehouse, Mary. 1999. 'Physical Movement and Personality (1963).' In *Authentic Movement: A Collection of Essays by Mary Starks Whitehouse, Janet Adler & Joan Chodrow*, edited by Patrizia Pallaro. London: J. Kingsley Publishers.

Starzynski, Laura L., S.E. Ullman, Stephanie M. Townsend, LaDonna M. Long, and Susan M. Long. 2007. 'What Factors Predict Women's Disclosure of Sexual Assault to Mental Health Professionals?' *Journal of Community Psychology* no. 35 (5):619–638.

Starzynski, Laura L., Sarah E. Ullman, Henrietta H. Filipas, and Stephanie M. Townsend. 2005. 'Correlates of Women's Sexual Assault Disclosure to Informal and Formal Support Services.' *Violence and Victims* no. 20 (4).

Stein, Gertrude. 1990. *The Autobiography of Alice B. Toklas*. New York: Vintage Books.

Stenzel, Cheryl L., and Patricia A. Rupert. 2004. 'Psychologists' use of touch in individual psychotherapy.' *Psychotherapy: Theory, Research, Practice, Training* no. 41 (3):332–345.

Stromsted, Tina. 2007. 'The Dancing Body in Psychotherapy: Reflections on Somatic Psychotherapy and Authentic Movement.' In *Authentic Movement: Moving the Body, Moving the Self, Being Moved*, edited by Patrizia Pallaro. London: Jessica Kingsley Publishers.

Stromsted, Tina. 2009. 'Authentic Movement: A dance with the divine.' *Body, Movement and Dance in Psychotherapy* no. 4 (3):201–213.

Tamas, Sophie. 2009. 'Writing and righting trauma: Troubling the autoethnographic voice.' *Forum: Qualitative Social Research* no. 10 (1).

Tarczon, Cindy, and Antonia Quadara. 2012. 'The nature and extent of sexual assault and abuse in Australia.' ACSSA Resource Sheet. edited by Australian Institute of Family Studies: Australian Government.

Thomas, Suzanne. 2001. 'Reimagining Inquiry, Envisioning Form.' In *The Art of Writing Inquiry*, edited by Lorri Neilsen, Ardra L. Cole and J. Gary Knowles. Nova Scotia: Backalong Books.

Thompson, Kevin M., and Stephen A. Wonderlich. 2004. 'Child sexual abuse and eating disorders.' In *Handbook of Eating Disorders and Obesity*, edited by J.K. Thompson. Hoboken, NJ: John Wiley and Sons.

Thompson, Kevin M., Stephen A. Wonderlich, Ross D. Crosby, and James E. Mitchell. 2001. 'Sexual Violence and Weight Control Techniques Among Adolescent Girls.' *International Journal of Eating Disorders* no. 29:166–176.

Thompson, Martie, Ileana Arias, Kathleen C. Basile, and Sujata Desai. 2002. 'The Association Between Childhood Physical and Sexual Victimization and Health Problems in Adulthood in a Nationally Representative Sample of Women.' *Journal of Interpersonal Violence* no. 17 (10):1115–1129.

Tjaden, Patricia, and Nancy Thoennes. 2008. 'Extent, Nature & Consequences of Rape Victimization: Findings from the National Violence Against Women Survey.' Edited by United States Department of Justice.

Tong, Rosemarie. 1992. *Feminist Thought: A Comprehensive Introduction*. London: Routledge.

Toronto, Ellen L.K. 2001. 'The Human Touch: An Exploration of the Role and Meaning of Physical touch in Psychoanalysis.' *Psychoanalytic Psychology* no. 18 (1):37–54.

Tortora, Gerard. J., and Bryan Derrickson. 2009. *Principles of Anatomy and Physiology (12th Edition)*. Hoboken: John Wiley & Sons, Inc.

Toronto Police Service. 2013. 'Statistics'. Toronto Police Service.

Trimble, Michael. 2004. *Somatoform Disorders: A medicolegal guide*. Cambridge, UK: Cambridge University Press.

Trinh, T. Minh-ha. 1999. 'Write Your Body and The Body in Theory.' In *Feminist Theory & the Body: A Reader*, edited by J. Price and M. Shildrick. Edinburgh: Edinburgh University Press.

Ullman, Sarah E. 1996. 'Correlates and Consequences of Adult Sexual Assault Disclosure.' *Journal of Interpersonal Violence* no. 11. doi: 10.1177/088626096011004007.

Ullman, Sarah E., and Leanne R. Brecklin. 2002. 'Sexual assaualt history, PTSD, and mental health service seeking in a national sample of women.' *Journal of Community Psychology* no. 30 (3):261–279.

Ullman, Sarah E., and H.H. Filipas. 2001. 'Correlates of Formal & Informal Support Seeking in Sexual Assault Victims.' *Journal of Interpersonal Violence* no. 1028e (16).

Ullman, Sarah E., Stephanie M. Townsend, H.H. Filipas, and Laura L. Starzynski. 2007. 'Structural Models of the Relations of Asssault Severity, Social Support, Avoidance Coping, Self-Blame, and PTSD Among Sexual Assault Survivors.' *Psychology of Women Quarterly* no. 31:23–37.

UN. 2007. 'Violence Against Women. Facts and Figures. Sexual Violence.' UN Development Fund For Women. <http://www.unifem.org/attachments/gender_issues/violence_against_women/facts_figures_violence_against_women_2007.pdf>.

Ussher, Jane. 1989. *The Psychology of the Female Body*. London: Routledge.

van der Kolk, Bessel A. 1994. 'The Body Keeps the Score: Memory and the Evolving Psychobiology of Posttraumatic Stress.' *Harvard Review of Psychiatry* no. 1:253–265.

van der Kolk, Bessel A. 1998. 'Trauma and memory.' *Psychiatry and Clinical Neurosciences* no. 52 (S1):52–64. doi: 10.1046/j.1440-1819.1998.0520s5S97.x.

van der Kolk, Bessel A. 2007. 'Trauma and Memory.' In *Traumatic Stress: The Effects of Overwhelming Experience on Mind, Body and Society*, edited by Bessel A. van der Kolk, Alexander C. McFarlane and Lars Weisaeth. New York: The Guilford Press.

van der Kolk, Bessel A., Onno van der Hart, and Charles Marmar, R. 2007. 'Dissociation and Information Processing in Posttraumatic Stress Disorder.' In *Traumatic Stress*, edited by Bessel A. van der Kolk, Alexander C. McFarlane and Lars Weisaeth. New York: The Guilford Press.

van der Kolk, Bessel A., Lars Weisaeth, and Onno van der Hart. 2007. 'History of Trauma in Psychiatry.' In *Traumatic Stress: The Effects of Overwhelming Experience on MInd, Body, and Society*, edited by Bessel A. van der kolk, Alexander C. McFarlane and Lars Weisaeth. New York: The Guildford Press.

van der Tuin, Iris. 2011. '"New feninist materialisms".' *Women's Studies International Forum* no. 34:271–277.

van der Tuin, Iris, and Rick Dolphijn. 2010. 'The Transversality of New Materialism.' *Women: A Cultural Review* no. 21 (2):153–171. doi: 10.1080/09574042.2010.488377.

Vidal, Maria Elena, and Jenny Petrak. 2007. 'Shame and adult sexual assault: a study with a group of female survivors recruited from an East London population.' *Sexual and Relationship Therapy* no. 22 (2):159–171. doi: 10.1080/14681990600784143.

Waldinger, Robert J., Marc S. Schulz, Arthur J. Barsky, and David K. Ahern. 2006. 'Mapping the Road From Childhood Trauma to Adult Somatization: The Role of Attachment.' *Psychosomatic Medicine* no. 68:129–135.

Warr, Deborah J. 2004. 'Stories in the Flesh and Voices in the Head: Reflections on the Context and Impact of Research with Disadvantaged Populations.' *Qualitative Health Research* no. 14:578–587.

Weedon, Chris. 1992. *Feminist Practice and Poststructuralist Theory*. Cambridge: Blackwell.

Weiss, Karen G. 2010. 'Too Ashamed to Report: Deconstructing the Shame of Sexual Victimisation.' *Feminist Criminology* no. 5 (3):286–310.

Whitehouse, Mary 1995. 'The Tao of the Body (1958).' In *Bone, Breath and Gesture: Practices of Embodiment*, edited by Don Hanlon Johnson. Berkeley, CA: North Atlantic Books.

WHO. 2002. 'World Report on Violence and Health.' Chapter 6. Sexual Violence. <http://www.who.int/violence_injury_prevention/violence/global_campaign/en/chap6.pdf>.

WHO and PAHO. 2012. 'Understanding and addressing violence against women.' <http://apps.who.int/iris/bitstream/10665/77434/1/WHO_RHR_12.37_eng.pdf>.

Wilson, Elizabeth A. 1998. *Neural Geographies: Feminism and the Microstructure of Cognition*. New York: Routledge.

Wilson, Elizabeth A. 2004a. 'Gut Feminism.' *Differences* no. 15 (3):66–94.

Wilson, Elizabeth A. 2004b. *Psychosomatic: Feminism and the Neurological Body*. Durham: Duke University Press.

Wilson, Elizabeth A. 2008. 'Organic Empathy: Feminism, Psychopharmaceuticals, and the Embodiment of Depression.' In *Material Feminisms*, edited by Stacy Alaimo and Susan Hekman, 373–399. Bloomington: Indiana University Press.

Wonderlich, Stephen A., Ross D. Crosby, James E. Mitchell, Kevin M. Thompson, Jennifer Redlin, Gail Demuth, Joshua Smyth, and Beth Haseltine. 2001. 'Eating Disturbance and Sexual Trauma in Childhood and Adulthood.' *International Journal of Eating Disorders* no. 30:401–412.

Woolf, Virginia. 1953. *A Writer's Diary*. Orlando: Harcourt, Inc.

Woolf, Virginia. 2008. *Virginia Woolf: Selected Essays*. Oxford: Oxford University Press.

Wright, Miller, Gill, Pat Etheridge, and Kate Tarlow Morgan, eds. 2011. *Exploring Body-Mind Centering: An Anthology of Experience and Method*. Berkeley: North Atlantic Books.

Yodanis, Carrie L. 2004. 'Gender Inequality, Violence Against Women, and Fear: A Cross-National Test of the Feminist Theory of Violence Against Women.' *Journal of Interpersonal Violence* no. 19 (6):655–675.

Young, Courtenay. 2006. 'One hundred and fifty years on: The history, significance and scope of body psychotherapy today.' *Body, Movement and Dance in Psychotherapy* no. 1 (1):17–28.

Yuan, Nicole P., Mary P. Koss, and Mirto Stone. 2006. 'The Psychological Consequences of Sexual Trauma.' <http://www.vawnet.org>.

Appendix 1

> Cells are a microcosm of our individual self. Each cell is an aspect of our self, of our unconscious and conscious behaviour.
>
> — BONNIE BAINBRIDGE COHEN

As a practice with a philosophy grounded in materiality, embodied consciousness, and experiential learning, and with a deep regard for the intelligence of the body, Body-Mind Centering provided me with a framework of understanding which informed my research praxis as well as provided an access point for my research method. This appendix provides an explication of the Body-Mind Centering philosophy and approach.

***

The School for Body-Mind Centering was established in New York City in 1973 by founder, Bonnie Bainbridge Cohen. The philosophy that underpins the Body-Mind Centering approach grew out of her research in a range of body-focused fields including dance, occupational therapy, neurodevelopmental therapy, Western medicine, and the sciences (anatomy, physiology, kinesiology). The philosophy additionally draws on Bainbridge Cohen's interests in Eastern body-centred movement and healing practices, the arts, and eastern philosophical traditions and practices, including yoga and tai chi (Wright Miller, Etheridge, and Tarlow Morgan 2011).

Body-Mind Centering is not 'a random amalgamation of information but a coherent understanding that can be systematically taught, verbally articulated, and personally experienced' (Wright Miller, Etheridge, and Tarlow Morgan 2011, xii–xiii). While the use of the word *systematically* suggests a deliberate and methodical pedagogy, Alice points out that the teaching is not prescriptive: 'Body-Mind Centering is an *approach*, not a technique. It is philosophically different from other systems of learning such as Alexander Technique and Feldenkrais Method' (A. Cummins, personal communication, February 20, 2013). Body-Mind Centering offers a fluid and porous approach to learning. By valuing the uniqueness of the practitioner's, student's or client's experiential and embodied understandings, the practice locates these centrally and encourages self-focused and self-directed learning. As Alice observes, 'The person structures the Body-Mind Centering material, the material doesn't structure them. Each person creates the form the material takes' (A. Cummins, personal communication, February 20, 2013).

In common with other somatic practices, the Body-Mind Centering approach begins from the central premise that body and mind are not separate entities. Rather, they are 'integrally connected and mutually interactive expressions of being' (Hartley 1995, xxx). An important point of difference however, between Body-Mind Centering and other body-based practices, is that its approach is grounded in a philosophy which values 'the specificity with which each of the body systems can be personally embodied and integrated, the fundamental groundwork of developmental repatterning, and the utilization of a body-based language to describe movement and body-based relationships' (BMC 2012). It is this philosophical grounding in these areas of attention that combine to make Body-Mind Centering a sophisticated and creative approach to somatic exploration and self-discovery. For individuals interested in developing the capacity to become active, engaged and embodied human beings, Body-Mind Centering positions itself as an experiential study with the potential to be 'transformative' (Wright Miller, Etheridge, and Tarlow Morgan 2011, xiii).

What does it mean to claim Body-Mind Centering as transformative?

The concept of transformation implies personal growth and adaptation to new ways of perceiving and experiencing ourselves and others. The Body-Mind Centering argument is that transformation is possible by working directly with the bodymind; by attending deeply to the cellular body; by freeing entrenched holding and movement patterns; by learning to develop and trust our intuition; and by embodying new states of being and moving in the world (Hartley 1995). In relation to this, Bainbridge Cohen (2008) states, 'We are the material, our bodies and minds the medium of our exploration. The research is experiential as is the material. We are each the study, the student, the teacher' (1). Bainbridge Cohen's argument here is that transformation is possible when it is self-directed and that, through experiential learning and the embodiment of that learning, we become both the instrument of learning and the instrument of change.

Somatic psychotherapist, Body-Mind Centering teacher, and writer Linda Hartley (1995) expands on Bainbridge Cohen's argument. By including the role of process in the enablement of change, Hartley's argument runs that 'the work is [also] about learning *how* [author's own emphasis] we learn – how we access information, make transitions from one state to another, and develop the awareness of this process' (xxx). My experiential understanding at the end of this project is that the work is all about the embodiment of these states of understanding and each are enhanced through self-reflexivity. The work does not involve memorising facts as one might when studying geography or history. Experiential anatomy forms a key component of the practice, so that, while the body systems can be *systematically taught,* due to the 'integrated and embodied approach to movement, the body and consciousness' (BMC 2012), *memorising* the material is simply not enough. Both experiential discovery *and* self-reflexivity are integral components of learning. It is for this reason that Bainbridge Cohen argues that the Body-Mind Centering approach 'includes both the cognitive and experiential learning of the body systems [...]' (2008, 2).

The *cognitive* and the *experiential* are the *thinking* and the *doing* of Body-Mind Centering and other somatic practices, distinguishing them from other non-experiential systems of learning. Within Body-Mind Centering, bringing together intellectual understandings with the visual imagery of the anatomical systems and encouraging the embodiment of these through guided imagination and movement (BMC 2012), facilitates the integration of the material. However, as Hartley (1995) observes 'The nature of learning is that we stand in a state of unknowing in relation to what it is that will be learned' (xxxv).

Gill Wright Miller et al (2011, xiii) suggest that one of the guiding principles of Body-Mind Centering, 'support precedes movement', reflects the philosophical underpinning of the work which values individuals for their humanity and their right to make decisions that alter their lives. This guiding principle 'requires a willingness to rest in unknowing and allow its nature to be revealed' (Wright Miller, Etheridge, and Tarlow Morgan 2011, xiii). The argument is that it is this preparedness to *rest in unknowing*, of one's own volition, that feeds and supports change; one cannot move towards change unless desire for change is present. The approach argues therefore that to begin to expand human potential there must be a propensity to move beyond preconceived ideas and beliefs and a willingness to move into the realm of the unknown, receptive to new ways of learning and open to new states of being.

Within a teaching and therapeutic context, in addition to the transmission of somatic knowledge through verbal instruction and the use of materials to support the learning (such as anatomical diagrams and texts), movement plays a crucial role. Bainbridge Cohen (2008, 1) applies the term somatisation[1] to the engagement of 'kinaesthetic experience directly, in contrast to "visualisation" which utilises visual imagery to evoke a kinaesthetic experience.' She notes it is through somatisation that 'the body cells are informing the brain as well as the brain informing the body cells' (1) and thus forms an important component of learning.

Movement plays a vital role in helping to facilitate our first experience of learning in utero. If we turn our attention to the developing foetus in the womb, in, what could be argued, the ultimate state of unknowing and self-discovery, it is possible to perceive the importance of movement to learning. As the foetus moves and grows in the uterine space surrounded by amniotic fluid, it brushes up against and presses the mother's organs. It is in this connection through movement that kinaesthetic information is received. As Bainbridge Cohen (2008, 106) argues, 'In the beginning, movement is perception.' Hartley (1995, 4) additionally notes that 'It is through movement that we first learn and establish a foundation for further growth at other levels of our being'.

1 In a footnote to her 'Introduction to Body-Mind Centering', Bonnie Bainbridge Cohen (2008) tells us she derived the term *somatisation* from the word 'soma' to 'designate the experienced body in contrast to the objectified body'. *Somatisation* can also be thought of as *guided movement* (A. Cummins, personal communication, December 26, 2013).

In terms of the value of the Body-Mind Centering philosophy to my feminist research, Susan Aposhyan (2008, vii) acknowledges the value of an approach that doesn't artificially separate body and mind intelligence. She states in the foreword to Bainbridge Cohen's (2008) text, *Sensing, Feeling, and Action*:

> For me the most precious aspect of BMC is the uncompromising belief that consciousness pervades *all* [authors emphasis] of the body. This leads one to a very intimate, almost microscopic, experience of the body. From this level, all tissues and fluids, each and every cell, are clearly intelligent, can perceive and take action. Not only can we be aware *of* [authors emphasis] each part of our physical self, we can be aware *with* [authors emphasis] each part of our physical self. (vii)

Aposhyan gives a clear example here of the ways the Body-Mind Centering approach avoids the oppositional binary by pivoting on the concept of a fluid non-hierarchical and reciprocal relationship between the body and mind. In Bainbridge Cohen's (2008, 13) words, the conscious and the unconscious are not discreet entities; rather, they 'are a continuum of one mind. They are each the shadow or support of the movement and expression of the other'. As in other somatic practices, it is this principle that grounds the Body-Mind Centering approach and provides a critical framework of guidance. This inclusivity of body and mind supports an increased consciousness of kinaesthetic experience through movement, with movement also providing a means for the bodily expression and storying of experience through non-verbal and creative articulation.

As mentioned in the body of the book, touch plays an important role in somatic practices. In Body-Mind Centering, touch offers both a means of discovery and a means of facilitating repatterning (Bainbridge Cohen 2008). The use of touch through hands-on work facilitates access to unconscious material that permeates the body systems at a cellular level and helps increase awareness of the 'subtle interplay between body and mind' (Sellers 2002, 6). Within the therapeutic and educative setting, touch facilitates a close encounter with our cellular selves. Bainbridge Cohen (2008, 6) notes:

> In hands-on work, through touching in different rhythms, through placement of attention within specific layers of the body, through following the existing lines of

> force and suggesting new ones, and through changes in the pressure and quality of our touch, we come into harmony with the different tissues and their associated qualities of mind. (6)

The *tissues* Bainbridge Cohen refers to here are the tissues that make up the systems of the body and include the skeletal, ligamentous, muscular, organs, endocrine, nervous, fluid and fascia systems (Bainbridge Cohen 2008). Hands-on work enables the quality of mind and intelligence of all the body systems to be felt, explored and interpreted. Touch, as a central bodywork skill then, invites increased awareness of the nuance and subtlety of the cells throughout the entire body. As already noted, the practice of Body-Mind Centering offers a *very intimate* (Bainbridge Cohen 2008, vii) micro experience of the patterns and processes of the body. Aposhyan (Bainbridge Cohen 2008) argues that it is this forensic attention that enables the self-identification of vulnerability and disequilibrium and opens up possibilities for the illumination of ability and potentiality.

Appendix 2

Global under-reporting and victimisation rates

Global research conducted by the World Health Organisation (2012) supports the Australian research which argues that statistics relating to sexual violence offer an estimate only of the actual prevalence of gendered sexual violence. When compared with survey data (which reaches other populations of girls and women), information drawn from sources such as crime reports, reflects the reality that only a minority of crimes are formally reported to police and therefore the data available from these sources 'produce[s] under-estimates of prevalence' (2012, 1). The World Health Organisation information cites the example of a study conducted in Latin-America in which 'only around 5% of adult victims of sexual violence reported the incident to police'. Results from the International Crime Victims Survey conducted in 1997 also found that countries whose sexual violence victimisation rates were high experienced low levels of reporting to police (Cook, David, and Grant 2001). Low rates of reporting are consistently identified from research conducted in countries such as the United States (Ahrens and Campbell 2000, Starzynski et al. 2005, Kaukinen and DeMaris 2009, Fanflik 2007, Holcomb and Holcomb 2011), the United Kingdom (Corry, Pouwhare, and Vergara 2008, Beckford 2012, Anderson and Doherty 2008, Ministry of Justice 2013), Canada (TPS 2013), and New Zealand (Jordan 2001).

Despite high levels of under-reporting globally, research on sexual assault victimisation rates, by age, in Canada found children under 12 (female and male) accounted for 25 per cent of all rapes with 81 per cent of offences targeting girls (Brennan and Taylor-Butts 2008). Another study found rates peak for girls at age 13 (Kong et al. 2003). Research from the United States found two thirds of all reported sexual violence crimes are against girls less than 17 years of age with those less than 12 years representing one third of those victimised (Snyder 2000). The findings on the youth of the victims in these studies are consistent with the findings of the British Crime Survey conducted in 2000. Although this survey only focused on participants aged 16 years and older, it found that young women aged 16–19 years were more likely to be victimised (Myhill and Allen 2002). Findings from other studies in sub-Saharan Africa, the Caribbean and Peru also indicate high rates of sexual violence against adolescent girls (WHO 2002).

Index

Adler, Janet 71–72
agency, loss of 126, 127, 174
Alaimo, Stacy 171
Astbury, Jill 83
Authentic Movement 65, 70, 71, 72, 192, 202, 208, 209, 228, 230, 251, 259, 260, 286
autoethnography 8, 75, 167, 180, 185, 186, 187, 197, 261, 262
autonomic nervous system 98, 99, 100, 106
autonomic rhythm 100

Bainbridge-Cohen, Bonnie 64, 75, 198
Barad, Karen 171, 200
Body-Mind Centering 3, 5, 7, 21, 33, 50, 63, 65, 97, 99, 100, 101, 134, 136, 137, 181, 191, 192, 193, 195, 196, 198, 199, 201, 202, 206, 210, 215, 216, 217, 219, 221, 222, 223, 226, 231, 245, 251, 252, 258, 285, 286, 315, 316, 317, 318, 319, 320
bodywork 50, 55, 58, 63, 64, 66, 68, 69, 70, 117, 121, 135, 136, 137, 138, 195, 207, 287, 320
Brison, Susan 18, 19, 43, 51, 76, 77, 78, 79, 80, 89, 91, 111, 120, 151, 152, 187, 188, 284
Brown, Brene 75, 86, 87

Caruth, Cathy 23, 225
Charcot, Jean-Martin 59, 128
Cheever, Olivia 56, 66, 67, 68, 181, 207
Cixous, Hélène 7, 9, 35, 49, 75, 149, 153, 158, 159, 160, 161, 162, 163, 164, 167, 173, 179, 181, 189, 190, 191, 197, 249, 278
Culbertson, Roberta 103, 104
Cummins, Alice 3, 4, 21, 33, 191, 258

Descartes, Rene 53, 54
Dickinson, Emily 197
diffraction 177
disclosure,
- barriers to 42, 81
- fear of 81, 153
- negative responses to 42, 82, 141
- normalisation of 84
- plausibility of 78
- rates of 144, 145
- risks of 82
- time elapsed since 36, 121, 139, 142, 143
- to GP's 28, 45, 110, 113, 138, 139, 140, 141, 142, 144, 145
- cultural change and 80

discourse, dominant, impact of 132
dissonance 25, 94, 100, 115, 150, 216, 282

Easteal, Patricia 42, 44, 45, 297
Echo 25, 26
embodied methodology 167–178, 196, 215, 288
empathic engagement 146, 278, 279

empathy
somatic empathy 66, 67, 68, 207, 258
entanglement 177, 200, 215
enteric nervous system 99, 100, 234
essentialism 172, 175
ethics,
research and 8
of embodiment 167, 262

fear,
of rape 19, 41, 43, 79, 91, 110
disclosure 83
see also disclosure
Feldenkrais, Moshe 64, 67, 68
feminism,
ethics of practice 177
sexual violence and 35, 41, 76, 183, 258
fight, flight, freeze response 11, 22, 87, 96, 101
flashbacks *see* nightmares
Freedman, Karyn L 43
Freud, Sigmund 59, 60, 90, 91, 127, 284

Gindler, Elsa 55
globus hystericus 234
Green, Jill 57
Greenberg, Judith 25
Grosz, Elizabeth 50, 53, 54, 65, 176, 181, 182, 212

hands-on 21, 22, 58, 64, 65, 100, 101, 192, 193, 196, 199, 202, 203, 204, 205, 206, 207, 208, 211, 212, 213, 227, 229, 230, 254, 259, 278, 285, 319, 320
Hanna, Thomas 49, 56, 57
Hartley, Linda 98, 99, 223, 317
Hekman, Susan 171, 176, 281
Herman, Judith 23, 26, 107, 232
Hielbrun, Caroline 155
Hird, Myra 175
Hirsch, Marianne 17, 18, 79, 224, 225
hypervigilance 76, 122, 123, 210, 211, 216
hysteria 58, 59, 60, 61, 108, 127, 128, 129, 130, 131, 234, 279, 284
aetiology of 127, 131, 280

Janet, Pierre 59
Juhan, Dean 64, 65, 66

Ker Conway, Jill 156
Kirby, Vicki 5, 171, 175, 279, 282, 284
van der Kolk, Bessel 108, 144

Levine, Peter 92, 94, 96, 98, 100, 101, 102, 103

masculinist language 7, 155, 156, 157
difficulties of 157, 183, 231
materialism 57, 132
memory,
cellular 5, 7, 65, 99, 100, 101, 102, 150, 153, 164, 189, 197, 207, 224, 231; *see also* memory, somatic
explicit 11, 95, 96, 104
frozen 5, 11, 63, 98, 99, 101
implicit 11, 12, 95
post-rape re-integration of 5, 60, 90, 92, 137, 206, 207, 213, 259, 288
sensory 92, 95, 96, 204, 282
somatic 5, 7, 12, 23, 25, 76, 94, 95, 96, 101, 103, 105, 110, 180, 204, 205, 212, 237, 286; *see also* memory, cellular
trauma 2, 4, 5, 7, 17, 23, 24, 25, 31, 75, 76, 91, 92, 94, 96, 102, 103, 104, 105, 106, 107, 109, 117, 137, 150, 153, 167, 168, 170, 199, 206, 213, 232, 244, 245, 264, 272, 277
unresolved 5, 25, 94, 101, 104, 107, 150, 167, 168, 180, 201, 232

Merleau-Ponty, Maurice 56, 196, 205
Michaels, Anne 7, 113, 161, 241
Mobius strip 19, 67, 68, 181, 182, 212
Modjeska, Drusilla 7, 121, 156, 188, 306

Neilsen Glenn, Lorri 241, 243, 244, 249, 277
nightmares 93, 232, 264

parasympathetic nervous system 99, 100
performance,
  as method of research 259
  making-as-inquiry 8, 32, 161, 241, 254, 257
Pert, Candace 5, 10, 100, 201
Philomela 7, 9, 12, 13, 14, 15, 16, 17, 19, 20, 159, 277, 283
Plato 50, 51, 52, 54, 56, 94, 175
Post Traumatic Stress Disorder 25, 82, 91, 92, 93, 105, 106, 122, 123, 125, 128, 280
postmemory 17, 18, 19, 79
postmodernism 175
poststructuralism 175
prememory 18, 19, 43, 91
PTSD *see* Post Traumatic Stress Disorder

rape,
  definitions of 35, 37, 40
  identity and 76, 174, 208
  impacts of 30, 33, 98, 130, 219, 280
  self-blame and 81, 82, 85, 89, 111, 134, 135, 144, 283
the raped body,
  as site of resistance 127, 265
  as archive 181
  as subversive 2, 279, 284
  as agentic 90, 91, 281
  as disseminator 265
  disconnection from 144, 210, 217
  detachment from 5, 28, 53, 210, 211, 216, 219, 254
  feelings towards 2, 40, 54, 60, 62, 68, 132, 133, 134, 161, 194, 198, 218, 231, 254
re-victimisation 82
Reich, Wilhelm 60, 61
Rothschild, Babette 92, 94

self-blame 81, 82, 85, 89, 111, 134, 135, 144, 283
sensitive research
  autoethnography and 75, 197, 261
  conducting 39
  interviews, electronic, and 114, 117, 124, 132, 134, 135, 139, 140, 282, 283
  surveys, electronic, and 39, 45, 46
sexual assault *see* rape
shame 2, 7, 17, 25, 36, 53, 75, 76, 78, 82, 83, 84, 85, 86, 87, 88, 89, 90, 91, 92, 110, 111, 132, 133, 134, 141, 143, 144, 146, 168, 257, 264, 268, 283
Showalter, Elaine 309
silence,
  externally imposed 20, 24, 144, 153, 282
  impacts of 30, 33, 98, 130, 132, 153, 207, 219, 280
  rape and cultural 3, 4, 6, 9, 16, 20, 24, 30, 36, 75, 79, 80, 143, 146, 170, 260, 264, 268, 277
  self-silencing 20, 23, 24, 82, 89, 111, 141, 144, 146, 152, 168, 224
Soma 50, 54, 56, 57, 129
somatic,
  awareness 5, 24, 55, 56, 57, 58, 64, 68, 69, 191, 211, 226, 237

disturbance, post-rape 106, 107, 109, 280
empathy 66, 67, 68, 118, 207, 238, 258
narratives 7, 26, 84, 108, 113, 114, 121, 153, 165, 259, 279
psychology/psychotherapy 58
symptoms, post-rape 5, 6, 12, 23, 25, 26, 93, 98, 106, 108, 109, 122, 123, 124, 125, 129, 130, 131, 139, 142, 143, 145, 282, 283
somatic inquiry,
autoethnographic 4, 5, 21, 76, 118, 134, 181, 188, 189, 191, 192, 193, 197, 199, 202, 207, 215, 226, 238, 255, 265, 285, 288
participant 5, 7, 113, 117, 121, 129, 281, 284, 288
somatic symptoms,
examples of 19, 54, 96, 196, 211, 232, 245, 252
medically unexplained 6, 58, 93, 110, 129, 130
somatics (the field of) 49, 56, 57, 58, 62, 68, 73, 297
somatoform disorders 108, 128, 234
somatophobia 50
Spry, Tami 32, 75, 151, 152, 187, 257, 258, 259, 260, 261, 262
sympathetic nervous system 99, 100, 101

temporal disruption 232
touch,
being touched 39, 66
difficulties surrounding touch, post-rape 5, 32, 82, 85, 93, 94, 104, 109, 126, 134, 138, 201, 207, 210, 287
healing and touch 61, 79
therapeutic touch 62
trauma memory *see* memory

victim-blaming 83
victimisation,
determinants of 43
rates of 44
secondary victimisation 82, 83, 141
vulnerability 37, 75, 77, 87, 88, 89, 90, 123, 150, 228, 253, 261, 262, 268, 269

Whitehouse, Mary Starks 65, 69, 70, 71
Wilson, Elizabeth A. 119, 131, 171, 176
witnessing,
Authentic Movement and 71, 72, 286
performance-making and 241, 254, 255
Woolf, Virginia 7, 155, 156, 242, 248, 251
writing,
-as-inquiry 8, 88, 96, 167, 198, 241
embodied writing 75, 190, 250, 252
inadequacies of language 102
journal writing 184, 205, 232, 242, 251, 252
reflective writing 196, 199, 210

www.ingramcontent.com/pod-product-compliance
Ingram Content Group UK Ltd.
Pitfield, Milton Keynes, MK11 3LW, UK
UKHW020201290926
15471UKWH00005B/1003

9 783034 319706